PERFORMING FINANCIAL STUDIES
A METHODOLOGICAL COOKBOOK

Michael J. Seiler

Associate Professor of Finance
Hawaii Pacific University

Prentice Hall

UPPER SADDLE RIVER, NJ 07458

Library of Congress Cataloging-in-Publication Data

Seiler, Michael J.
      Performing financial studies : a methodological cookbook / Michael J. Seiler.
          p. cm.
      Includes index.
      ISBN 0-13-047981-0
      1. Finance—Study and teaching. 2. Finance—Statistics. I. Title.

HG152.S45 2003
332'.01'5195—dc21   2002190878

Executive Editor: Mickey Cox
Managing Editor (Editorial): Gladys Soto
Editorial Assistant: Francesca Calogero
Assistant Editor: Erika Rusnak
Media Project Manager: Victoria Anderson
Executive Marketing Manager: Kathleen McLellan
Marketing Assistant: Christopher Bath
Managing Editor (Production): John Roberts
Production Editor: Kelly Warsak
Production Assistant: Joe DeProspero
Permissions Coordinator: Suzanne Grappi
Associate Director, Manufacturing: Vincent Scelta
Production Manager: Arnold Vila
Manufacturing Buyer: Michelle Klein
Cover Design: Bruce Kenselaar
Cover Illustration: Getty Images Inc.
Composition: BookMasters, Inc.
Full-Service Project Management: BookMasters, Inc.
Printer/Binder: Courier-Westford
Cover Printer: Phoenix Color Corp.

Credits and acknowledgments borrowed from other sources and reproduced, with permission, in this textbook appear on appropriate page within text.

Microsoft Excel, Solver, and Windows are registered trademarks of Microsoft Corporation in the U.S.A. and other countries. Screen shots and icons reprinted with permission from the Microsoft Corporation. This book is not sponsored or endorsed by or affiliated with Microsoft Corporation.

Pearson Education LTD.
Pearson Education Australia PTY, Limited
Pearson Education Singapore, Pte. Ltd.
Pearson Education North Asia Ltd.
Pearson Education, Canada, Ltd.
Pearson Educación de Mexico, S.A. de C.V.
Pearson Education–Japan
Pearson Education Malaysia, Pte. Ltd.

10 9 8 7 6 5 4 3 2 1
ISBN 0-13-047981-0

*I would like to dedicate this book
to my wife Vicky,
my parents, and my brothers and sisters,
Kelly, Paul, Steve, Amber, and Danielle.*

CONTENTS

PREFACE

Business schools, especially finance departments, around the world require students at the undergraduate and graduate levels to employ financial methodologies to perform research, analyze data, solve cases, or complete a thesis or dissertation. Unfortunately, it is the experience of most professors that students are not familiar with the procedures and format to follow when completing these requirements. Even though statistics books can be used as references for methodological procedures, the examples used in most statistics texts rarely relate to finance and the specific problems presented by financial data. So although students can follow an example in a statistics book, when it comes time to apply that example to their financial research, the students invariably get hung up on details. In addition, many of the procedures we use in finance are not found in statistics books. Instead, they have evolved through academic journals. Anyone who has ever read an academic journal knows that the methodology presented is often void of the necessary details for replication.

To make up for the lack of financial statistics textbooks, a few professors have written extremely advanced books in financial econometrics. These texts are truly worthy of the authors' Herculean intellectual capabilities. Although these books work well for their intended purpose, the material is so advanced that it is only accessible to other finance professors and a select few students who have years of top-notch training in finance. Unfortunately, the number of people who can read and understand these books represents a very small percentage of the students who are required to employ financial methodologies in their studies.

A second gap is left not only by advanced financial econometric texts, but also by every other statistics book. Although many statistics and econometrics texts explain how a particular procedure should be performed, they do not actually show the students how to do it. Therefore, students leave the class thinking they know statistics. Then, when asked to carry out the methodology in a research setting, they invariably cannot.

My goal in this book is to break down some of the statistical procedures used in finance to a level truly accessible to the remaining 99.9 percent of students. Instead of just pontificating from an ivory tower, I actually present each methodological procedure to the reader step by step. No detail is left out. I even include the raw datasets used in each example. To help this step-by-step process, the raw datasets are available for students and professors to download from, *www.prenhall.com/seiler*. To make it even easier, in addition to the written instructions, this book shows each step by presenting the corresponding action in Excel, SPSS, or EViews, whichever is appropriate, through a series of screen captures so the students can match the example in the book with their computer screens at home. I refer to this cookbook approach as enabling the students to follow a recipe.

In conclusion, whereas past texts have placed a premium on the breadth of topics covered, I understand that in order to show each methodology in such great detail, it is necessary to focus on only a few key financial procedures. So, instead of writing a 10,000-page definitive text that is all things to all people, I hope this book finds that optimal balance between breadth and illustration. Finally, my goal is not to create or invent cutting-edge financial innovations, but to bring those that already exist to a wider, more mainstream, audience.

ACKNOWLEDGMENTS

I would like to extend a special thanks to Sorin A. Tuluca of Fairleigh Dickinson University and Arnold R. Cowan of Iowa State University. These two professors, as well as numerous students, provided valuable feedback on various chapters. I would also like to thank SPSS and EViews for providing the software that was used to write this book.

My students should also be acknowledged for asking, up to the point of demanding, me to write this text. Along these lines, I would like to thank Joseph Murray of Prentice Hall for encouraging me to step forward and write the book I have been saying for several years needs to be written.

The entire Prentice Hall team is acknowledged for their assistance in producing this book. A special thank you is extended to Mickey Cox, Executive Editor of Finance; Gladys Soto, Managing Editor; Kelly Warsak, Production Editor; and John Roberts, Managing Editor of Production. I would also like to thank Angie Campbell and Jennifer Welsch, Project Directors at BookMasters, Inc.

I would like to extend my appreciation to the reviewers who provided Prentice Hall with reviews on this book: Mikhail Smirnov of Columbia University; Barry Oliver of The Australian National University; Jacky Yuk-chow So of Southern Illinois University–Edwardsville; Tom Arnold of Louisiana State University; and Chumning Zhang of the University of Wisconsin–Madison.

ABOUT THE AUTHOR

Dr. Michael J. Seiler is an associate professor of finance at Hawaii Pacific University. He has published over 50 studies in professional and academic journals as well as three books and has served as a special edition editor for five journals and a reviewer for another four.

Dr. Seiler has been written about in *Fortune* magazine and has appeared on NBC news as a financial expert to discuss "online day trading and its effect on individuals, the stock market, and the overall economy." Dr. Seiler also discussed one of his books, *Becoming Fiscally Fit: How to Control Your Financial Future,* and various other investing concepts on the television program *The Free Money Show.* In addition, Dr. Seiler explained the history of the New York Stock Exchange on the TV series, *Financing Your Future: Finding Your Way in the Market.*

1

UNDERSTANDING
YOUR DATA

Before you can perform statistical procedures, you must first understand the characteristics of your data. Data are either *metric* or *nonmetric*. Metric data can be further classified as either *continuous* (ratio) or *interval* data. Nonmetric data can be broken down into *ordinal* or *nominal* data. This chapter will introduce these four general types of data and illustrate their differences, primarily by referring to the dataset titled "Home Values - 1."

The dataset "Home Values - 1" contains cross-sectional data relating to home (residential property) attributes for 1,172 properties located in Cuyahoga County, Ohio. Although each variable discussed in this chapter will be explained in the text, additional information on each variable can be found in the Appendix.

1.1   NONMETRIC DATA

1.1.1   NOMINAL DATA

A nominal variable is one to which numbers are arbitrarily assigned to identify or classify categories. For example, consider the numbers assigned to football players. If you are number 40 and your teammate is number 80, it does not mean that he is twice as good a player as you are. If his number were changed to 89, it would have no effect on his statistics. The number 80 is just a number used to identify a player. The same thing can be said about a Social Security number; it is simply a way for the government to identify a person.

In a financial setting, consider an IPO (initial public offering) database where one of your variables is "Lead Underwriter." Assume that you have four lead underwriters: Merrill Lynch, Goldman Sachs, Morgan Stanley, and Charles Schwab. You could assign value to each underwriter as follows:

Merrill Lynch = 1
Goldman Sachs = 2
Morgan Stanley = 3
Charles Schwab = 4

However, you could also assign the values as

Morgan Stanley = 1
Charles Schwab = 2
Merrill Lynch = 3
Goldman Sachs = 4

As you can see, the number you assign to each firm is completely arbitrary. Your goal is simply to distinguish one firm from another.

As a final example, in the dataset "Home Values - 1," the variable "view" measures whether a home has a view of Lake Erie or not. If the home does have a view of Lake Erie, a value of "1" is assigned. If the home does not have a view of Lake Erie, a value of "0" is assigned. However, we could have just as easily assigned the values the other way. That is, we could have assigned the value of "1" if the home did not have a view of Lake Erie and a value of "0" if the home did have a view of Lake Erie. Moreover, we could have used the numbers "1" and "2" for each case.

When a nominal variable has only two classifications or categories, as is the case for the variable "view," it is also known as a *dummy variable*. Traditionally, dummy variables are assigned the values "0" and "1."

1.1.2   ORDINAL DATA

When you think of ordinal data, think of the word *order*. Ordinal data indicate the relative position of each observation but do not consider the magnitude of the differences between them. That is, ordinal data might give you a ranking from best to worst, but the ranking will not distinguish how much better or worse.

As an example, consider the ranking of the top 100 performing mutual funds.

Ranking	1-Year Performance
1	210.6%
2	95.5%
3	94.2%
.	.
.	.
100	74.9%

A higher ranking corresponds to a higher 1-year performance return. However, the differences between rankings are not consistent. For example, between the first and second ranking the difference is 115.1% (210.6% − 95.5%), yet the difference between the second and third ranking is only 1.3% (95.5% − 94.2%).

In sum, ordinal data provide the order or ranking of observations, but the data do not tell you how much higher or lower one observation is relative to another.

1.2   METRIC DATA

1.2.1   INTERVAL DATA

Interval data are ordinal data where the differences between each observation are constant. In the dataset "Home Values - 1," the variable "constrql" indicates a rating of the home's construction quality ranging from 1 (lowest quality) to 6 (highest quality). Moving from a construction quality rating of 2 to 3 is the same amount of improvement as going from 3 to 4, or 4 to 5, and so on. What distinguishes interval data from ordinal data is that with interval data, the values are set equally apart.

The most commonly referred to nonfinancial example of interval data is temperature. The increase in temperature from 70 to 71 degrees is the same amount as an increase from 80 to 81 degrees. Thus, each degree is spread equally apart.

One restriction associated with interval data is that it has what is referred to as an arbitrary zero point. In the construction quality example, this means that a home with a value of 2 is not twice as well built as a home with a value of 1. Moreover, a home with a value of 6 is not three times as sturdy as a home with a value of 2. In the temperature example, this simply means that you cannot say that 80 degrees is twice as hot as 40 degrees. Similarly, 25 degrees is not three times colder than 75 degrees.

1.2.2 CONTINUOUS (RATIO) DATA

What sets continuous (or ratio) data apart from interval data is that continuous data have a fixed zero point. Common financial examples of continuous data include the market capitalization of a firm, total assets, sales, GDP, returns, and so on. Nonfinancial examples include population, age, weight, salary, number of children, and so on.

In the "Home Values - 1" dataset, the variable "value" refers to the assessed value (or price) of a home. A home priced at $400,000 is twice as valuable as a home priced at $200,000. The variable "homesqft" is defined as the total square feet of living space in the home. A value of 4,500 means that the home is three times larger than a home with 1,500 square feet.

PREPARING YOUR DATA FOR ANALYSIS

2.1 GETTING DATA OFF THE INTERNET AND INTO EXCEL

In recent years, the Internet has become a tremendous source of data for all types of research. No matter what you are looking for, run a search on the Internet and you will likely find it. Although some Web sites sell access to their data, save your money. You will most likely be able to find the data you need for free. This section shows you in great detail how to download free data off the Internet and get it into Excel.

Let's get the historical monthly data for five time series: the yield on Aaa rated corporate bonds, Baa rated corporate bonds, 3-month Treasury Bills, 30-year Treasury Bonds, and the Consumer Price Index (CPI). After performing a search on the Internet, we quickly find the first series. The URL address is www.federalreserve.gov/releases/H15/data/m/aaa.txt.

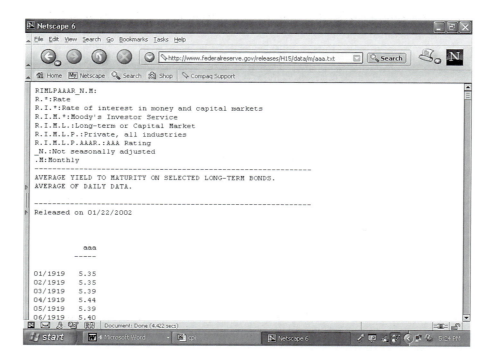

As you can see, the monthly data series begins in January 1919. We likely will not care about data going back that far, but let's capture it all for now. To do so, simply place your mouse pointer on the first observation, left-click, and while holding down the button, drag all the way down to the bottom of the data series.

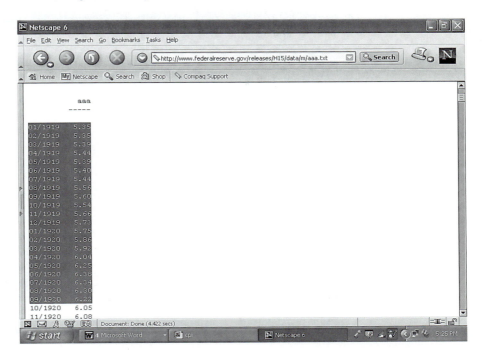

After you have highlighted the entire series, you can release the left mouse button. You will see that you have successfully highlighted all the data. Right-click on your mouse, then select "Copy."

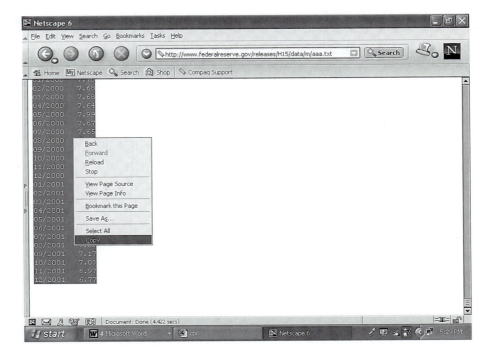

Enter Excel and paste the information into a blank spreadsheet.

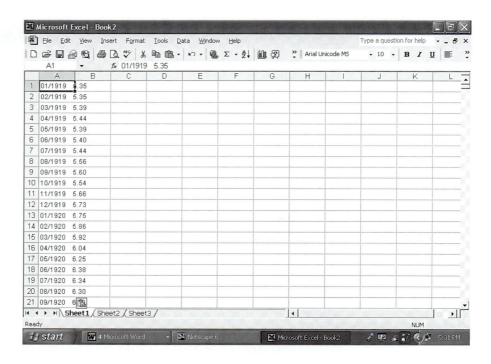

You will notice that both the date and the yield appear in column "A." What you want is for the date to appear in column "A" and the yield to appear in column "B." One way to separate them is to click "File," "Save As."

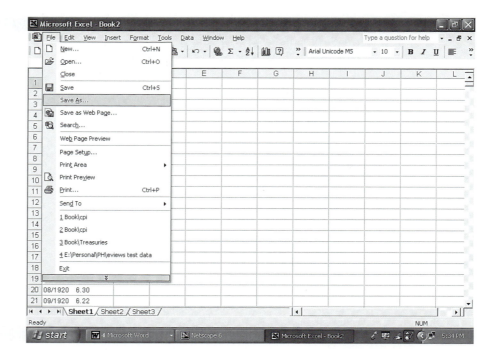

Type in the name of the new file as "Internet Data - 1." Instead of saving it as a "Microsoft Excel Workbook," save it as a "Text (Tab delimited)" file.

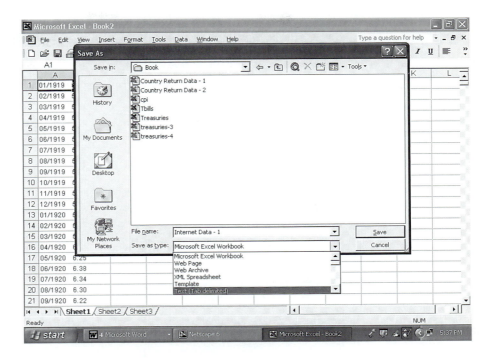

You will be given two warning screens. The first will look like this.

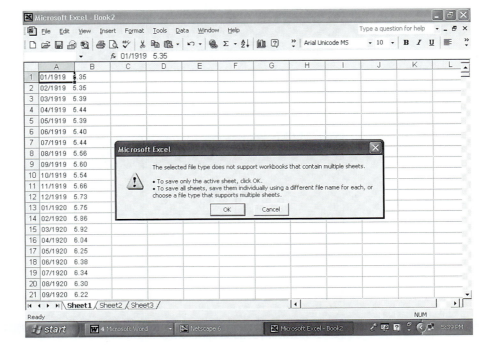

Click "OK" and "OK" again to get through both warning screens. Now close out of the Excel worksheet by clicking "File" and then "Close" or by clicking on the smaller "X" right below the big red "X" in the top-right corner of your Excel window.

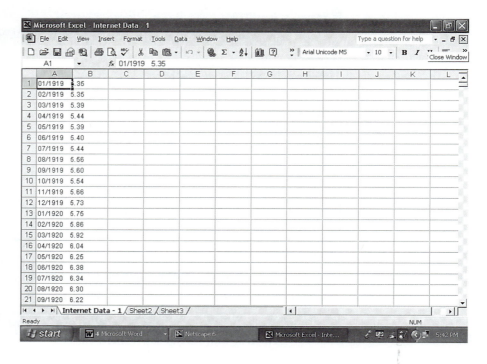

When asked if you want to save changes, click "No."

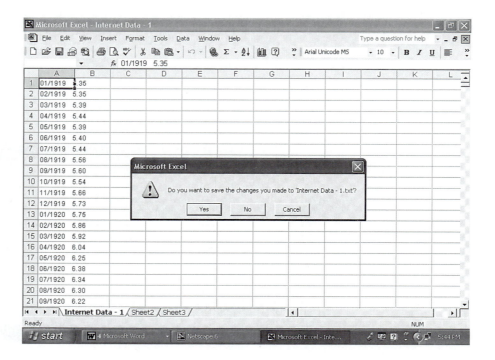

Click "File" and then "Open" to open a new file. Under the option "Files of type," select "All Files." Double-click on "Internet Data - 1" to open it.

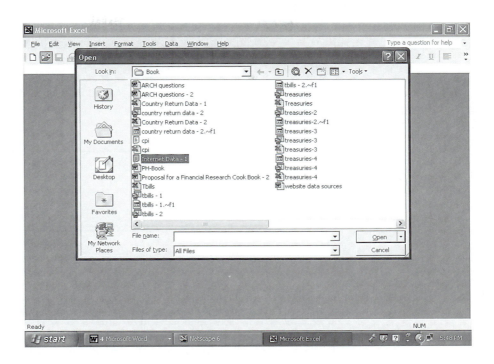

Select "Fixed width," then click "Next."

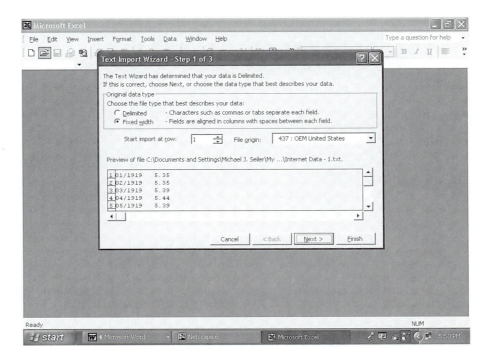

Click "Next" again, then click "Finish."

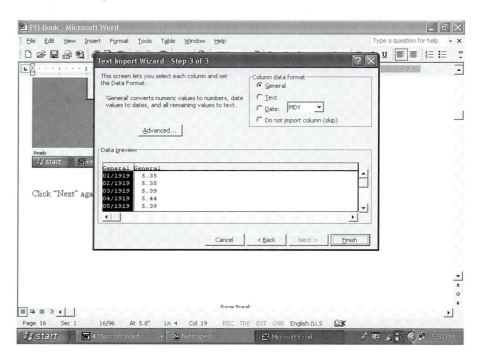

The date and yield will now appear in two different columns, "A" and "B."

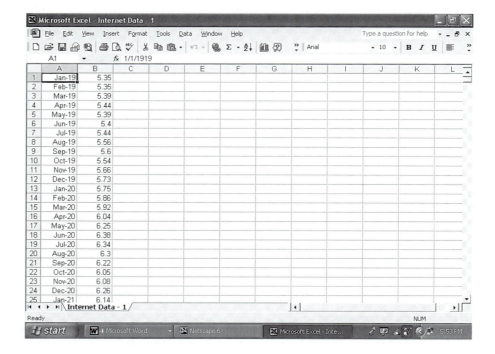

Save the file as a "Microsoft Excel Workbook" and use the same file name—"Internet Data - 1."

You are now ready to go back to the Internet and pull down the four remaining series. Use the same procedure that was just described. The URL addresses for the other four series are as follows:

www.federalreserve.gov/releases/H15/data/m/baa.txt
www.federalreserve.gov/releases/H15/data/m/tcm30y.txt
www.federalreserve.gov/releases/H15/data/m/tbsm3m.txt
ftp.bls.gov/pub/special.requests/cpi/cpiai.txt

When you are done downloading the data for all five series, simply cut and paste each series into the common Excel Workbook, "Internet Data - 1." Be sure to line up the dates correctly, because each series may begin on a different date. After you finish, your Excel Workbook should look like the following screen.

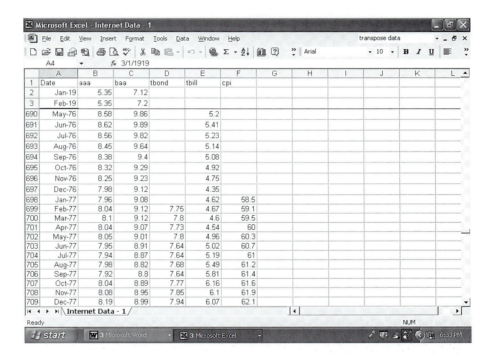

Notice that the "Freeze Panes" setting has been activated so that you can view the series titles (row 1) and the data at the beginning of 1977 (row 698). This shows that the five series do not all begin at the same point in time. This is normal.

When performing any type of analysis, researchers will often go back in time only as far as they have data for all the series. In this example, our monthly series should begin in February 1977 and end in December 2001, because all five series have observations for all months within this range.

After cutting the data before February 1977 and moving the rest to row 2, your spreadsheet should look as follows.

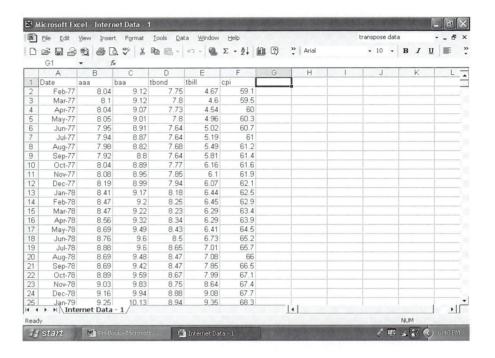

You are now ready to analyze the data.

2.2 PREPARING DATA IN EXCEL

It is often easier to perform certain calculations in Excel before importing the data into one of the more powerful statistical packages. To illustrate this concept, open the Excel file titled "Country Return Data - 1." Your computer screen should look like this.

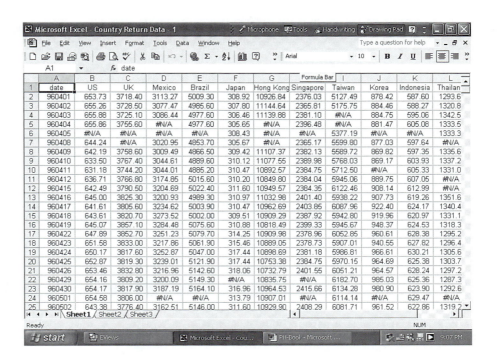

This file contains the stock market index values of 13 markets around the world. The name of each country is given in row 1. For more details, see the Appendix, where each dataset is described in detail.

Let's convert each index series into a return series. Go to cell "O1." Type in the label "rUS" to denote that this column will represent the return on the U.S. stock market. In cell "P1," type in the label "rUK" to denote that this column will represent the return on the UK stock market. Do this for all 13 world stock markets. As a shortcut, you may find it easier to copy and paste the titles. Then all you have to do is go back and insert an "r" in front of each label to signify that it represents a return. Using the "Copy" and "Paste" functions will also reduce the chance of accidentally labeling the countries out of order.

If you use the "Copy" and "Paste" commands, your sequence of screens will be as follows. First, highlight the names in row 1. Next, click "Copy."

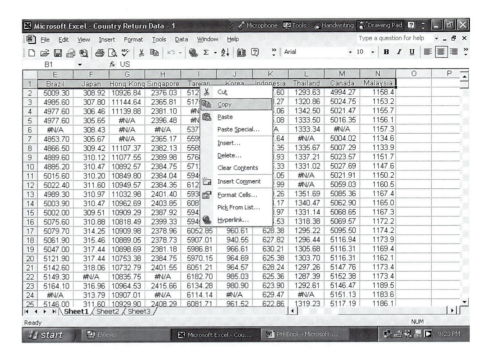

Go to the blank cell "O1." Now click "Paste."

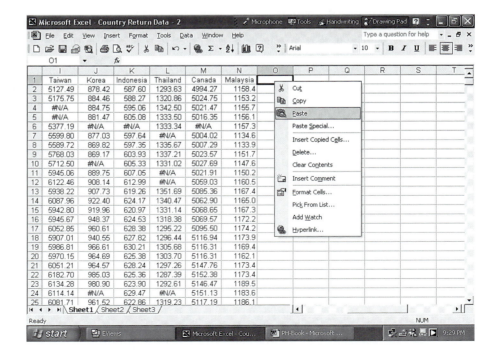

You should see the names of each country repeated. To indicate that these new cells will represent returns, place an "r" in front of each label. For example, go to cell "O1" and type "rUS." Now go to cell "P1" and type "rUK."

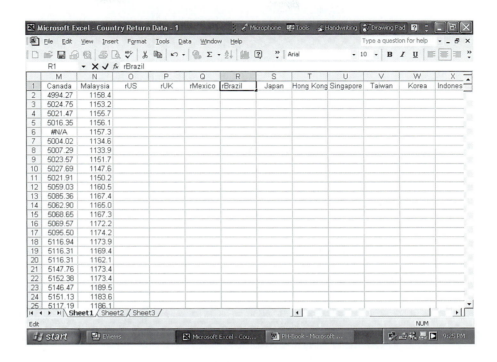

You are done when you finish putting "r" in front of each country label.

To calculate the return on the U.S. index, go to cell "O3." Stock returns are known to follow a log normal distribution. Therefore, the formula you want to use is "LN (1 + (B3 − B2)/B2)." A less intuitive, yet equivalent, way to write the formula is to simply write "LN (B3/B2)." Try both equations and you will see that they result in the exact same value.

Note that the return series actually starts one row below the start of the index values. That is, the index values start in row 2, whereas the returns start in row 3. This is always the result when taking the return of an index. You will lose one observation.

You will want to copy this formula all the way down to cell "O761." The easiest way to do this is to place your mouse pointer on the lower-right-hand corner of cell

"O3." Left-click and hold down the button as you move your mouse downward to fill down to cell "O761." Your screen will look like this.

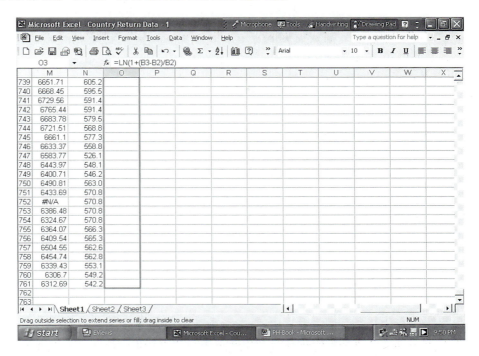

When you reach cell "O761," release your left mouse button and the column will be filled with returns.

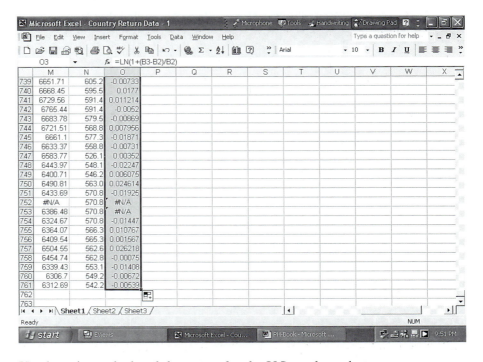

You have just calculated the return for the U.S. stock market.

You can repeat these steps to calculate the return for all 13 world markets. To make the task quicker, highlight the area between cells "O3" and "O761." Then click "Copy." Now highlight the area "P3" through "AA3," then click "Paste." Your screen will look like this.

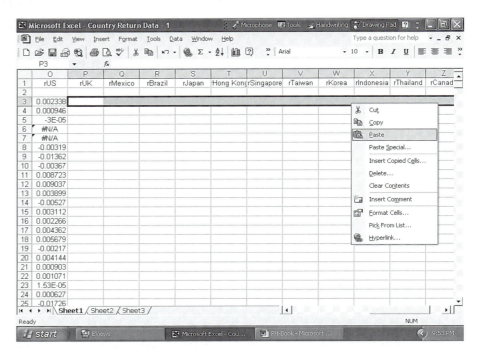

After the "Paste" function has been completed, you should have returns for all 13 countries. Your Excel file will look like this.

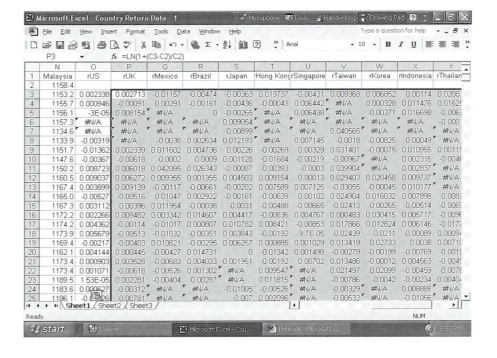

You can verify that the formulas in columns "P" through "AA" are correct by clicking on any one of their cells. The columns referred to in their formulas should correspond to the index values for the same country. For example, if you click on cell "S3," it should have a formula that refers to column "F," because column "S" is the return for Japan and column "F" is the index for Japan. Your verification should appear as follows.

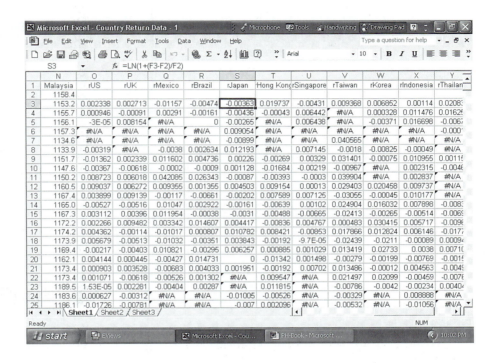

Save this completed file as "Country Return Data - 2" so you can use it in future applications.

2.3 GETTING DATA INTO EVIEWS

To work in EViews, we must first create a "Workfile." To do so, open EViews and click "File," "New," and then "Workfile." The screen appears as follows.

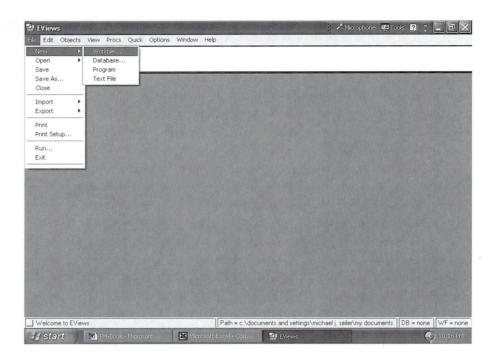

A "Workfile Range" screen will appear.

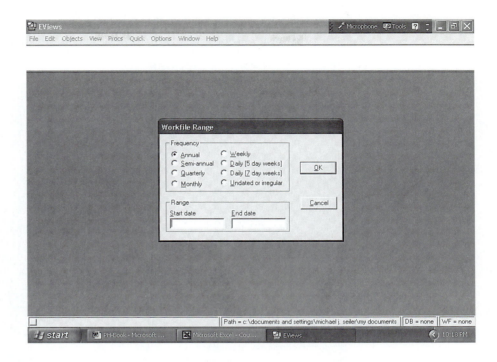

Type the start and end dates for your data. In our case, the start date is "04-01-96" and the end date is "02-26-99." Our data are daily, and the stock markets are not open on weekends. Therefore, under the heading "Frequency," you should mark the box

"Daily [5 day weeks]." Then click "OK." Your window should be marked as shown in the following screen.

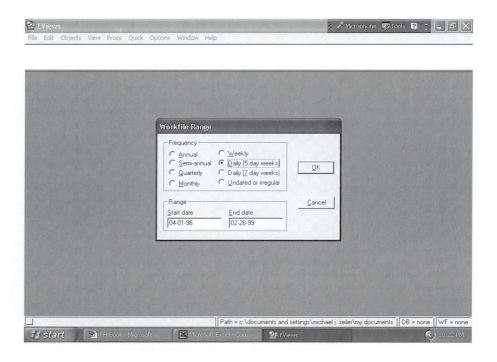

After clicking "OK," the untitled "Workfile" screen will appear.

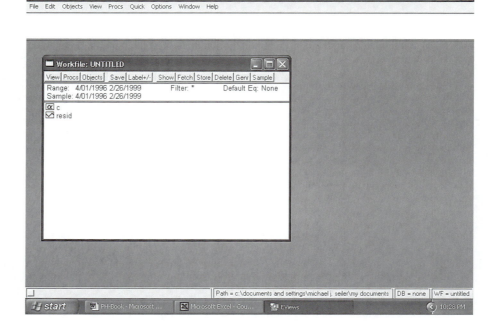

The variable "c" stands for the constant term. The variable "resid" stands for residual. These two variables will appear every time. Do not worry about them for now.

At this point, you are ready to import data from Excel into EViews. To do so, click "File," "Import," and then "Read Text-Lotus-Excel."

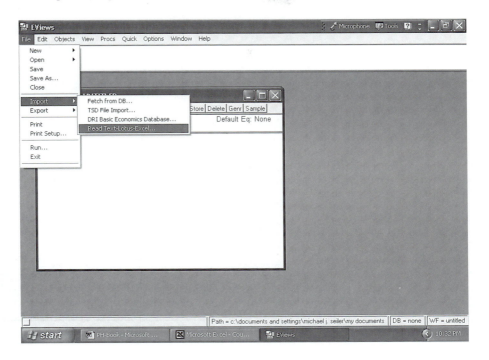

A screen will pop up as follows.

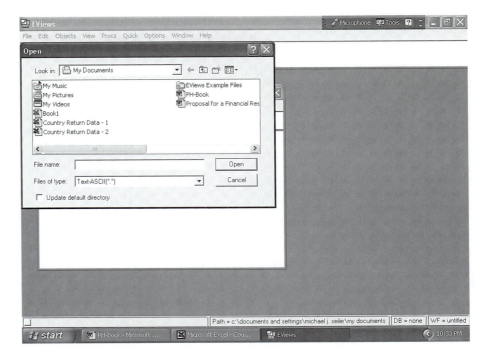

Simply double-click on the file you wish to import or single-click on it to highlight the file and then click "Open." The file we want to import is "Country Return Data - 2." Performing this sequence of steps results in the following screen.

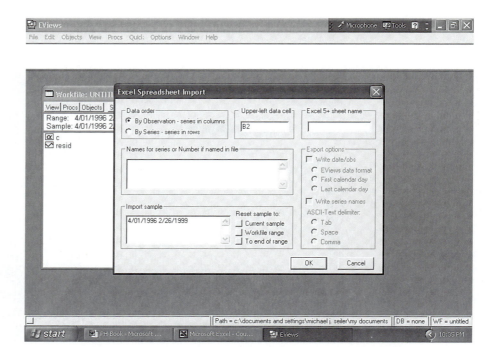

Under the section titled "Names for series or Number if named in file," type in the value "27" because we have 27 columns in our Excel file. Note that since we have already labeled our data (e.g., date, US, UK, Mexico, . . . , rThailand, rCanada, rMalaysia), all we have to do here is type in the number of columns we have. Another way to think of it is that there is no need for us to type in the "Names for series"

because we have already typed them in the Excel file. Instead, we tell EViews the "Number (of variables)." Our number of variables is 27.

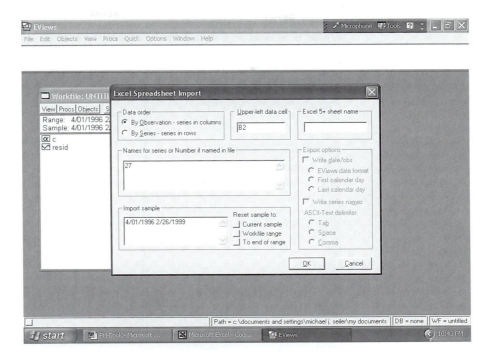

After typing in the number "27," click "OK." The following screen will appear.

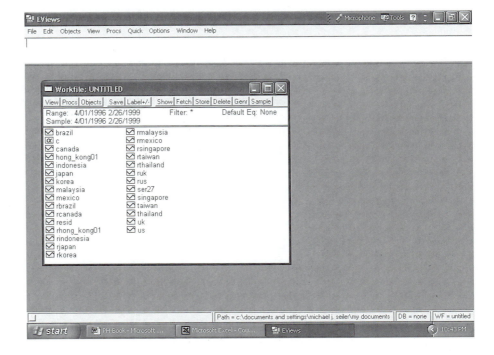

Any time you import data, it is a good idea to verify that nothing has gone wrong. To make sure EViews has made the transition correctly, view the data in the EViews "Workfile." To do this, click "View," and then "Select All (except C-RESID)."

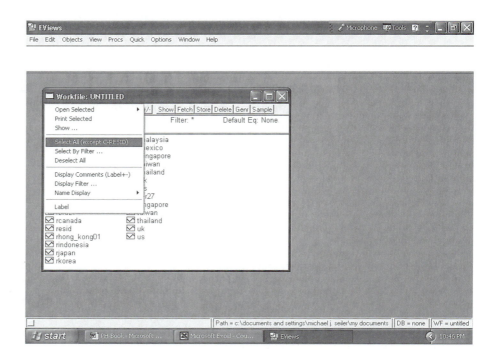

The following screen will appear.

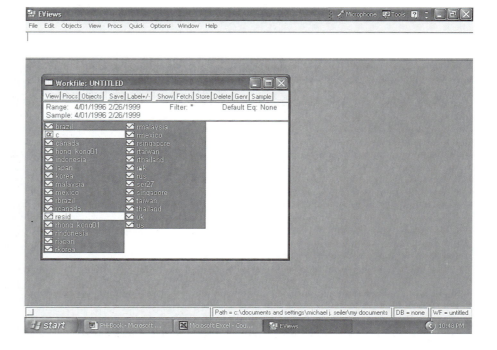

Note that everything has been highlighted except the variables "c" and "resid," which we still do not need to worry about for now.

Now click "View," "Open Selected," and then "One Window."

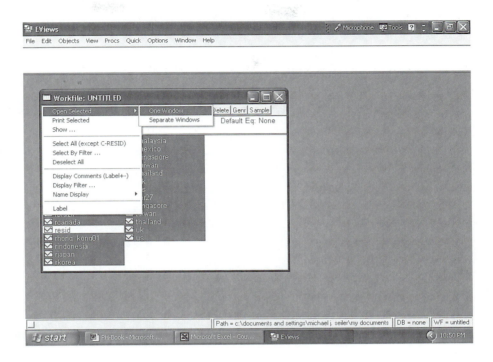

After the function finishes, a small screen will appear.

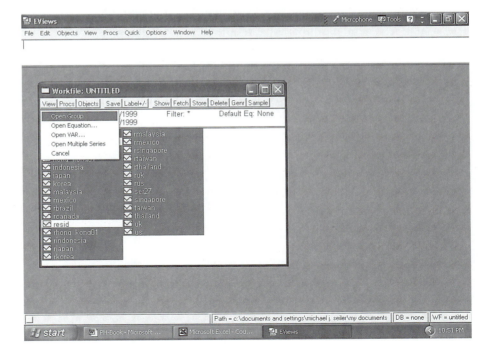

Another way to do this is to double-click in the highlighted area. Either way, you will see the same screen.

Click "Open Group." When the spreadsheet appears, click on the "Maximize" icon in the upper-right-hand corner to fill your computer screen.

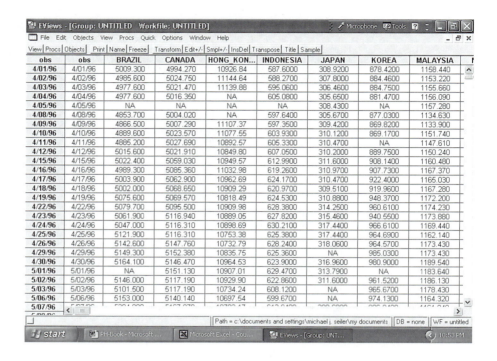

Notice that the order of the variables is now alphabetical instead of in the order we created in Excel. This, of course, makes no difference. Impressively, EViews correctly matched the dates it generated with the dates we already had listed in the Excel file. I say this is impressive because even though the stock market is typically open 5 days a week, there are numerous weekdays over which it is closed (e.g., regular holidays, as well as unexpected closings for things such as fires, power outages, etc.). EViews had no problem controlling for these events.

Now that we have created a file in EViews, we should name it and save it. Simply click "File" and then "Save" or "Save As." It makes no difference, because we are saving the file for the first time.

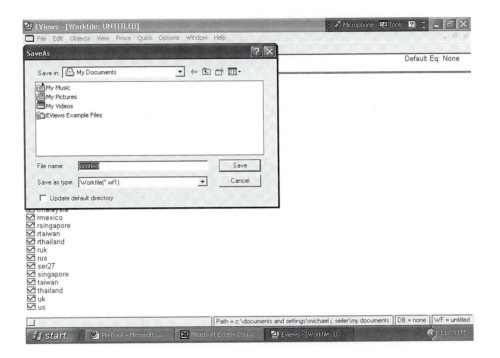

Let's choose the same name as our Excel file, "Country Return Data - 2." We will not confuse the two files because Excel documents have the extension "*.xls" while EViews files have the extension "*.wf1."

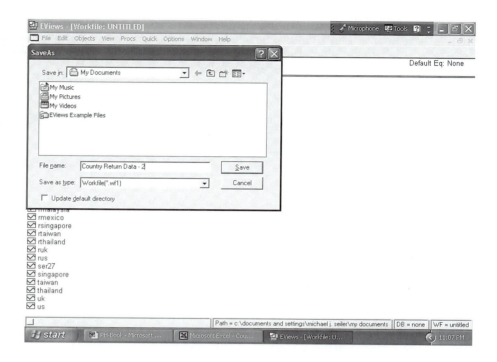

Click the "Save" button.

2.4 GETTING DATA INTO SPSS

SPSS does a great job of reading all types of data. In a previous section, we created an Excel Workbook called "Internet Data - 1." Let's open this file in SPSS. After opening SPSS, click "File," "Open," and then "Data."

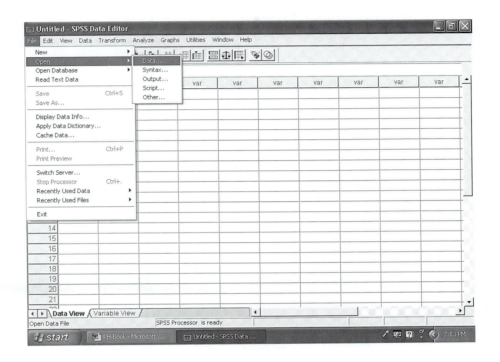

Under the box labeled "Files of type," select "All Files (*.*)." Double-click on the Excel file "Internet Data - 1."

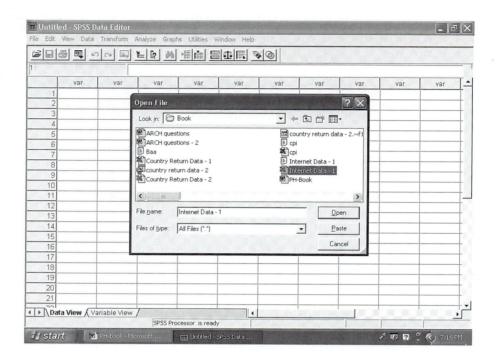

In SPSS, you will see a window pop up titled "Opening Excel Data Source." Because our series titles appear in row 1 of our Excel file and the data start in row 2, you should leave the box labeled "Read variable names from the first row of data" checked. Under the tab marked "Worksheet," the default is to import everything in the Excel file. If you wish, you can select a subset of data to import. This range would be entered into the tab titled "Range." Because we would like to import all the data, all we need to do is click "OK."

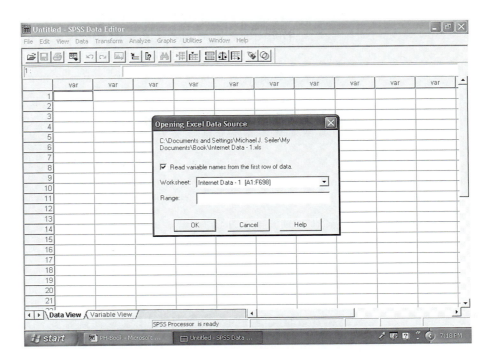

You have just successfully imported your data into SPSS. Your SPSS window will appear as follows.

Save the newly created SPSS file by clicking "File" and then "Save."

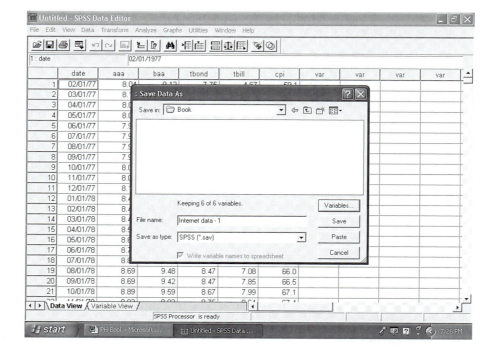

The "Save Data As" screen will appear. Type in the file name "Internet Data - 1." The default in SPSS is to save the file with the extension "*.sav." Click "Save." This is now an SPSS file.

2.5 SCREENING THE DATA FOR TYPOS AND OUTLIERS

The first time you work with a dataset, you should always check it for typos and outliers. The accidental inclusion of an extra "0" or the omission of a decimal point can severely throw off your results and lead you to make false conclusions. To avoid this pitfall, this section describes easy ways to screen your data.

To illustrate the steps involved in screening data, we will examine the SPSS file "Faculty Evaluations - 1." This file contains the student evaluations of 11 professors in the Department of Finance at a 4-year university in the Midwest. Each row corresponds to a different student. Each column represents the response to a different question. A complete description of all of the variables is given in the Appendix.

To open this file, click "File" and then "Open" or simply click on the "Open File" icon. Then select the file "Faculty Evaluations - 1" by double-clicking on it.

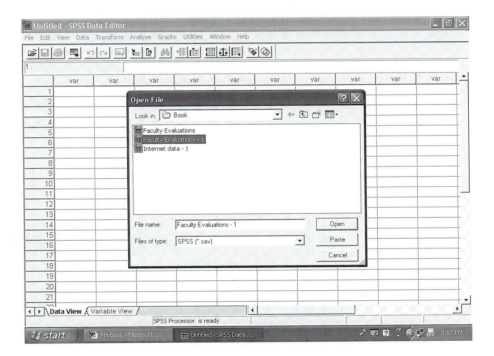

The opening screen will appear.

The first 34 columns are generically titled "q01, q02, q03, . . . , q33, q34." These are the 34 questions each student answers when completing the evaluation. To find out what the question asked, click "View" and then "Variables." You could also simply click on the "Variable View" tab at the bottom of the window.

This gives you a behind-the-scenes look at the variable labels, values, and other characteristics that might be of interest.

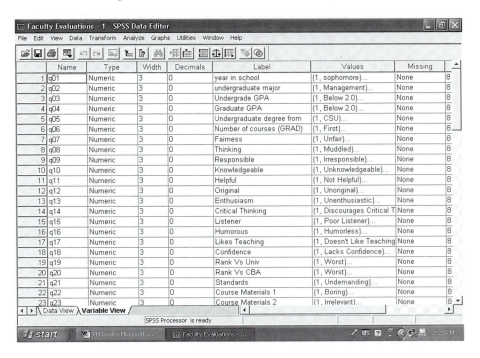

For example, if you click anywhere in the column "Values," you will highlight that particular cell. Notice the small gray box in the right-most part of that cell. Now click on the gray box.

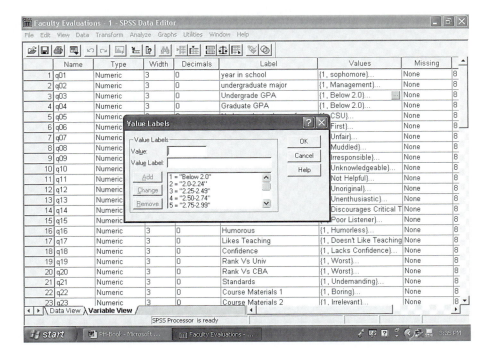

In this example, I clicked in the cell associated with question 3 (q03). Under the column with the heading "Label," I can see that this question asks the student about their undergraduate GPA. The "Value Labels" window shows a "Value" assigned to each student response. For example, if a student had a GPA of 2.61, they would have filled in the bubble next to "2.50-2.74" on the evaluation form. The person who created this file would have coded the student response as a "4."

If you click on the downward-pointing blue arrow under the scroll bar, you can see the assigned values associated with GPAs above 2.99.

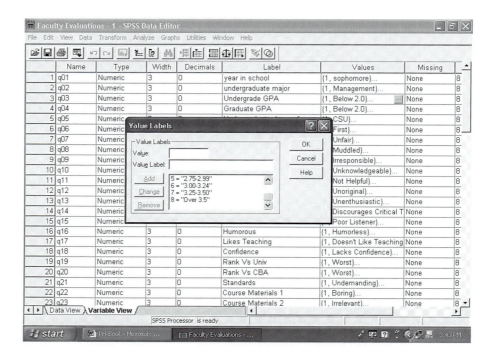

You can now see that any GPA over 3.5 has been coded as an "8." Because the values associated with student responses can only range from 1 through 8, any value outside that range must be an error.

Using this logic, we want to screen question 3 to see if all responses are integers between the values of 1 through 8. To do so, click "Cancel" to get out of the "Value Labels" window. Now click "Analyze," "Descriptive Statistics," and then "Descriptives."

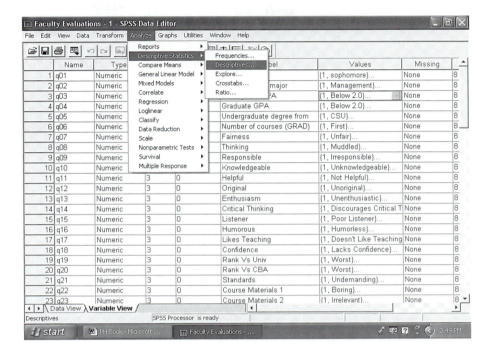

The following "Descriptives" window will appear.

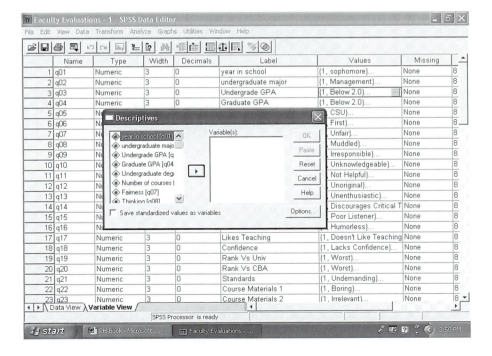

Each variable is listed on the left-hand side. The list is provided in the order the variables appear in the "Data" window from left to right. The variable label is provided first, followed by the variable's name in brackets. For example, "year in school [q01]" is the first variable listed because it appears in the first column of the "Data" window. The variable is listed by stating its label (year in school) followed by its name (q01).

Because question 3 is in the third column of the "Data" window, it should be in the third row here. You might find it easier to locate the question by looking for the label "Undergrad GPA." Once you find it in the variable list, double-click on it to move it into the empty box titled "Variable(s)."

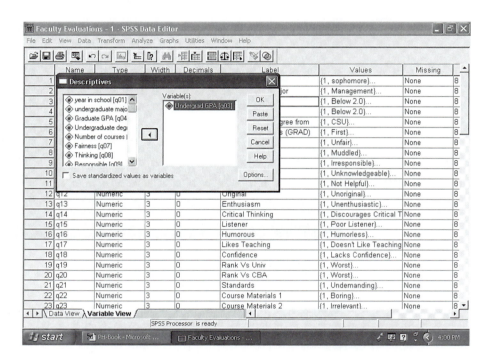

You could click "OK" at this time, but the default is to give you a lot of information you do not need right now. Instead, click on the "Options" tab. The window "Descriptives: Options" will appear.

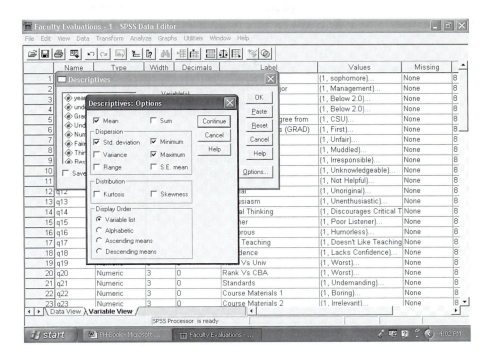

Uncheck all boxes (except the minimum and maximum) by clicking on them.

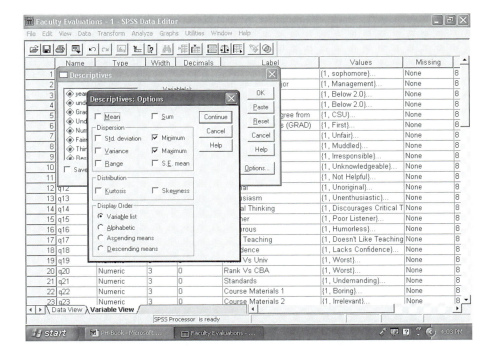

Now click "Continue." After you return to the previous screen, click "OK" to run the test. An SPSS "Output" window will appear showing you the results of your test.

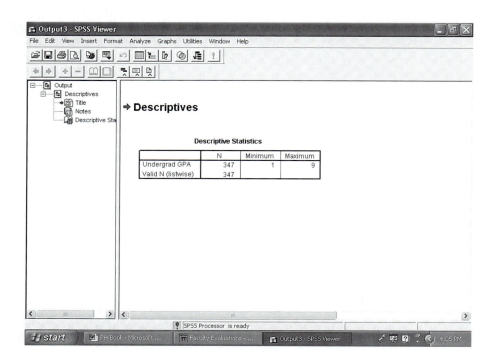

Of the 352 students who completed the evaluation, only 347 answered this question. You know this by looking at the value of "N." The minimum value of "1" is good, but the maximum value of "9" is outside our range. Therefore, you have identified an error.

To correct this error, go back to the "Data" window. Click in the first row of q03. Now select "Edit" and then "Find."

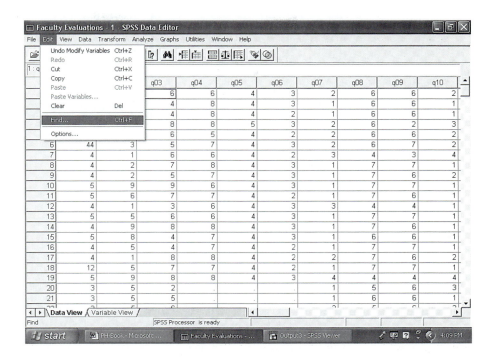

Under the area marked "Find what," type in the number "9."

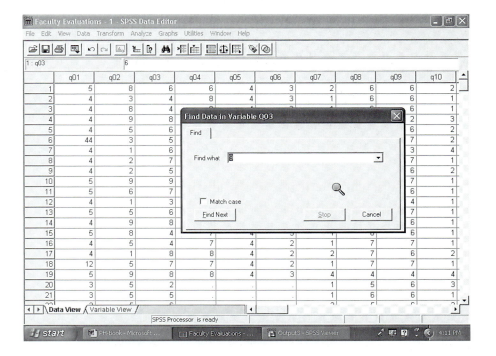

Now click "Find Next" to begin the search. You will see that row 10 is highlighted with a box around it.

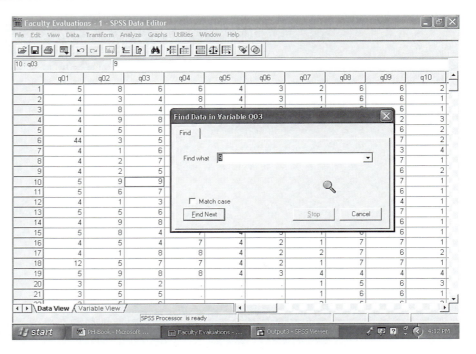

This is certainly an error, but is it the only time q03 was assigned a value of "9"? To make sure the error was not repeated elsewhere, click "Find Next" again. You will need to repeat this step until all outliers have been identified and corrected. You will know you are done when you see this screen.

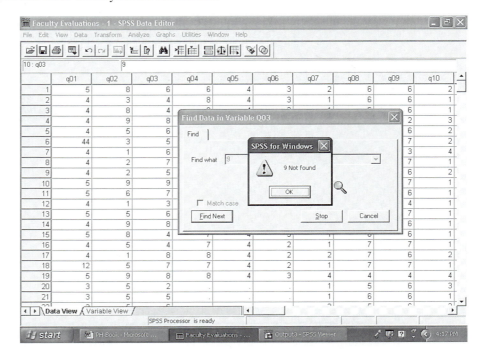

You must decide what to do with this input error. My advice is to simply remove the score without trying to guess what the number should have been. Unless you can pull the original student evaluations and identify the actual response with 100% certainty, you should leave the cell blank. The default in performing SPSS procedures is to ignore the case. The result is just one less observation. This is much better than the alternative, which is for you to guess what the number might have been. If you are wrong, you will bias your analysis/results and therefore risk reaching erroneous conclusions. You should never make up data.

This method of identifying outliers is efficient if only a few exist. If you suspect your dataset has many coding errors in it, you may want to check it using the following procedure.

Consider question 1 (q01). The range for this variable is between 1 and 6. In the SPSS "Data" window, click "Analyze," "Descriptive Statistics," and then "Frequencies."

The "Frequencies" window will appear.

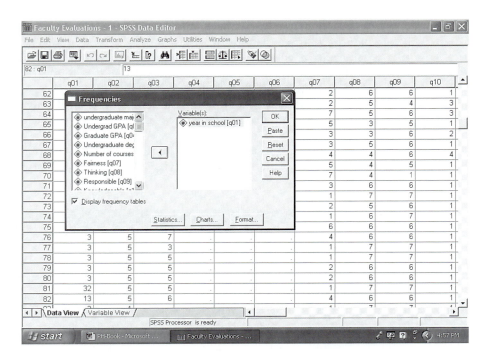

Select "year in school [q01]" and then click "OK." The following output screen will appear.

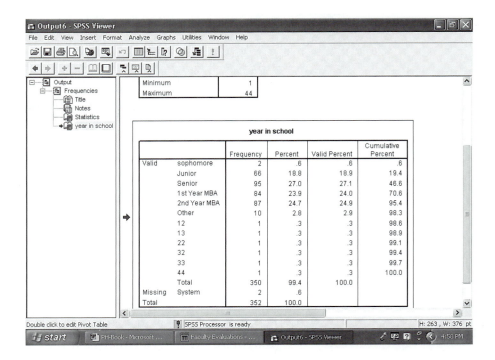

You will see a minimum value of "1," which is good, and a maximum value of "44," which is an outlier. If you look in the lower table, you will see a list of "Frequencies" associated with each value that appears in q01. The values "1" through "6" are not shown. Instead, their "labels" are given. For example, the value of "1" is associated with "Sophomore." The value of "2" represents "Junior," and so forth. Finally, the value of "6" corresponds to the student response "Other," meaning that they did not fit into any of the other choices. The remaining values, "12," "13," "22," "32," "33," and "44," all represent errors in the dataset. To find and remove these errors, use "Edit" and "Find" as previously described.

This procedure was performed on just one variable at a time to keep the demonstration simple and easy to follow. However, it is far more efficient to perform the procedure on the entire dataset at once. Only one extra step is needed. Instead of selecting just one variable, as shown here, simply select them all.

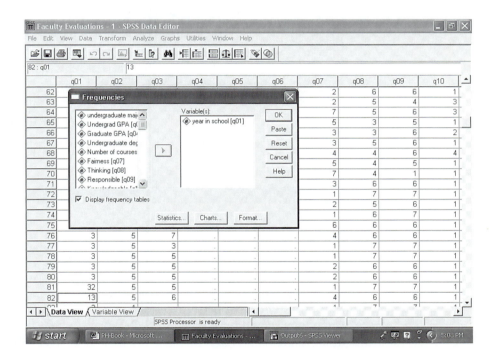

To select all the variables, click in the left window. While holding down the "Shift" key, use your "down arrow" key to highlight all the variables. Then click on the "right arrow" button in the SPSS "Frequencies" box to move all the variables to the box on the right.

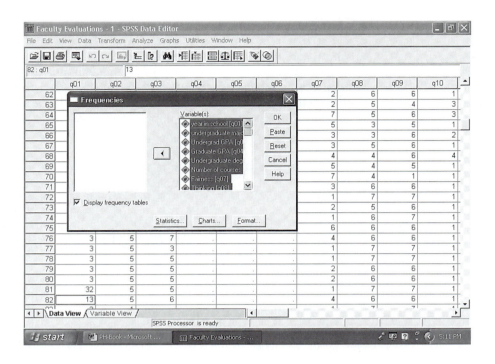

Click "OK." The rest of the procedure is the same. When you have finished screening the data for outliers, save the SPSS file under the title "Faculty Evaluations - 2." This file will be free from identifiable errors. I am careful to use the qualifier "identifiable" because we have removed all the erroneous values outside the range for each variable. However, we still cannot be sure that the person who coded this file did not type in a "1" when they should have typed in a "2." To verify that these types of errors do not exist, you would have to go back to the original source (the student evaluation sheets).

2.6   TRANSFORMING/COMPUTING FINANCIAL VARIABLES

It is often necessary to compute new variables or adjust existing variables once in SPSS. This section walks you through some of the most common and more basic transformations/calculations in financial research.

To demonstrate these concepts, we will consider the dataset "Beta Data - 1." To open the "Beta Data - 1" file in SPSS, click "File" and then "Open" or simply click on the "Open File" icon. Then select the file "Beta Data - 1" by double-clicking on it.

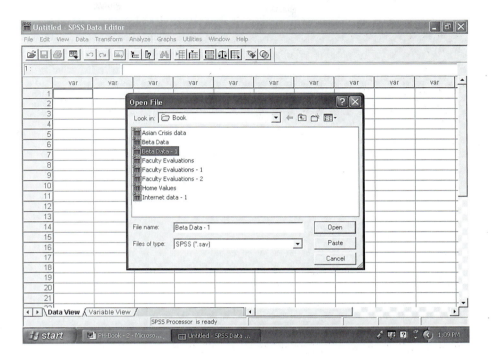

You should now see the data in SPSS.

	date	sp500	tbill	microsft	netegrit	var	var	var	var	var
1	01/01/98	980.28	5.04	37.2969	1.0417					
2	02/01/98	1049.34	5.09	42.3750	1.1667					
3	03/01/98	1101.75	5.03	44.7500	1.2917					
4	04/01/98	1111.75	4.95	45.0625	1.4583					
5	05/01/98	1090.82	5.00	42.4062	1.4375					
6	06/01/98	1133.84	4.98	54.1875	1.6875					
7	07/01/98	1120.67	4.96	54.9688	2.0000					
8	08/01/98	957.28	4.90	47.9688	1.2500					
9	09/01/98	1017.01	4.61	55.0312	1.0417					
10	10/01/98	1098.67	3.96	52.9375	1.0000					
11	11/01/98	1163.63	4.41	61.0000	2.3333					
12	12/01/98	1229.23	4.39	69.3438	2.8750					
13	01/01/99	1279.64	4.34	87.5000	4.5833					
14	02/01/99	1238.33	4.44	75.0625	4.1667					
15	03/01/99	1286.37	4.44	89.6250	7.4583					
16	04/01/99	1335.18	4.29	81.3125	10.0000					
17	05/01/99	1301.84	4.50	80.6875	8.0833					
18	06/01/99	1372.71	4.57	90.1875	11.0000					
19	07/01/99	1328.72	4.55	85.8125	14.0000					
20	08/01/99	1320.41	4.72	92.5625	14.8333					
21	09/01/99	1282.71	4.68	90.5625	16.2500					

To read the full description of each variable, click on the tab marked "Variable View" at the bottom of the SPSS "Data" window.

	Name	Type	Width	Decimals	Label	Values	Missing	Columns
1	date	Date	11	0	Date (month and year)	None	None	8
2	sp500	Numeric	11	2	S&P500 Index values	None	None	8
3	tbill	Numeric	11	2	Nominal T-Bill yield	None	None	8
4	microsft	Numeric	11	4	Microsoft's stock price	None	None	8
5	netegrit	Numeric	11	4	Netegrity's stock price	None	None	8
6								
7								
8								

Beta Data - 1 - SPSS Data Editor

File Edit View Data Transform Analyze Graphs Utilities Window Help

Data View / **Variable View** /

SPSS Processor is ready

start   PH-Book - 2 - Microso...   Beta Data - 1 - SPSS ...   1:11 PM

2.6.1 CALCULATING RETURNS

In a future chapter, we will want to compute "beta" for two stocks, Microsoft and Netegrity. Thus far, all we have in the dataset is the stock price for each firm. In order to calculate beta, we will need the return on both stocks as well as their excess returns.

Let's start by calculating the return on each stock, the S&P 500 Index, and the T-bill series. To calculate the return, we use the formula:

$$Return = \text{LN}(price_t \,/\, price_{t-1})$$

In words, this means that we will take the price this period (t) and divide it by the price from last period (t–1). Then, we will take the LN (natural log) of the result.

To do this in SPSS, go back to the data screen by clicking on the "Data View" tab at the bottom of your SPSS "Data" window.

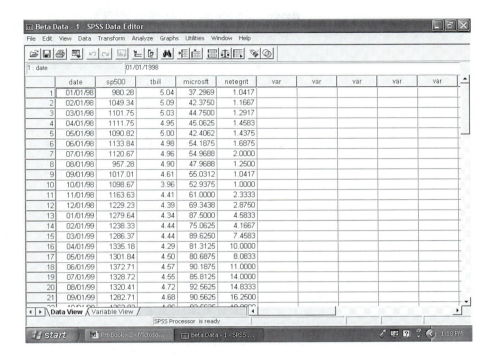

Select "Transform" and then "Compute."

You should now see this smaller window.

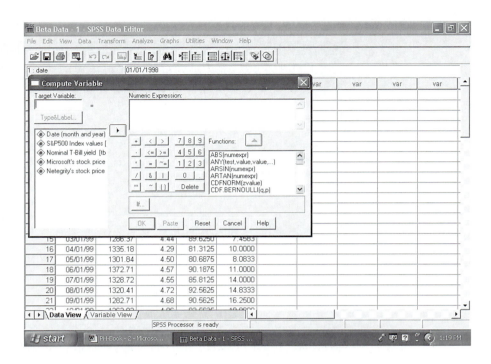

In the box marked "Target Variable," type in the new name for the variable you are about to create. Because we will calculate the return on the S&P 500, we will name the variable "rsp500." The "r" represents "return."

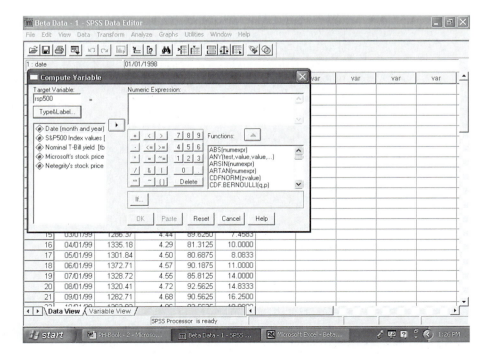

Now click on the button marked "Type&Label."

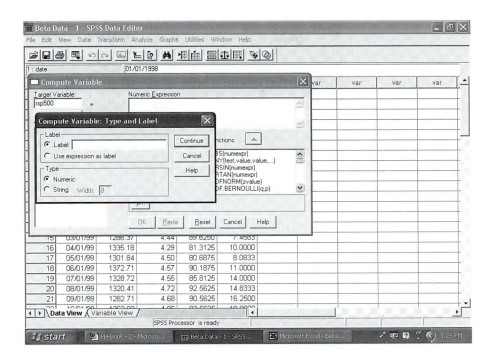

Type in the full description of the variable "rsp500" that we are about to create. Let's enter, "The return on the S&P 500 Index."

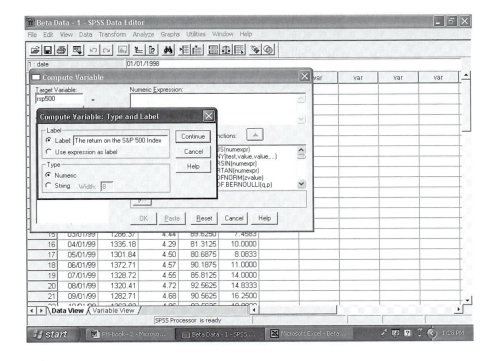

Click "Continue" to go back to the previous screen.

Under the box titled "Numeric Expression," we need to write the formula used to create this new variable. As previously discussed, the formula is given by

$$Return = \text{LN}(price_t / price_{t-1})$$

This means that we will take the price this period (t) and divide it by the price from the last period ($t-1$). Then, we will take the LN (natural log) of the result.

The "price this period (t)" is already a variable in the dataset. It is the existing variable "sp500." The formula states that we will also need this variable from the "last period." In finance, we refer to this as the "first LAG in the series." If we were looking for ($t-2$), it would be the second lag in the series, and so forth.

In SPSS, we will express the right-hand side of the equation as

$$\text{LN}(sp500 / LAG(sp500))$$

The steps involved in creating this equation are as follows.

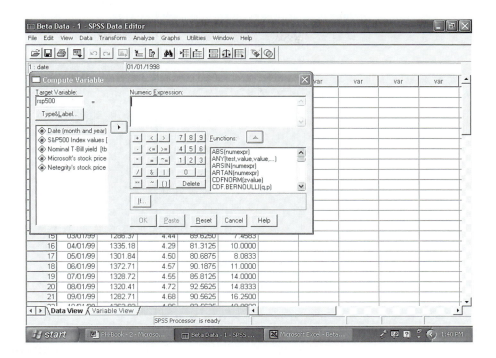

From the SPSS "Compute Variable" screen, type in the equation directly (manually) and click "OK." Alternatively, you can scroll down inside the box labeled "Functions" until you reach the function "LN(numexpr)."

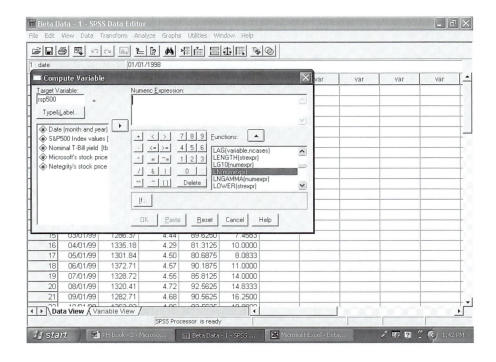

Select "LN(numexpr)" by double-clicking it. Alternatively, you can single-click on it, then click on the "up arrow" button to move it to the "Numeric Expression" box. Either way, your screen should look like this.

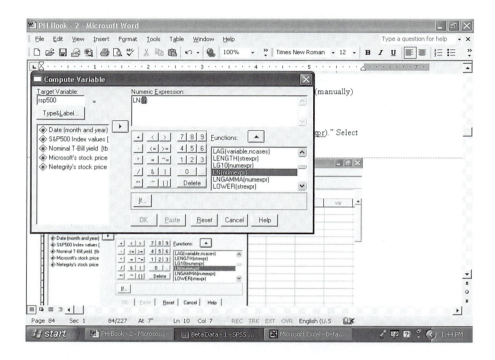

In the "Numeric Expression" box, you will notice a "?" inside the parentheses. SPSS is waiting for you to tell it what to take the natural log (LN) of. Again, you can either type in the variable "sp500" or you can highlight it in the list (in the lower-left-hand box) and then click the "right arrow" button to put it in the expression.

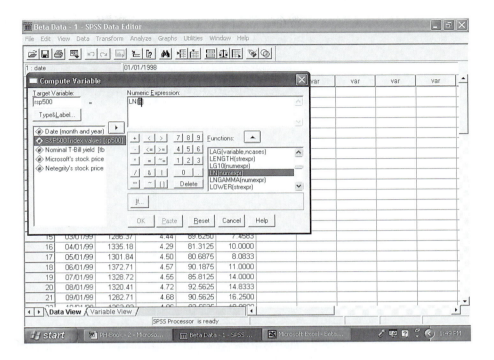

You can even simply double-click on the variable "sp500." Any way you do it, your screen will appear as follows.

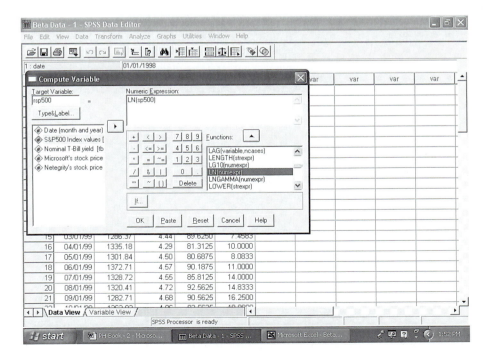

Now that we have the price at time t, we need to divide it by the price in time, $t - 1$. That is, we need to divide it by the *LAG* of the variable "sp500." To do this, click on the calculator's "divide" button. You should see the division sign appear in the box marked "Numeric Expression."

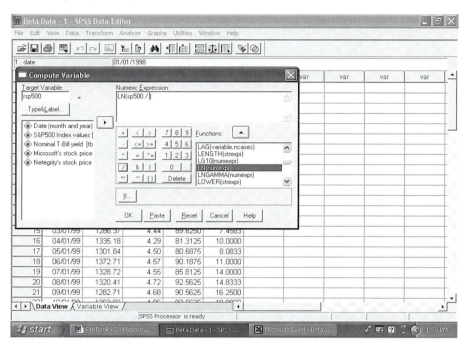

We just need to include the last term, "LAG(sp500)." Using the scroll bar under the "Function" box, select "LAG(variable)" by double-clicking on it.

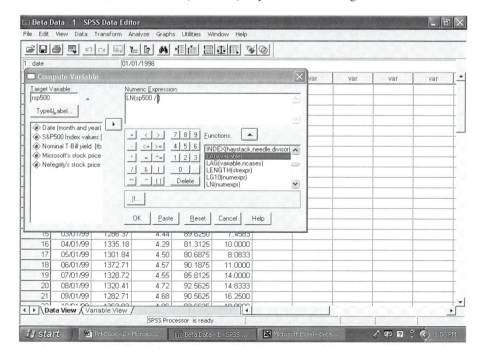

You will see that it now appears in the box "Numeric Expression."

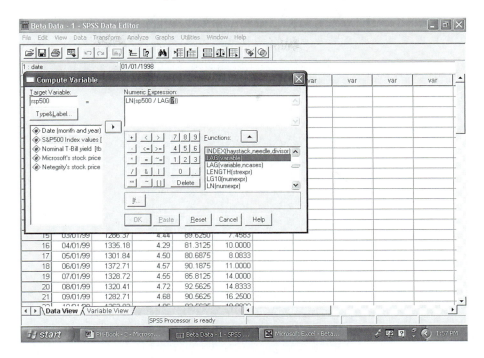

Again, the "?" is how SPSS asks which variable should be lagged. Select the variable "sp500" the same way you did before.

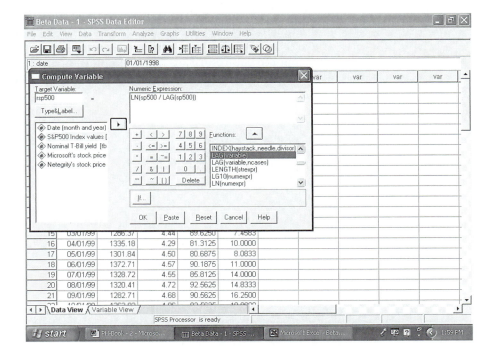

When you are done, click "OK."

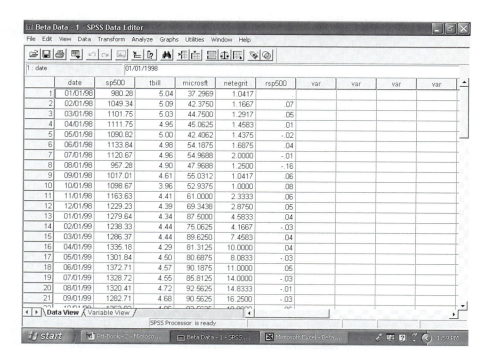

You should now see the newly created variable "rsp500." Notice that the series begins in the second row. This is correct because when you use the first lag, you lose the first observation in the series. Accordingly, if you used a lag of "2," you would have lost the first two observations in the series, and so forth.

Let's compute the return on the remaining three series. You can use the long method as previously explained or the shorter way demonstrated here. These steps will be done for the variable "tbill."

From the SPSS "Data" window, click "Transform" and then "Compute."

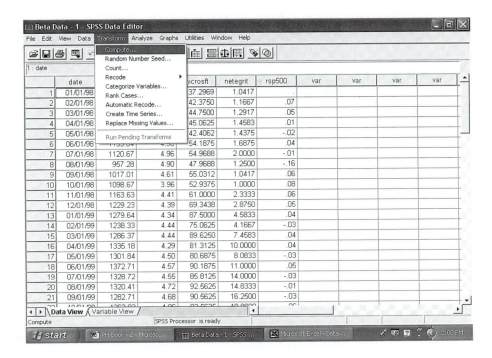

You will see the "Compute Variable" window.

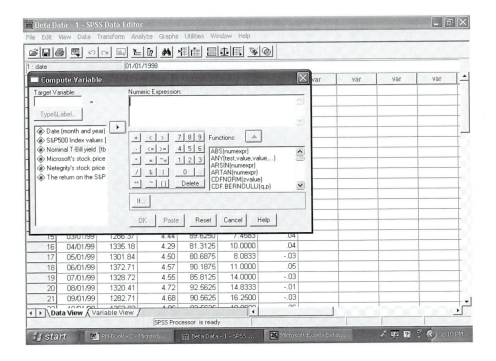

Under the box "Target Variable," type in the name "rtbill." Under the "Numeric Expression" box, type "LN(tbill / LAG(tbill))."

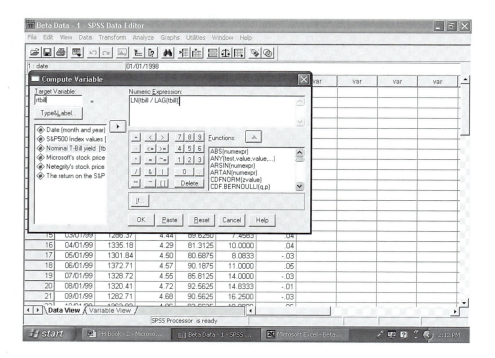

Now click "OK" to create the variable.

	date	sp500	tbill	microsft	netegrit	rsp500	rtbill	var	var	var	
1	01/01/98	980.28	5.04	37.2969	1.0417	.	.				
2	02/01/98	1049.34	5.09	42.3750	1.1667	.07	.01				
3	03/01/98	1101.75	5.03	44.7500	1.2917	.05	-.01				
4	04/01/98	1111.75	4.95	45.0625	1.4583	.01	-.02				
5	05/01/98	1090.82	5.00	42.4062	1.4375	-.02	.01				
6	06/01/98	1133.84	4.98	54.1875	1.6875	.04	.00				
7	07/01/98	1120.67	4.96	54.9688	2.0000	-.01	.00				
8	08/01/98	957.28	4.90	47.9688	1.2500	-.16	-.01				
9	09/01/98	1017.01	4.61	55.0312	1.0417	.06	-.06				
10	10/01/98	1098.67	3.96	52.9375	1.0000	.08	-.15				
11	11/01/98	1163.63	4.41	61.0000	2.3333	.06	.11				
12	12/01/98	1229.23	4.39	69.3438	2.8750	.05	.00				
13	01/01/99	1279.64	4.34	87.5000	4.5833	.04	-.01				
14	02/01/99	1238.33	4.44	75.0625	4.1667	-.03	.02				
15	03/01/99	1286.37	4.44	89.6250	7.4583	.04	.00				
16	04/01/99	1335.18	4.29	81.3125	10.0000	.04	-.03				
17	05/01/99	1301.84	4.50	80.6875	8.0833	-.03	.05				
18	06/01/99	1372.71	4.57	90.1875	11.0000	.05	.02				
19	07/01/99	1328.72	4.55	85.8125	14.0000	-.03	.00				
20	08/01/99	1320.41	4.72	92.5625	14.8333	-.01	.04				
21	09/01/99	1282.71	4.68	90.5625	16.2500	-.03	-.01				

This process should not take more than 30 seconds. It just seemed to take a long time because I explained how to do it using the "Functions" and "Calculator" buttons. After you repeat this process for the two stocks, your screen will look like this.

	date	sp500	tbill	microsft	netegrit	rsp500	rtbill	rmicrosf	rnetegr	var
1	01/01/98	980.28	5.04	37.2969	1.0417	.	.	.	.	
2	02/01/98	1049.34	5.09	42.3750	1.1667	.07	.01	.13	.11	
3	03/01/98	1101.75	5.03	44.7500	1.2917	.05	-.01	.05	.10	
4	04/01/98	1111.75	4.95	45.0625	1.4583	.01	-.02	.01	.12	
5	05/01/98	1090.82	5.00	42.4062	1.4375	-.02	.01	-.06	-.01	
6	06/01/98	1133.84	4.98	54.1875	1.6875	.04	.00	.25	.16	
7	07/01/98	1120.67	4.96	54.9688	2.0000	-.01	.00	.01	.17	
8	08/01/98	957.28	4.90	47.9688	1.2500	-.16	-.01	-.14	-.47	
9	09/01/98	1017.01	4.61	55.0312	1.0417	.06	-.06	.14	-.18	
10	10/01/98	1098.67	3.96	52.9375	1.0000	.08	-.15	-.04	-.04	
11	11/01/98	1163.63	4.41	61.0000	2.3333	.06	.11	.14	.85	
12	12/01/98	1229.23	4.39	69.3438	2.8750	.05	.00	.13	.21	
13	01/01/99	1279.64	4.34	87.5000	4.5833	.04	-.01	.23	.47	
14	02/01/99	1238.33	4.44	75.0625	4.1667	-.03	.02	-.15	-.10	
15	03/01/99	1286.37	4.44	89.6250	7.4583	.04	.00	.18	.58	
16	04/01/99	1335.18	4.29	81.3125	10.0000	.04	-.03	-.10	.29	
17	05/01/99	1301.84	4.50	80.6875	8.0833	-.03	.05	-.01	-.21	
18	06/01/99	1372.71	4.57	90.1875	11.0000	.05	.02	.11	.31	
19	07/01/99	1328.72	4.55	85.8125	14.0000	-.03	.00	-.05	.24	
20	08/01/99	1320.41	4.72	92.5625	14.8333	-.01	.04	.08	.06	
21	09/01/99	1282.71	4.68	90.5625	16.2500	-.03	-.01	-.02	.09	

You have just calculated the return on the four series.

2.6.2 CALCULATING EXCESS RETURNS

In the calculation of beta, it is necessary to calculate the excess return on a stock. Excess return is defined as the return in "excess" of the risk-free rate. The risk-free rate of return is approximated by the return on a 3-month T-bill. Therefore, the excess return on Microsoft is equal to the return on Microsoft minus the return on the 3-month T-bill.

This simple calculation can be expressed generically as follows:

$$Excess\ Return\ (Stock\ i) = Return\ (Stock\ i) - Return\ (T\text{-}bill)$$

We generically refer to stock "*i*," because the formula can apply to any stock. For Microsoft, we could specifically write:

$$Excess\ Return\ (Microsoft) = Return\ (Microsoft) - Return\ (T\text{-}bill)$$

This is a very simple computation in SPSS. From the SPSS "Data" window, click "Transform" and then "Compute."

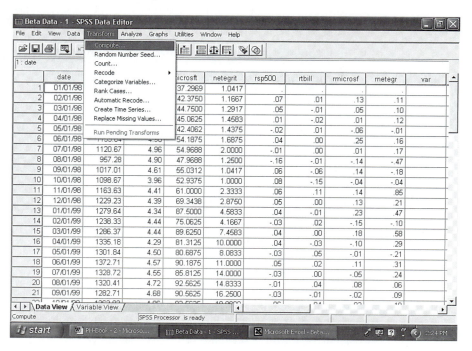

The "Compute Variable" window will appear.

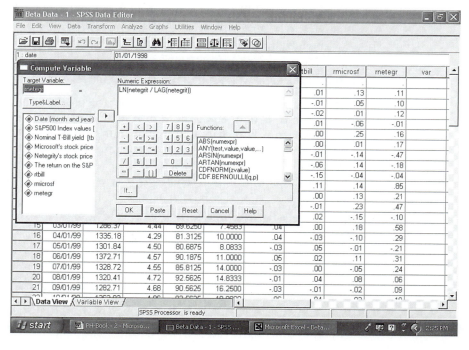

You will notice that it still contains all the inputs from our previous calculation. Usually, this is convenient, so we do not have to retype all the formulas. However, because we are changing the calculations, it is easier to start with a fresh screen. To start the screen over, click the "Reset" button.

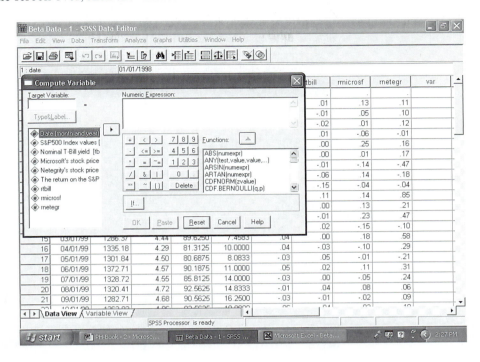

To calculate the excess return on Microsoft, we simply need to subtract the return on the T-bill from the return on Microsoft. To do this, double-click on the variable "rmicrosf" to get it into the "Numeric Expression" box.

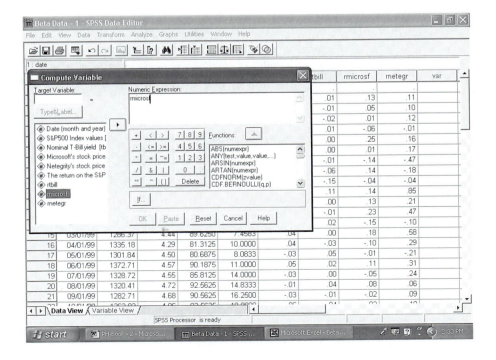

Now either type in the subtract sign or use the visual calculator on the screen and click the subtract symbol.

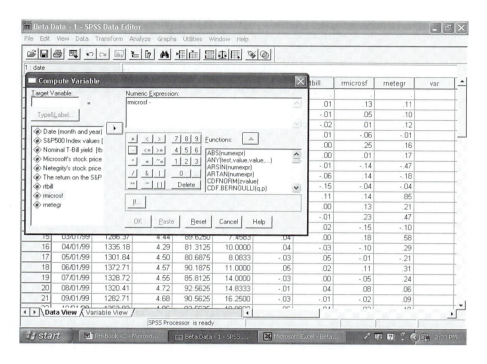

Complete the expression by selecting the variable "rtbill." After double-clicking it, your screen should look like this.

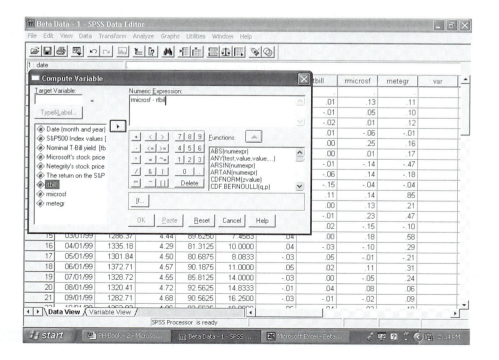

The final step is to name the new variable. Call it "ermicro," where the letters "er" stand for "excess return."

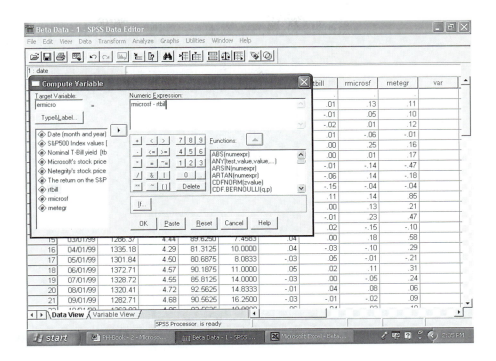

Click "OK" and you should see the SPSS "Data" window containing your new variable.

	date	sp500	tbill	microsft	netegrit	rsp500	rtbill	rmicrosf	rnetegr	ermicro
1		980.28	5.04	37.2969	1.0417					
2	02/01/98	1049.34	5.09	42.3750	1.1667	.07	.01	.13	.11	.12
3	03/01/98	1101.75	5.03	44.7500	1.2917	.05	-.01	.05	.10	.07
4	04/01/98	1111.75	4.95	45.0625	1.4583	.01	-.02	.01	.12	.02
5	05/01/98	1090.82	5.00	42.4062	1.4375	-.02	.01	-.06	-.01	-.07
6	06/01/98	1133.84	4.98	54.1875	1.6875	.04	.00	.25	.16	.25
7	07/01/98	1120.67	4.96	54.9688	2.0000	-.01	.00	.01	.17	.02
8	08/01/98	957.28	4.90	47.9688	1.2500	-.16	-.01	-.14	-.47	-.12
9	09/01/98	1017.01	4.61	55.0312	1.0417	.06	-.06	.14	-.18	.20
10	10/01/98	1098.67	3.96	52.9375	1.0000	.08	-.15	-.04	-.04	.11
11	11/01/98	1163.63	4.41	61.0000	2.3333	.06	.11	.14	.85	.03
12	12/01/98	1229.23	4.39	69.3438	2.8750	.05	.00	.13	.21	.13
13	01/01/99	1279.64	4.34	87.5000	4.5833	.04	-.01	.23	.47	.24
14	02/01/99	1238.33	4.44	75.0625	4.1667	-.03	.02	-.15	-.10	-.18
15	03/01/99	1286.37	4.44	89.6250	7.4583	.04	.00	.18	.58	.18
16	04/01/99	1335.18	4.29	81.3125	10.0000	.04	-.03	-.10	.29	-.06
17	05/01/99	1301.84	4.50	80.6875	8.0833	-.03	.05	-.01	-.21	-.06
18	06/01/99	1372.71	4.57	90.1875	11.0000	.05	.02	.11	.31	.10
19	07/01/99	1328.72	4.55	85.8125	14.0000	-.03	.00	-.05	.24	-.05
20	08/01/99	1320.41	4.72	92.5625	14.8333	-.01	.04	.08	.06	.04
21	09/01/99	1282.71	4.68	90.5625	16.2500	-.03	-.01	-.02	.09	-.01

You should repeat this process for the S&P 500 Index as well as for the stock, Netegrity. After doing so, your screen will look like this.

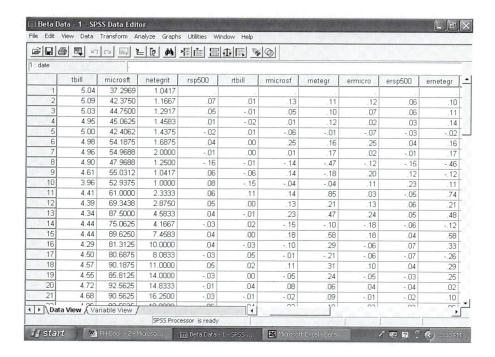

You have now calculated the excess return for three series.

2.6.3 TYING UP LOOSE ENDS: LABELS AND DECIMAL POINTS

To generate professional looking tables, you should go back and clean up your labels and decimal points to make sure they are presented in a clear and logical fashion. For example, when we referred to the stock prices for Microsoft, we titled the series "microsft." We had to leave out the second "o" because in SPSS, we are only allowed to have a title that is eight characters long. Then, when we calculated the return on Microsoft, we put an "r" in front, which meant we had to leave out another letter. We did our best and called the variable "rmicrosf." Finally, when we calculated the excess return, we added another letter to the front, which meant that some other letter had to go. We called our new variable "ermicro."

The purpose of naming variables is so that you (or the reader of your research) can quickly determine from the variable title what the variable represents. The names "microsft," "rmicrosf," and "ermicro" might be more user friendly if written as "micro," "r_micro," and "er_micro." This way of naming the series shows consistency. Moreover, it is easier to see what is different about each variable because the prefix is clearly separated from the rest of the name by an underscore.

Many researchers using SPSS find that it is faster to adjust the names of the series after all variables have been created. By waiting until the end, you are better able to create appropriate names, because only then are you aware of all the variables that will exist. The same can be said for providing labels for your variables.

Let's change our variable names and labels.

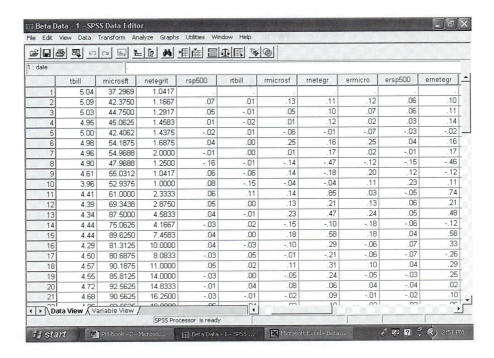

From the SPSS "Data" screen, click on the tab "Variable View" at the bottom of the window.

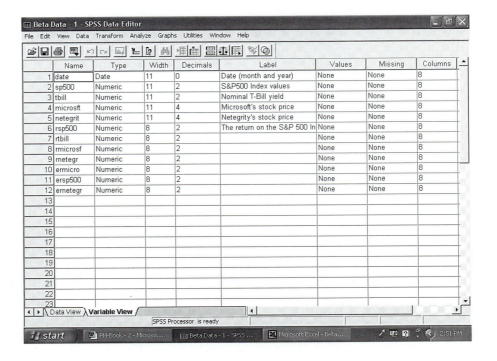

To change a variable name, just double-click on the cell.

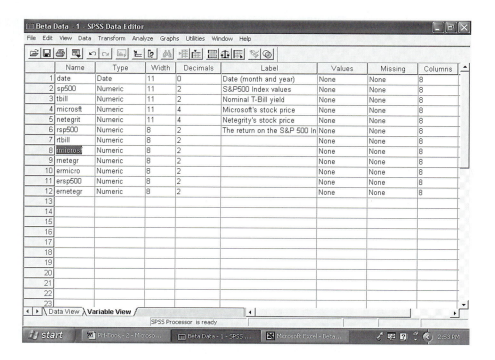

Type the new name. After you are done, just click on the next variable and repeat the process. Do this for all your variables.

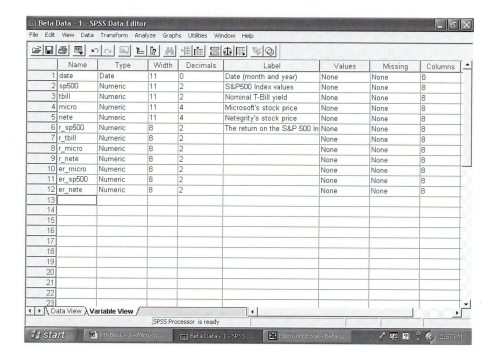

Notice that the "Label" column is not complete. Being consistent, type the labels as you want them to appear in your output. Do this for all the variables.

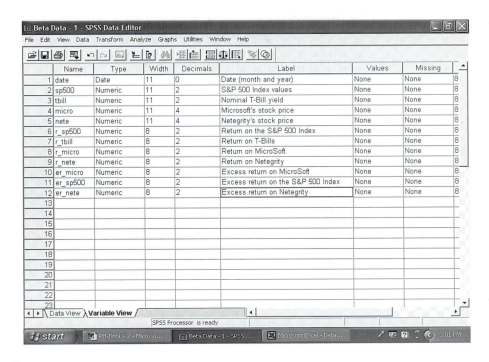

As a final step, you may want to see more than just two decimal places for each variable. To see more decimal places, simply click on the cell you want to change.

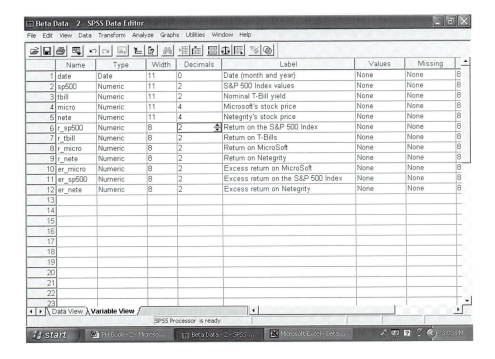

An "up and down" arrow will appear. Use the arrow to change the number of decimal places to whatever you want.

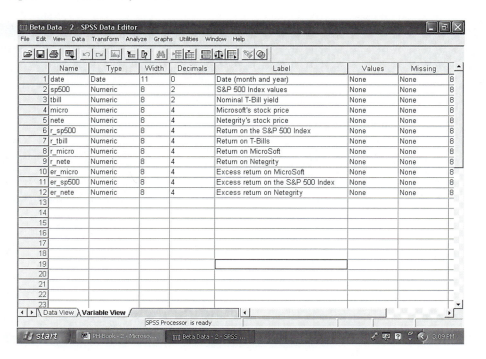

3

CORRELATION

3.1 PURPOSE OF A CORRELATION TEST

Correlation measures the degree to which two variables are associated with or relate to each other. However, correlation does not provide a test of "cause and effect." For example, even though there is a significant historical positive correlation between the NFC (National Football Conference) winning the Super Bowl and the stock market increasing in value, one clearly has nothing to do with the other. If you consider the thousands upon thousands of variables in existence, it is not surprising that there are significant correlations that are spurious (i.e., those that occur by chance and have no theoretical foundation). In fact, with all the data out there, it would be next to impossible not to find significant correlations that lack a cause-and-effect relationship.

A more useful (and theoretically grounded) application of correlation would be to examine the relationship between consumer sentiment and retail sales. However, even if you find a significant correlation, it does not mean that one variable necessarily caused the other. More advanced tests would be needed to confirm the relationship. In short, correlation simply measures the degree of association.

A correlation coefficient can take on any value between and including –1 and +1. A value of "–1" means that the two variables move in the opposite direction by the exact same magnitude. A correlation coefficient of "+1" means that the two variables move in the same direction by the exact same amount. These are the two extreme cases. In the middle is the case where the correlation coefficient is equal to "0." In this situation, the two variables move independently from one another. That is, if I tell you how one variable moves, it does not help you determine the direction or magnitude of the other.

To illustrate the concept of correlation, we will refer to the dataset "Home Values - 1." "Home Values - 1" contains cross-sectional data relating to home (residential property) attributes for 1,172 properties located in Cuyahoga County, Ohio.

3.2 PERFORMING A CORRELATION WITH METRIC VARIABLES

Recall from Chapter 1, "Understanding Your Data," that metric variables include both continuous (ratio) and interval data. When you perform a correlation test with two metric variables, the appropriate correlation measure is the Pearson's Product Moment Correlation.

To open the "Home Values - 1" file in SPSS, click "File" and then "Open" or simply click on the "Open File" icon. Then select the file "Home Values - 1" by double-clicking on it.

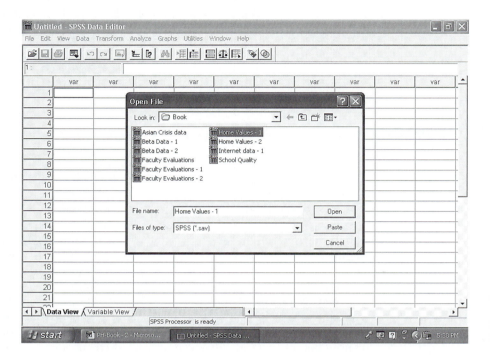

You should now see the data in SPSS.

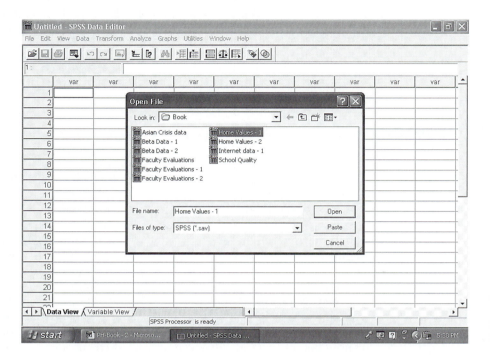

To perform the Pearson's Product Moment Correlation, click "Analyze," "Correlate," and then "Bivariate."

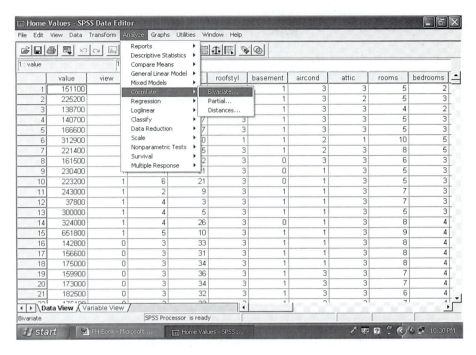

The "Bivariate Correlations" screen will appear.

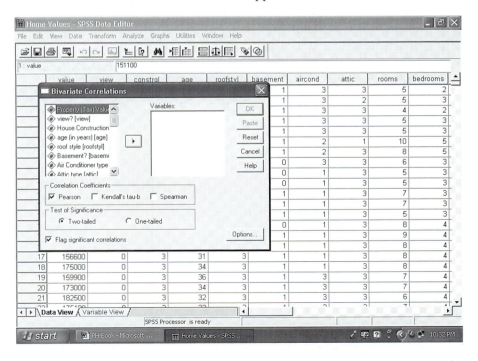

Under the "Correlation Coefficients" section in the "Bivariate Correlations" window, the "Pearson" box is already checked. All you have to do is select the two variables you want to test. Let's select the variables "Property (Tax) Value [value]" and "Square footage of house [homesqft]" by highlighting them and clicking the arrow button to move them over to the box on the right.

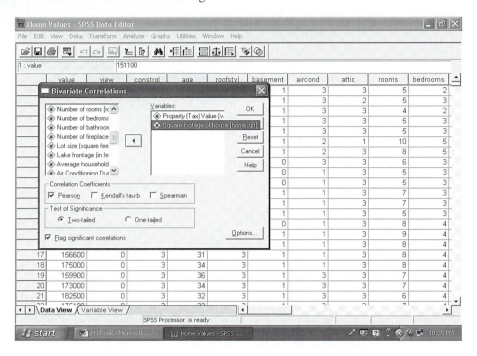

With this action, we are testing the association between the size of a home (as measured by square footage) and the value of a home. Click "OK." The results are shown automatically in the newly created SPSS "Output" window.

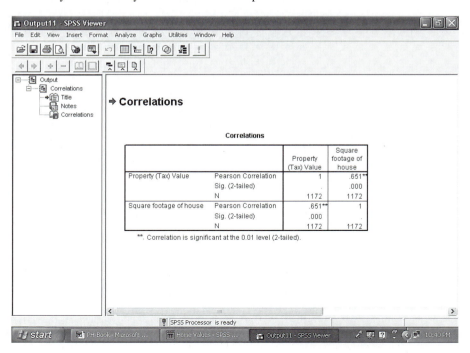

From the output, we see that the Pearson's Product Moment Correlation Coefficient is .651. The associated "Sig." value of .000 indicates that the results are significant beyond the 99% (or alternatively, .01) level. Another way to identify the significance of the results is to notice the two "**" marks next to the .651 value. The footnote below the table indicates that this means the results are significant at the .01 level.

This correlation test simply confirms an association between the size of the home and the value of the home. It does not allow you to reach the conclusion that a larger home causes the price to be higher. At the same time, it certainly does not imply that size does not affect home value. It simply measures the degree of association. If you want to determine if a cause-and-effect relationship exists, more advanced tests are needed. These tests will be discussed in future chapters.

3.3 PERFORMING A CORRELATION WITH NONMETRIC VARIABLES

Recall from Chapter 1 that nonmetric variables include both ordinal and nominal data. In order to perform a correlation test on nonmetric data, at least one of the variables must be nonmetric. For this example, consider the variables "House Construction Quality [constrql]" and "Air Conditioner Type [aircond]."

"House Construction Quality [constrql]" rates how well the home is built on a scale from 1 (lowest quality) to 6 (highest quality). "Air Conditioner Type [aircond]" contains three levels of progressive categories. A value of "1" means that the home has no air conditioner. A "2" indicates the presence of a window unit (better than no air-conditioning, but not as good as central air-conditioning). Finally, a value of "3" means that the home has central air.

To perform this test, you will begin the procedure the same way as you did with the Pearson's measure. Click "Analyze," "Correlate," and then "Bivariate."

You will arrive at the "Bivariate Correlations" screen.

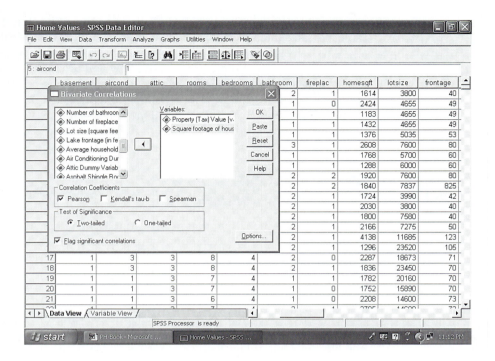

Notice that the procedure is set up to do the previous test. This is a useful default in SPSS, because researchers will often run several variations of a procedure over and over again. This default allows them to save time and prevent mistakes by not requiring them to set up the window from scratch every time.

In our case, we do not want to run the same test, nor do we want to include the same variables. Therefore, it is easier for us to start over. To do so, simply click the "Reset" button to clear the screen and start with a fresh blank screen.

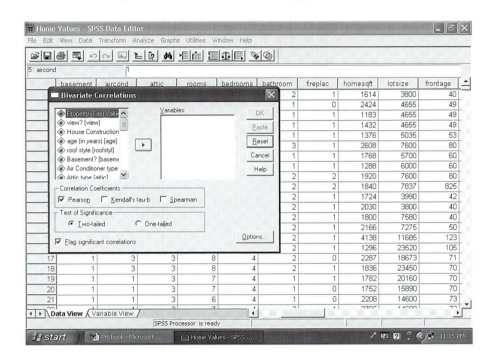

Start the procedure by selecting the two variables of interest. That is, highlight the variables and move them into the box to the right.

We must now decide which correlation coefficient to select. Because at least one of the variables is nonmetric, the parametric test, Pearson's Product Moment Correlation, is inappropriate. Instead, two nonparametric tests can be used. When a large number of observations fall into a small number of categories (thereby resulting in a large percentage of ties), a Kendall's tau-b is preferred. Otherwise, Spearman's rho should be used. If you want to focus on this distinction, you can examine the clustering of the data by clicking "Analyze," "Descriptive Statistics," and then "Crosstabs." However, to save time, you may want to consider running both tests. Only if the tests reach a different conclusion is it necessary to take the time to examine clustering. In most cases, you will find that the two tests generate very similar results.

To select both tests, simply click on the boxes next to "Kendall's tau-b" and "Spearman." Be sure to uncheck the "Pearson" box, because this test is not appropriate for our data.

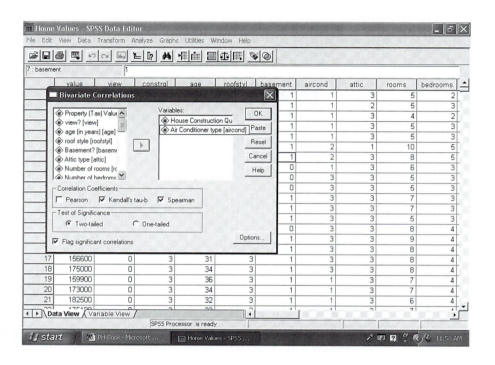

Click "OK" and the following SPSS "Output" window will appear.

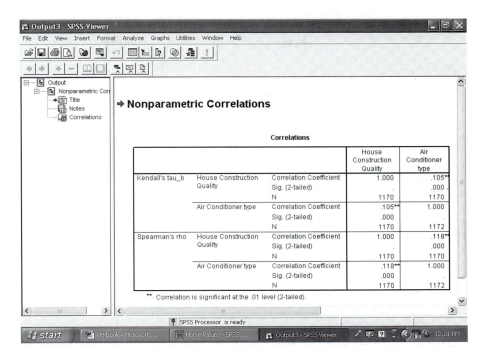

The interpretation of the results is the same as that for the Pearson's test. In our example, both the "Kendall's tau-b" and the "Spearman's rho" conclude that the two variables are significantly correlated (beyond the .01 level), as indicated by the "Sig." values.

4

AUTOCORRELATION

4.1 PURPOSE OF AN AUTOCORRELATION TEST

Correlation measures the degree to which two *different* series move relative to each other over time. Autocorrelation measures the degree to which a *single* series moves relative to its own lagged values over time.

First-order autocorrelation is defined as the degree of correlation between adjacent data values. Stated another way, it is the correlation coefficient when the same time series is measured against its own values that are lagged by exactly one period.

Accordingly, a second-order autocorrelation coefficient measures the correlation between the series' values and those lagged by exactly two periods. A third-order autocorrelation coefficient measures the correlation between series' values and those lagged by exactly three periods, and so forth.

There are several reasons why a researcher might want to measure autocorrelation in a time series. If autocorrelation is present, a future series can be successfully predicted using the recent past as explanatory variables. Moreover, knowing if autocorrelation exists will help you specify a model when performing more advanced tests such as ARCH/GARCH.

To demonstrate the autocorrelation test, we will use the dataset "Internet Data - 1." This dataset contains time series data on the yield on Aaa rated corporate bonds, Baa rated corporate bonds, 3-month Treasury Bills, 30-year Treasury Bonds, and the Consumer Price Index (CPI) from February 1977 through December 2001.

4.2 PERFORMING AN AUTOCORRELATION TEST

To open the "Internet Data - 1" file in SPSS, click "File" and then "Open" or simply click on the "Open File" icon. Then select the file "Internet Data - 1" by double-clicking on it.

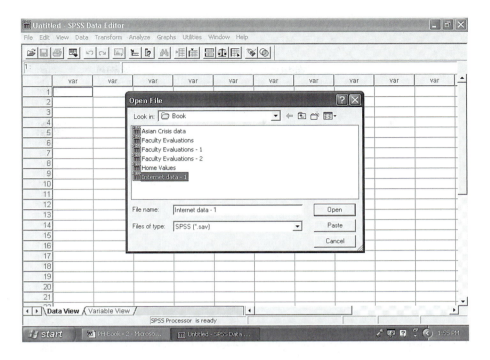

The SPSS "Data" screen will appear.

We will work with the series "tbill," which measures the nominal yield on a 3-month Treasury Bill for each month from February 1977 through December 2001.

To perform the test for autocorrelation, click "Graphs," "Time Series," and then "Autocorrelations."

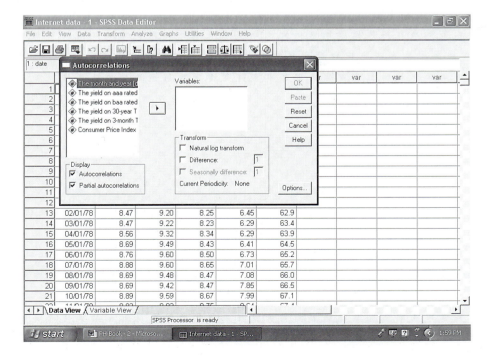

The "Autocorrelations" menu will pop up. Select the variable "the yield on 3-month Treasury Bills [tbill]" by double-clicking on it. Alternatively, you can single-click on it, then click on the right arrow button to move the variable into the box on the right labeled "Variables."

Your screen will appear as follows.

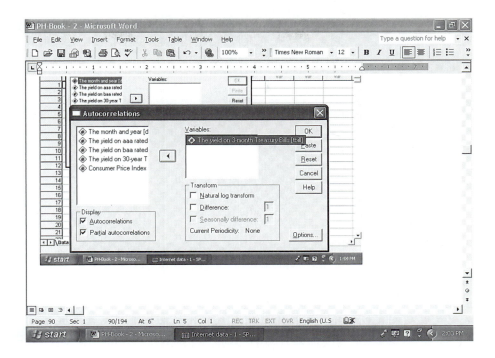

You only want to perform the autocorrelation test, so uncheck the box marked "Partial autocorrelations" by clicking on it.

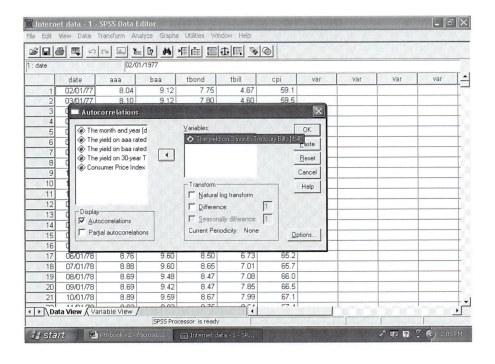

Click "OK" to perform the test.

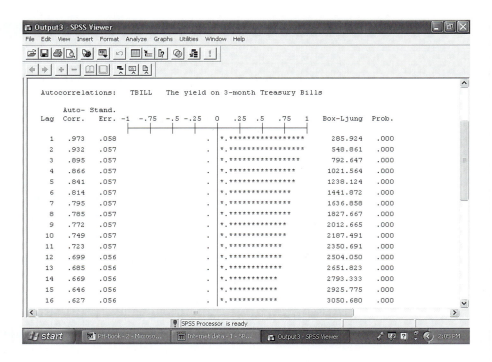

SPSS automatically uses 16 lagged values as the default. To determine if these lags are statistically significant, look at the "Prob." values associated with the "Box-Ljung" statistics. Because the "Prob." values are all below .01, the results are significant. That is, this series exhibits autocorrelation.

SPSS also presents the results visually. If you scroll down the SPSS "Output" screen, you will see the following graph.

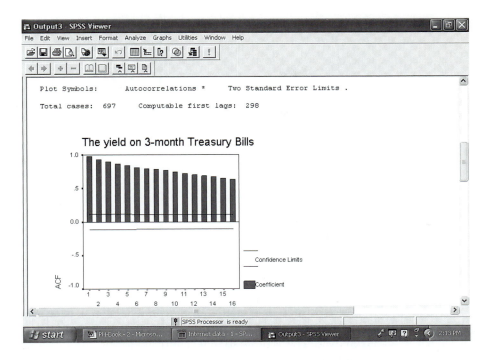

The two horizontal bars surrounding the "0.0" line represent confidence intervals. If the red bars stay within those two lines, autocorrelation is not present. In our example, you can clearly see that autocorrelation is present.

Autocorrelation can also be checked qualitatively. For example, if you plot the actual index (on the abscissa) against the same index with a one-period lag (on the ordinate), a straight line will result if the series is associated with perfect autocorrelation ($\rho = 1$). The less linear the plot, the less plagued are the data with autocorrelation. You can do this at any lag you wish. However, because this process is time-consuming and the results subjective, you should use the quantitative approach presented instead.

5

PARTIAL AUTOCORRELATION

———❧❧❧———

5.1 PURPOSE OF A PARTIAL AUTOCORRELATION TEST

An interesting extension of the autocorrelation analysis is the examination of partial autocorrelation coefficients. When first-order autocorrelation is present, the second-order coefficient also tends to be statistically significant. In order to remove the effects of lower-order coefficients, partial autocorrelation coefficients should be calculated. A partial autocorrelation coefficient analyzes correlation with lower-order effects removed. This is done so that significant lower-order coefficients cannot inflate higher-order coefficients.

Just to make sure this explanation is clear, partial autocorrelation analysis examines second-order autocorrelation after first-order correlation has been removed from the series. Further, it examines third-order autocorrelation after first-order and second-order autocorrelation have been removed. Moreover, it examines fourth-order autocorrelation after first-order, second-order, and third-order autocorrelation have been removed, and so forth.

To demonstrate the autocorrelation test, we will use the file "Internet Data - 1." This dataset contains time series data on the yield on Aaa rated corporate bonds, Baa rated corporate bonds, 3-month Treasury Bills, 30-year Treasury Bonds, and the CPI from February 1977 through December 2001.

5.2 PERFORMING A PARTIAL AUTOCORRELATION TEST

To open the "Internet Data - 1" file in SPSS, click "File" and then "Open" or simply click on the "Open File" icon. Then select the file "Internet Data - 1" by double-clicking on it.

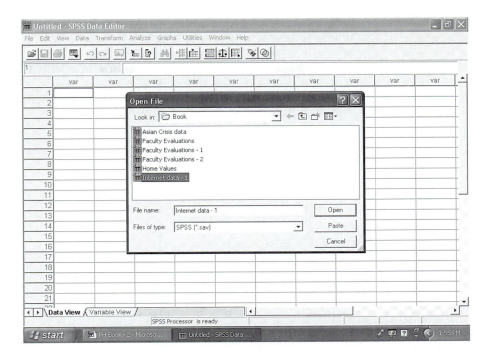

The SPSS "Data" screen will appear.

We will work with the series "tbill," which measures the nominal yield on a 3-month Treasury Bill for each month from February 1977 through December 2001.

To perform the test for autocorrelation, click "Graphs," "Time Series," and then "Autocorrelations."

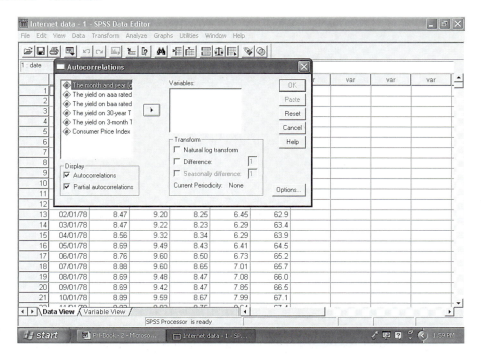

The "Autocorrelations" menu will appear. Select the variable "the yield on 3-month Treasury Bills [tbill]" by double-clicking on it. Alternatively, you can single-click on it, then click on the "right arrow" button to move the variable into the box on the right labeled "Variables."

Your screen will appear as follows.

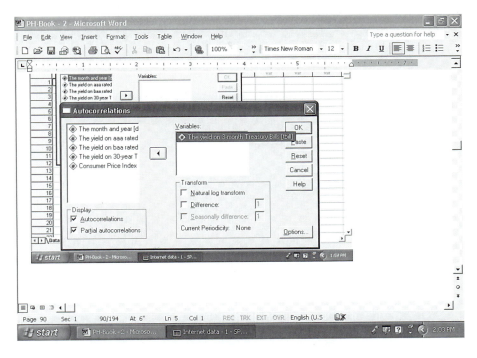

Because you only want to perform the partial autocorrelation test right now, check only the box marked "Partial autocorrelations." That is, be sure to deselect the box marked "Autocorrelations" if it is currently selected. Your screen should look like this.

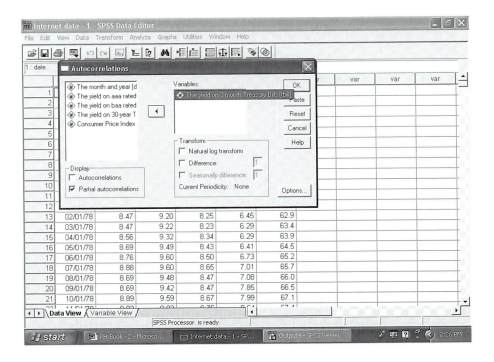

Click "OK" to perform the test. The SPSS "Output" window will appear.

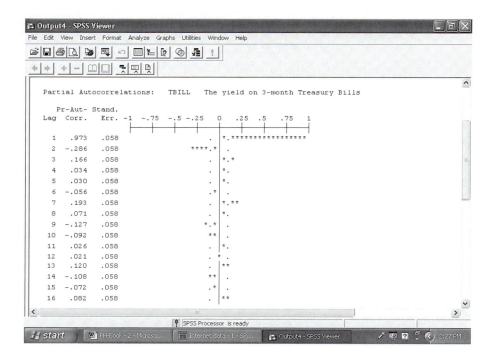

Graphically, the results are as follows.

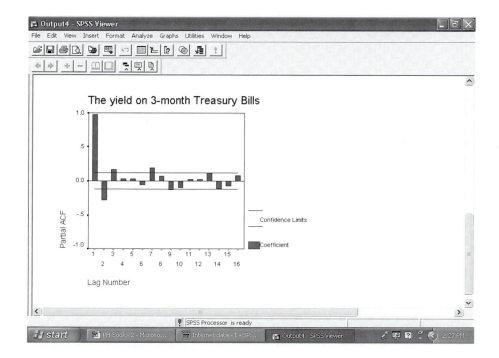

This graph shows the autocorrelation that exists after lower-order effects have been removed. Alternatively stated, it examines second-order autocorrelation after first-order correlation has been removed from the series. Further, it examines third-order autocorrelation after first-order and second-order autocorrelation have been removed, and so forth.

Because the red bars extend well beyond the horizontal confidence intervals, clearly the series "tbill" still exhibits autocorrelation even after the influencing effects of lower orders have been removed, particularly at the first three lags.

6

AUTOCORRELATION FOR NONPARAMETRIC DATA (WALD-WOLFOWITZ RUNS TEST)

6.1 PURPOSE OF A WALD-WOLFOWITZ RUNS TEST

The Wald-Wolfowitz Runs test is a nonparametric test for autocorrelation. It can be used to determine whether values in a time series affect subsequent values. This test defines a *run* as a sequence of like observations. Too many or too few runs indicate dependence among observations.

To illustrate the Wald-Wolfowitz Runs test, we will use the file "Internet Data - 1." This dataset contains time series data on the yield on Aaa rated corporate bonds, Baa rated corporate bonds, 3-month Treasury Bills, 30-year Treasury Bonds, and the CPI from February 1977 through December 2001.

6.2 PERFORMING A WALD-WOLFOWITZ RUNS TEST

To open the "Internet Data - 1" file in SPSS, click "File" and then "Open" or simply click on the "Open File" icon. Then select the file "Internet Data - 1" by double-clicking on it.

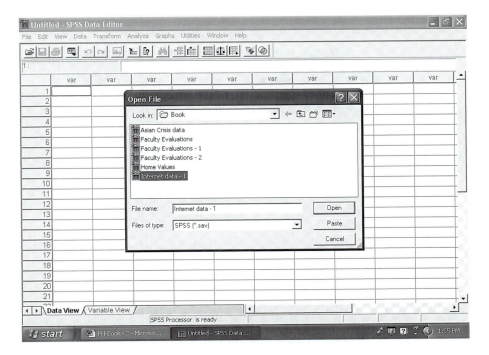

The SPSS "Data" screen will appear.

We will work with the series "tbill," which measures the nominal yield on a 3-month Treasury Bill for each month from February 1977 through December 2001.

To perform the test, click "Analyze," "Nonparametric Tests," and then "Runs."

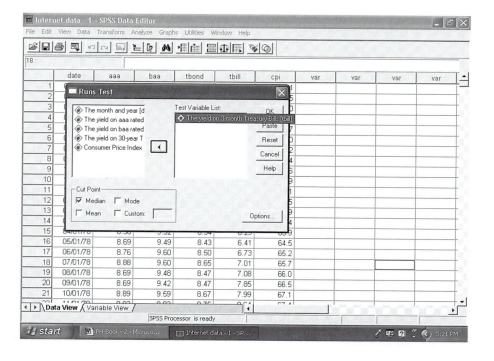

The "Runs Test" menu will pop up. Select the variable "the yield on 3-month Treasury Bills [tbill]" by double-clicking on it. Alternatively, you can single-click on the variable, and then click on the "right arrow" button to move the variable into the box on the right labeled "Test Variable List."

Click "OK." The SPSS "Output" window will appear.

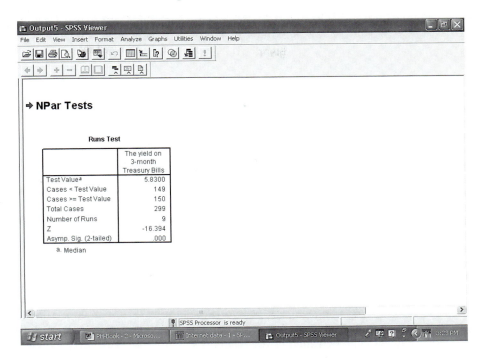

A run occurs when successive data points lie on the same side of the median (above or below). If the time series was random, you would expect there to be many runs, as observations would occur above, below, or on the median in no particular pattern. This is not what we observe here. Instead, we see that for the 299 observations, only nine runs occur. This means that when the series values are above the median, they tend to stay above the median. When they are below, they tend to stay below.

Another example of a run is the nominal yield on T-bills. The yield drifts over time due to the stable nature of the U.S. markets. For example, you would not likely observe the yield in January to be 4.36% and the yield in February to be 10.58%. Instead, the yields will stay almost the same from month to month and change will only occur gradually over time.

Getting back to our results, we want to know if nine runs are so few that we would conclude the series is autocorrelated. To make this assessment, consider the value for "Asymp. Sig. (2-tailed)." Because this number (.000) is below .01, we would conclude that the series is autocorrelated beyond the .01 level of significance.

7

T-TEST

7.1 PURPOSE OF A T-TEST

One of the most well-known statistical procedures is the t-test. A t-test is simply a test to determine if the means (averages) of two variables are significantly different from each other. The t-test has three common variations: one sample, independent samples, and paired samples. This chapter describes each type of t-test and demonstrates its use.

To demonstrate the first two types of t-tests, the one-sample t-test and the independent samples t-test, we will refer to the dataset "Home Values - 1." "Home Values - 1" contains cross-sectional data relating to home (residential property) attributes for 1,172 properties located in Cuyahoga County, Ohio. Although each variable discussed in this chapter will be explained in the text, additional information on each variable can be found in the Appendix.

To open the "Home Values - 1" file in SPSS, click "File" and then "Open" or simply click on the "Open File" icon. Then select the file "Home Values - 1" by double-clicking on it.

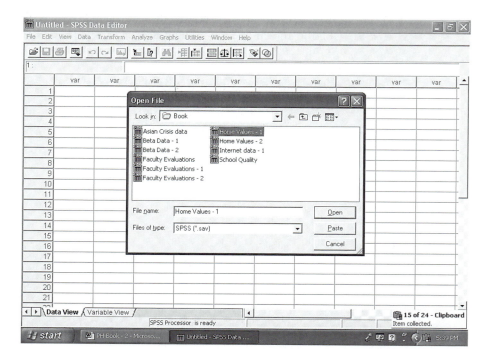

You should now see the data in SPSS.

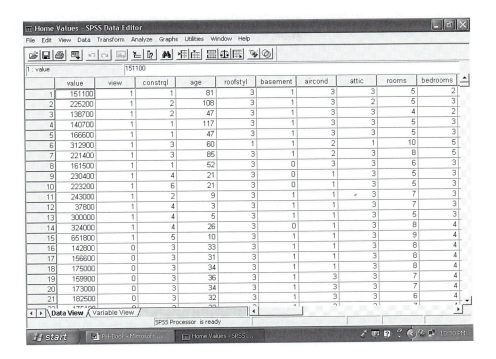

7.2 PERFORMING A ONE-SAMPLE T-TEST

As the name implies, with a one-sample t-test, only one variable is involved. The goal is to determine if the mean of that variable is significantly different from some fixed value (a constant).

To demonstrate the test, consider the variable "value," which represents the value of the homes in the sample. Let's perform an analysis to see if the average home value is significantly different from $200,000. To perform this test, click "Analyze," "Compare Means," and then "One-Sample T Test."

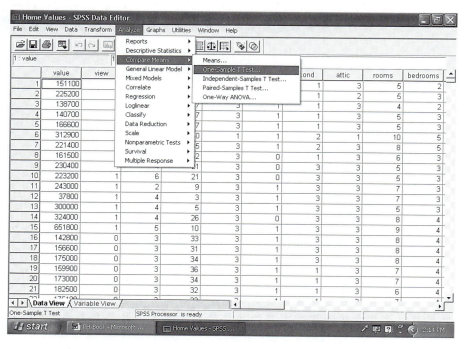

The "One-Sample T Test" screen will appear.

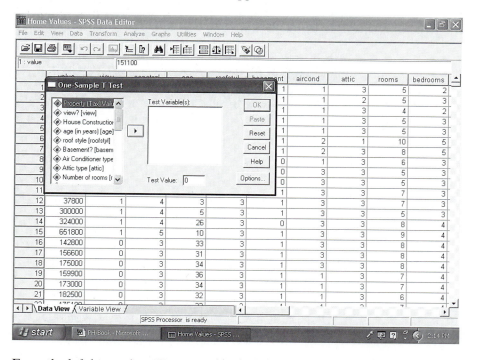

From the left box, select "Property (Tax) Value [value]" by double-clicking it or by single-clicking on it and then clicking on the "right arrow" button.

In the box labeled "Test Value," enter the number we are comparing the variable against. In our example, the number is "200000." Dollar signs and commas are not necessary. Notice that our number is so large we cannot see all of the digits at once. This is perfectly acceptable.

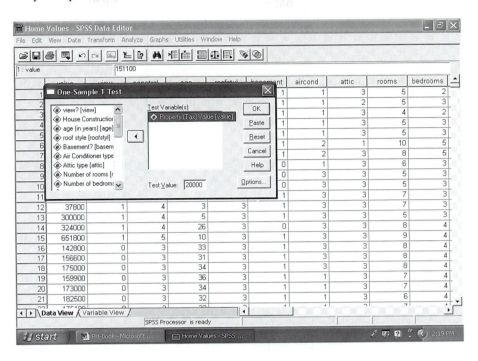

Click "OK." You will arrive at the following SPSS "Output" screen.

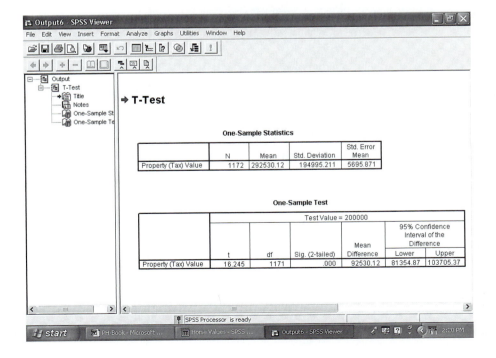

One-Sample Statistics

	N	Mean	Std. Deviation	Std. Error Mean
Property (Tax) Value	1172	292530.12	194995.211	5695.871

One-Sample Test

	Test Value = 200000					
					95% Confidence Interval of the Difference	
	t	df	Sig. (2-tailed)	Mean Difference	Lower	Upper
Property (Tax) Value	16.245	1171	.000	92530.12	81354.87	103705.37

The top box, "One-Sample Statistics," provides you with summary measures of the variable "Property (Tax) Value [value]." You can see that the mean of this variable is $292,530.12. Therefore, the test compares this amount to $200,000. The one-sample t-test will determine if the two values are significantly different from each other.

In the lower table, "One-Sample Test," find the letter "t" in the second column. This stands for the "t-statistic" associated with our test. In our example, the t-statistic is equal to 16.245. To know whether this is significant or not, simply look under the column with the heading "Sig. (2-tailed)." Because the number (.000) is below .01, the difference between the sample mean and $200,000 is significant at the .01 level.

To test the mean of the variable "Property (Tax) Value [value] against another value, simply enter a different "Test Value." For example, let's test whether or not the average value of homes in the sample is different from $282,000. To do so, click "Analyze," "Compare Means," and then "One-Sample T Test."

Home Values - SPSS Data Editor

File Edit View Data Transform Analyze Graphs Utilities Window Help

Analyze menu: Reports ▶ | Descriptive Statistics ▶ | Compare Means ▶ | General Linear Model ▶ | Mixed Models ▶ | Correlate ▶ | Regression ▶ | Loglinear ▶ | Classify ▶ | Data Reduction ▶ | Scale ▶ | Nonparametric Tests ▶ | Survival ▶ | Multiple Response ▶

Compare Means submenu: Means... | One-Sample T Test... | Independent-Samples T Test... | Paired-Samples T Test... | One-Way ANOVA...

	value	view				ond	attic	rooms	bedrooms
1	151100					1	3	5	2
2	225200					1	2	5	3
3	138700					1	3	4	2
4	140700		7		3	1	1	3	5	3
5	166600		7		3	1	1	3	5	3
6	312900		0		1	1	2	1	10	5
7	221400		5		3	1	2	3	8	5
8	161500		2		3	0	1	3	6	3
9	230400		1		3	0	3	3	5	3
10	223200	1	6	21	3	0	3	3	5	3
11	243000	1	2	9	3	1	3	3	7	3
12	37800	1	4	3	3	1	3	3	7	3
13	300000	1	4	5	3	1	3	3	5	3
14	324000	1	4	26	3	0	3	3	8	4
15	651800	1	5	10	3	1	3	3	9	4
16	142800	0	3	33	3	1	3	3	8	4
17	156600	0	3	31	3	1	3	3	8	4
18	175000	0	3	34	3	1	3	3	8	4
19	159900	0	3	36	3	1	1	3	7	4
20	173000	0	3	34	3	1	1	3	7	4
21	182500	0	3	32	3	1	1	3	6	4

Data View / Variable View

One-Sample T Test   SPSS Processor is ready

start | PH-Book - Microsoft... | Home Values - SPSS...   2:26 PM

Everything else will be the same as in the previous test. Just change the "Test Value" from "200000" to "282000," remembering to ignore dollar signs and commas. Again, you will not see all the digits at once because the number is so large.

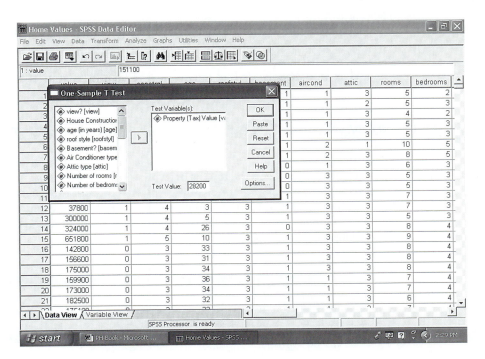

Click "OK" and the SPSS "Output" screen will appear.

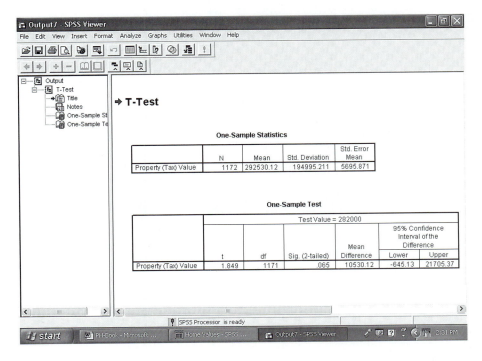

In the lower table, "One-Sample Test," you can see that the "Sig." value is .065. Most researchers use .05 and .01 as the required level of significance. Some rely on only .10. In our example, the results are significant at the .10 level, but not at the more stringent .05 level.

When interpreting a "Sig." value of .065, we would say that we are 93.5% (100% − 6.5%) confident that the mean home value is different from $282,000. For most researchers (those who require the results to reach at least .05), this is not stringent enough. They would conclude that the average value is *not* significantly different from $282,000.

7.3 PERFORMING AN INDEPENDENT-SAMPLES T-TEST

As the name implies, the independent-samples t-test determines if there is a significant difference between the means of two variables that belong to separate groups (or independent samples). In our example, we will consider the variables "Property (Tax) Value [value]" and "Air Conditioning Dummy Variable [ac_dum]."

To perform the test, click "Analyze," "Compare Means," and then "Independent-Samples T Test."

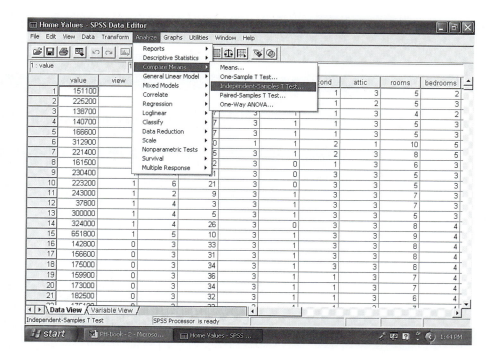

The "Independent-Samples T Test" window will appear.

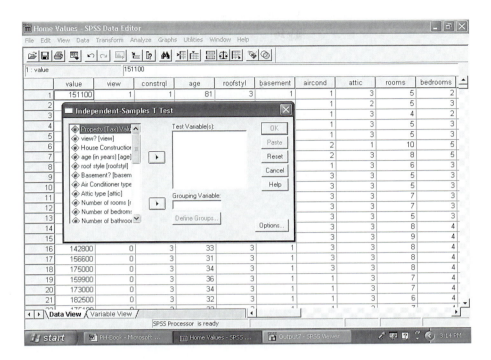

Select the variable "Property (Tax) Value [value]" and place it in the box on the right by single-clicking on it, and then clicking the "right arrow" button next to the "Test Variable(s)" box.

Select the variable "Air Conditioning Dummy Variable [ac_dum]" by single-clicking on it. Now click the "right arrow" button next to the "Grouping Variable" box. Your screen should look like this.

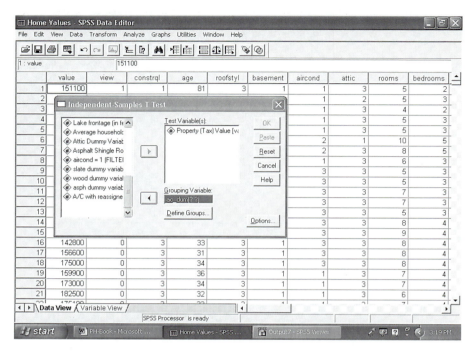

You must now define the values assigned to the variable "Air Conditioning Dummy Variable [ac_dum]." To do so, click on the "Define Groups" button. The following small window will appear.

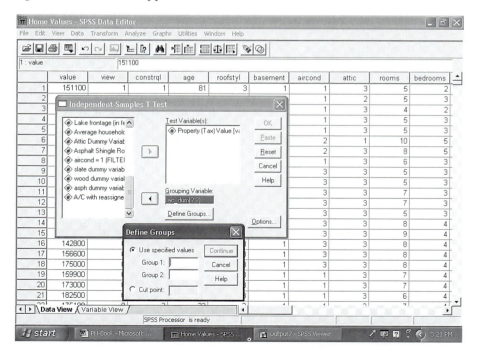

When the "ac_dum" variable was created, a value of "0" was assigned to homes without an air conditioner. Homes with an air conditioner were assigned a value of "1." For this reason, under the new window, "Define Groups," enter the values "0" for "Group 1" and "1" for "Group 2." You could even reverse these. As long as you specify that the groups are assigned a value of either "0" or "1," the results will be the same.

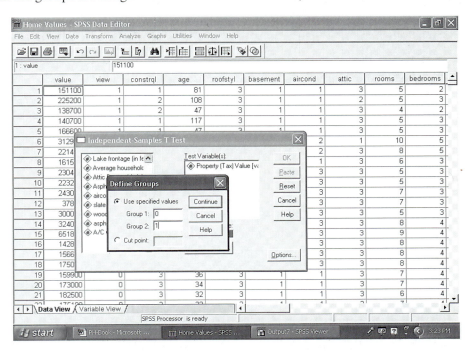

Click "Continue" to get back to the "Independent-Samples T Test" screen.

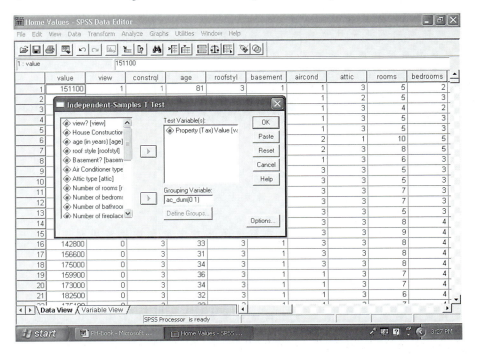

Click "OK" to perform the test. The following SPSS "Output" screen will appear.

From the upper table, "Group Statistics," you can see that the 764 homes without an air conditioner have an average value of $257,149.61. The 408 homes with an air conditioner have an average value of $358,781.86.

To determine if this difference is statistically significant, look at the lower table, "Independent Samples Test." The "Sig." value is ".000," which indicates that the means are significantly different beyond the .01 level.

7.4 PERFORMING A PAIRED-SAMPLES T-TEST

The purpose of a paired-samples t-test is to determine if there is a significant difference between the means of two groups that are linked (or paired) in some way. We can use a paired-samples t-test to examine the effects of a recession on world markets. The Asian financial crisis of 1997 caused major shifts in the return patterns of many world markets as several of the Pacific Rim countries fell into recession. We can use the paired-samples t-test to see if returns before the crisis are similar to those after the crisis.

To demonstrate the concept of a paired-samples t-test, we will refer to the dataset "Asian Crisis Data." "Asian Crisis Data" contains daily return data (a time series) for three world stock markets: the United States, Japan, and Hong Kong. For each market, returns leading up to the Asian crisis are listed first. Returns after the Asian crisis are listed second. Although each variable discussed in this section will be explained in the text, additional information on each variable can be found in the Appendix.

To open the "Asian Crisis Data" file in SPSS, click "File" and then "Open" or simply click on the "Open File" icon. Select the file "Asian Crisis Data" by double-clicking on it.

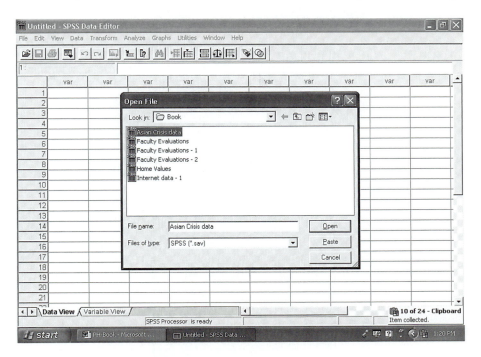

You should now see the data in SPSS.

To perform the test, we will consider the returns on the U.S. stock market both before ("rusb") and after ("rusa") the Asian crisis. In SPSS, click "Analyze," "Compare Means," and then "Paired-Samples T Test."

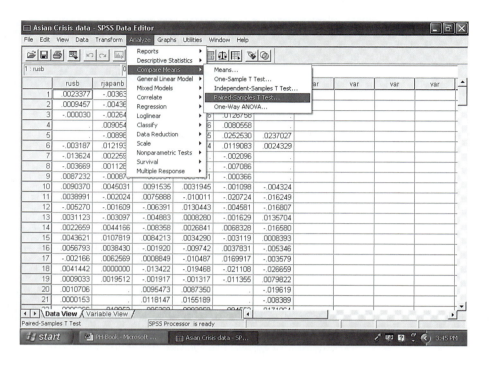

The "Paired-Samples T Test" window will open.

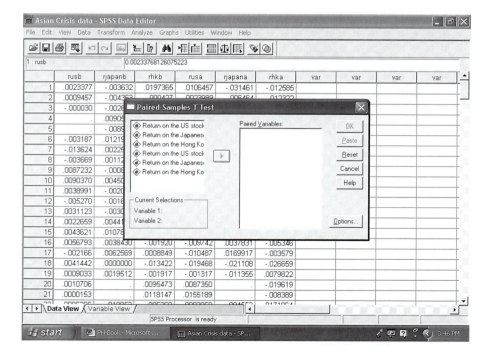

Select the variable "Return on the US stock market before the crisis [rusb]" by single-clicking on it. Before it can be moved into the "Paired Variables" box, it must be paired up with another variable. Single-click on the second variable, "Return on the US stock market after the crisis [rusa]."

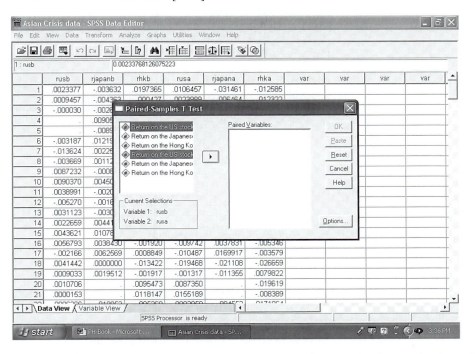

Click the "right arrow" button to move the paired (or matched) samples into the "Paired Variables" box.

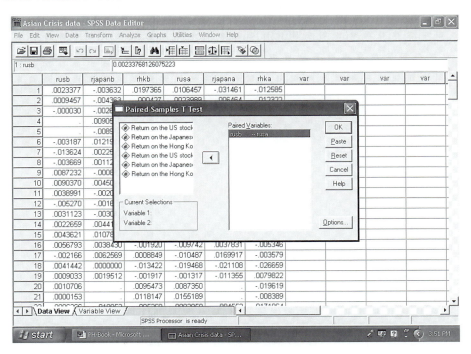

Click "OK" to perform the test. You will see the following SPSS "Output" window.

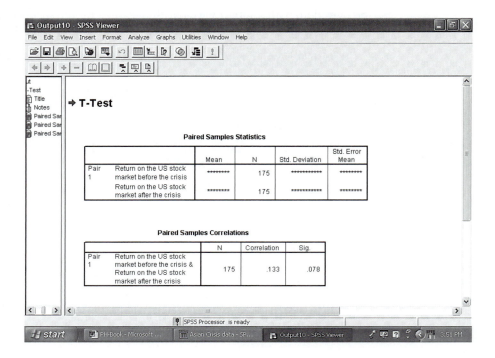

Notice that no values are shown under the "Mean" box. Instead, "*******" appears. This just means that the number is too long to be displayed. To make the column wider, double-click on the table "Paired Samples Statistics." Now place your mouse pointer on the vertical line separating the column "Mean" from the column "N." Click and hold your left mouse button as you drag to the right. When you are satisfied that the column is wide enough, release your left mouse button.

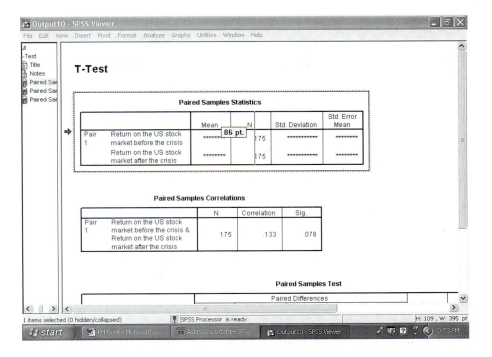

You should now see the table with a wider "Mean" column.

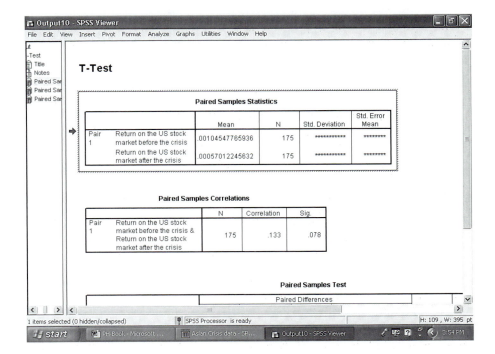

If you like, you can adjust the other columns for more desirable viewing using the same procedure. The reason the means are so small is because the data are daily and the numbers are in decimal form rather than percentages.

The number you are most interested in is found in the last table. To see the last table, simply scroll down the window to the "Paired Samples Test" table.

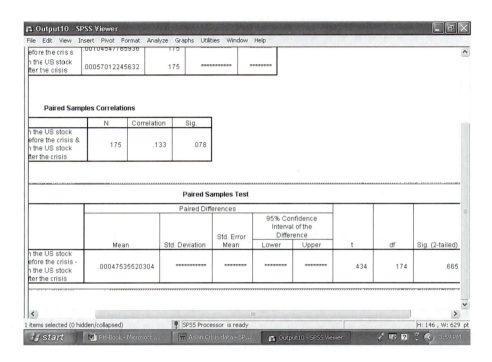

The "Sig." value of .665 indicates that the results are *not* statistically significant. That is, there is no significant difference between the daily mean of the U.S. stock market return before versus after the Asian financial crisis.

8

ANALYSIS OF VARIANCE

8.1 PURPOSE OF AN ANALYSIS OF VARIANCE

The purpose of an analysis of variance (ANOVA) is to determine if the means of more than two variables are the same as the overall mean. For example, consider the variables within the dataset "Home Values - 1." Within this file, the variable "value" represents the value of a home. The variable "roofstyl" indicates the type of roof covering a home. There are three types of roofs: (1) slate and tile, (2) wood shingle, and (3) asphalt shingle. It may be of interest to know if the type of roof on a home has any association with the value of that home.

To demonstrate the ANOVA test, we will refer to the dataset "Home Values - 1." "Home Values - 1" contains cross-sectional data relating to home (residential property) attributes for 1,172 properties located in Cuyahoga County, Ohio. Although each variable discussed in this chapter will be explained in the text, additional information on each variable can be found in the Appendix.

8.2 PERFORMING AN ANOVA

To open the "Home Values - 1" file in SPSS, click "File" and then "Open" or simply click on the "Open File" icon. Then select the file "Home Values - 1" by double-clicking on it.

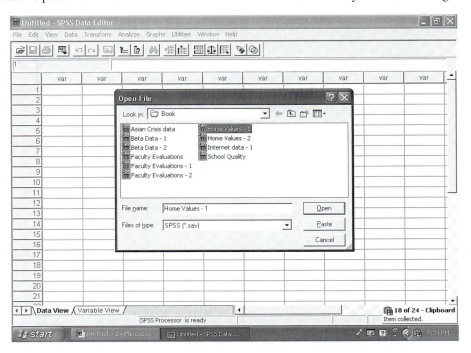

You should now see the data in SPSS.

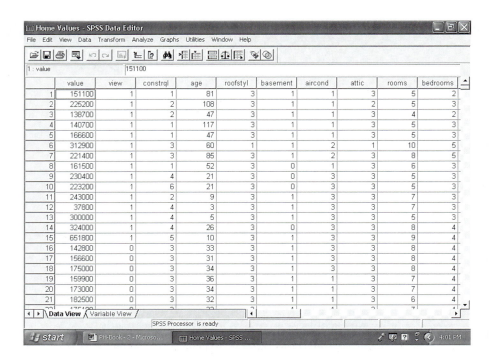

To perform an ANOVA in SPSS, use the pull-down menus by clicking on "Analyze," "Compare Means," and then "One-Way ANOVA."

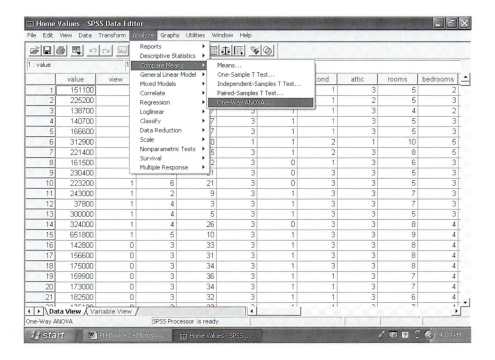

You will then see the following screen.

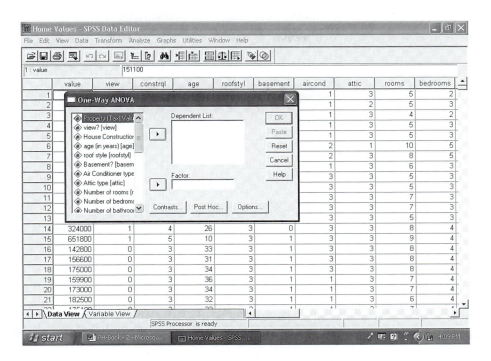

For now, move "Property (Tax) Value [value]" into the "Dependent List:" and specify "roof style [roofstyl]" as the "Factor." Your SPSS screen should appear as follows.

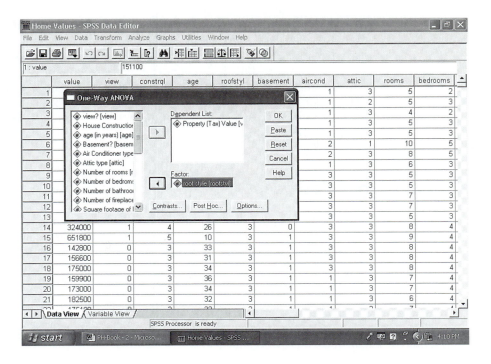

Click "OK" and the SPSS "Output" window will appear as follows.

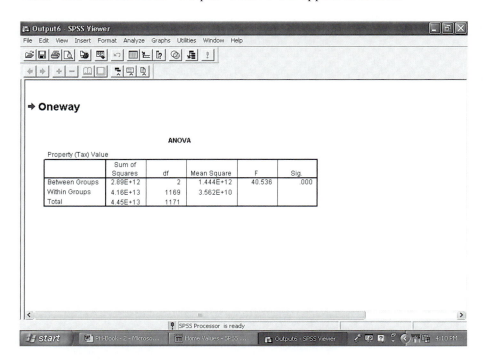

The output of most interest is the "Sig." value. Values below 0.05 indicate that the results are statistically significant beyond the 95% confidence level. Values below 0.01 mean that the results are statistically significant beyond the 99% confidence level. These are the two most common statistical significance cutoffs.

Notice that the "Sig." number reported in this example is .000. Therefore, our interpretation is that roof style is associated with significant differences in home values. What the results do not tell us is which roof styles are more valuable than others. We also do not yet know if the more valuable roof types are slightly (not significantly) more valuable or statistically significantly more valuable. That is, are homes with wood shingle roofs associated with higher values than homes with asphalt shingle roofs? Moreover, is this difference statistically significant?

To answer these specific questions, we must perform what are known as *post hoc multiple comparison* tests.

8.3 POST HOC TESTS

Post hoc tests perform pairwise comparisons of each of the categorical variables to measure if each variable is significantly different from each other variable. To perform a pairwise analysis, click "Compare Means," and then "One-Way ANOVA."

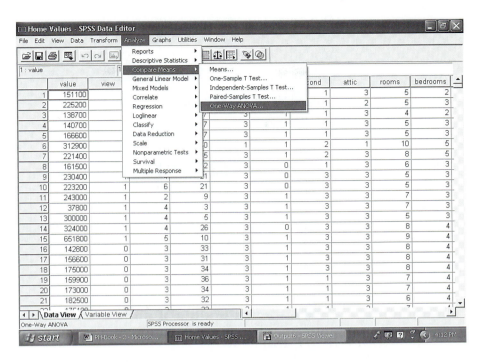

The "One-Way ANOVA" screen will appear, just as it did before. If you have followed the example, the screen will appear as follows.

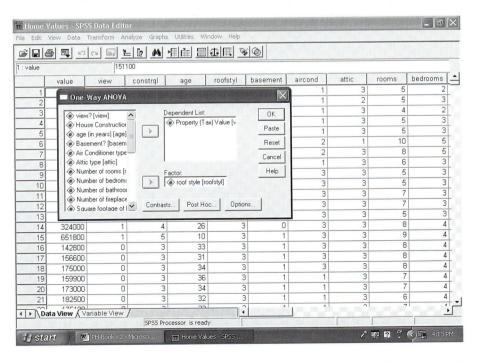

The variable "Property (Tax) Value [value]" is already in the "Dependent List:" and the variable "roof style [roofstyl]" is in the box labeled "Factor:" If the variables do not already appear in the boxes, just repeat the steps presented earlier.

Now click on the button labeled "Post Hoc." You will see the following screen.

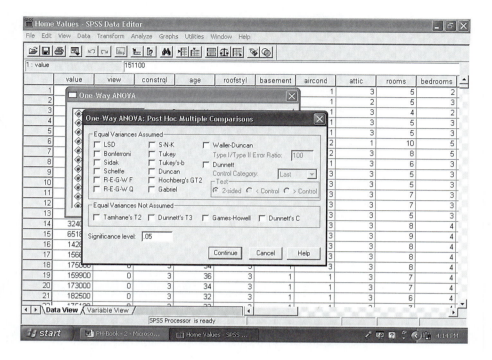

8.3.1 EQUAL VARIANCES ASSUMED VS. UNEQUAL VARIANCES ASSUMED

You will notice that there are 14 statistical measures that assume the variance of the three different roof types are equal and four that do not. Therefore, to determine which set of measures is appropriate for your data, you must first determine if the variances of your three roof types are equal or not. To do this, use the following procedure.

From the previous screen, titled "One-Way ANOVA," click on the "Options" button.

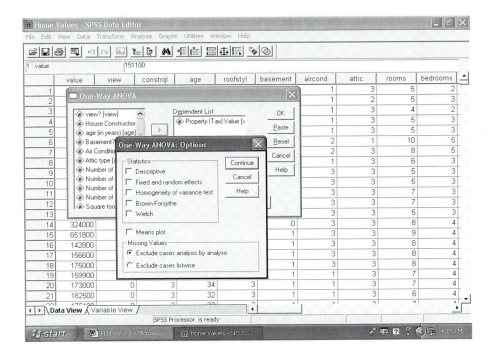

Check the box marked "Homogeneity of variance test."

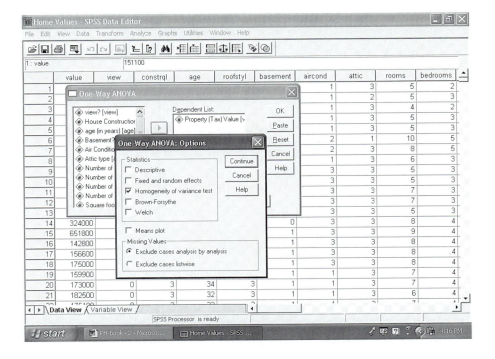

Click "Continue." You will return to the previous "One-Way ANOVA" screen.

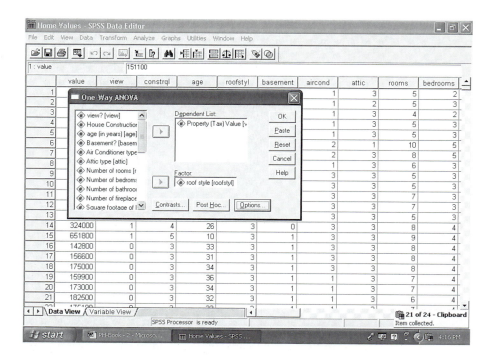

Click "OK" and the following SPSS "Output" screen will appear.

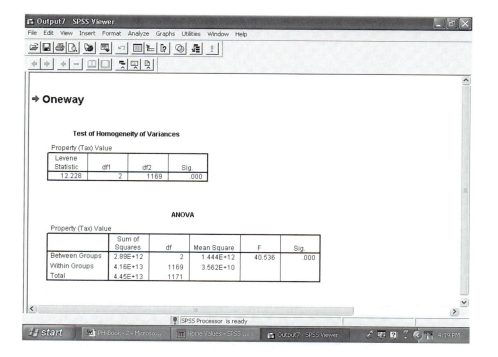

In the table "Test of Homogeneity of Variances," you want to focus on the value of "Sig.," which is associated with your calculated Levene statistic. Notice that the value of "Sig." is .000. This means that the variances are not equal.

Generically, "Sig." values below .05 mean that you are at least 95% confident that the variances are not equal. Accordingly, "Sig." values below .01 mean that you are at least 99% confident that the variances are not equal.

Because the variances are not equal, one of the four measures that do not assume equal variances should be used. It is beyond the scope of this text to provide a detailed discussion of when to use which specific type of measure and the implicit assumptions each one makes. For more information on these measures, consult an advanced statistics book.

We will use the first measure, "Tamhane's T2" test. Because we have taken a slight aside here to determine which set of measures to use, let's take it from the top and perform the multiple comparisons assuming unequal variances. From the SPSS "Data" window, click "Analyze," "Compare Means," and then "One-Way ANOVA."

The following window will appear.

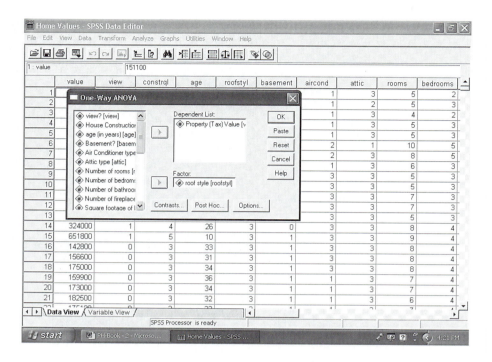

Now click on the "Post Hoc" button. The following window will appear.

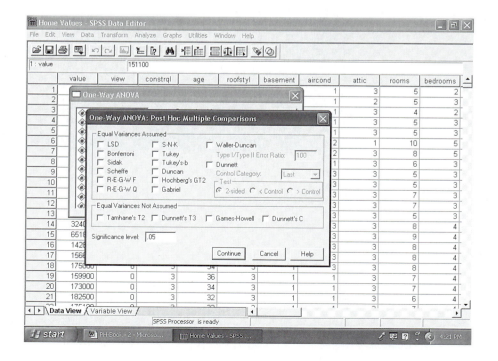

Check the box marked "Tamhane's T2."

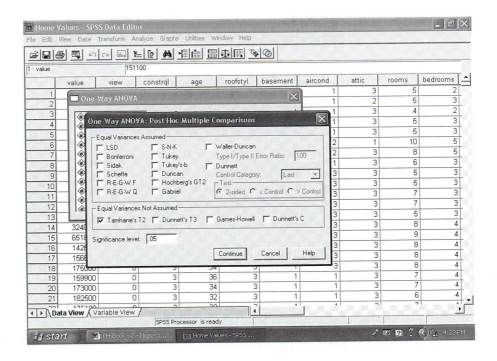

Click "Continue" and you will arrive at the following menu.

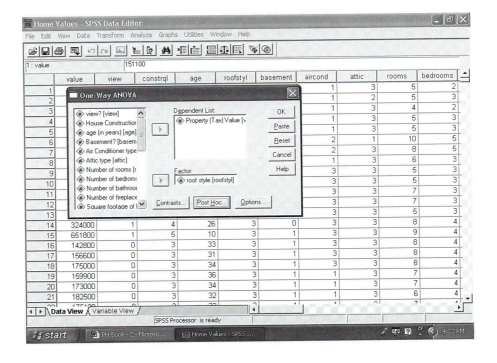

Click "OK" and the SPSS "Output" window will appear. Scroll down to the bottom to see the "Multiple Comparisons" table.

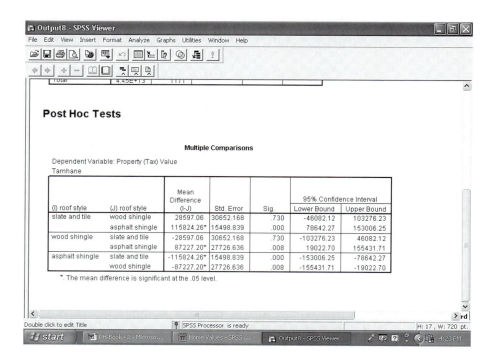

Each row in the "Multiple Comparisons" table shows the comparison of one roof type to the other two. The column "Mean Difference (I-J)" reveals that slate and tile roofs are associated with homes valued $28,597.06 higher than the value of homes with wood shingle roofs. Similarly, slate and tile roofs are associated with homes valued $115,824.26 higher than the value of homes with asphalt shingle roofs. Moreover, this difference is statistically significant at the 95% confidence level, as indicated by the asterisk. To know exactly how robust the differences are, examine the "Sig." values associated with each row. Again, values below .05 are significant beyond the 95% level of confidence.

To be sure that you understand how to interpret the "Mean Difference (I-J)" column, consider the next two rows in the table. These results are interpreted to mean that wood shingle roofs are associated with homes valued $28,597.06 *lower* than homes with slate and tile roofs. Likewise, wood shingle roofs are associated with homes valued $87,227.20 *higher* than homes with asphalt roofs. (Note that this difference is significant beyond the 99% level.) Be sure to observe both the sign and the magnitude of the difference in the column.

In closing, an ANOVA will simply tell you whether or not the means of more than two variables are the same as the grand (or overall) mean. It will not tell you which variable has the highest mean, nor will it tell you which variable means are significantly different from each other. To answer these questions, you must perform post hoc tests. Doing so will enable you to make pairwise comparisons between all variables.

Even after performing these tests, you must be very careful when interpreting the results. Notice that I have chosen my words very carefully throughout this demonstration. I have never said that different roof types *cause* higher home values. Instead, I have simply explained that different roof types *are associated with* higher home values. The former statement is much more powerful than the latter and should not be made after performing only an ANOVA test.

The reason I cannot yet definitively conclude that different roof types cause higher home values is because there are a number of additional home attributes that have not been considered in the analysis. For example, construction quality, view, age of the home, number of fireplaces, square footage, and whether or not the home has a basement, an attic, and/or air-conditioning, all affect a home's value. More tests are required before cause-and-effect conclusions can be drawn.

9

REGRESSION

9.1 PURPOSE OF A REGRESSION

Regression is one of the most versatile and popular statistical procedures. The primary goal of regression is to predict or explain one variable (the dependent variable) using one or more known variables (the independent variables). If only one independent variable is used in the regression, we refer to it as a simple regression. Multiple regression describes the technique if more than one independent variable is used.

To illustrate the concept of regression, we will refer to the dataset "Home Values - 2." "Home Values - 2" contains cross-sectional data relating to home (residential property) attributes for 1,170 properties located in Cuyahoga County, Ohio. Although each variable discussed in this chapter will be explained in the text, additional information on each variable can be found in the Appendix.

9.2 PERFORMING A LINEAR REGRESSION

To open the "Home Values - 2" file in SPSS, click "File" and then "Open" or simply click on the "Open File" icon. Then select the file "Home Values - 2" by double-clicking on it.

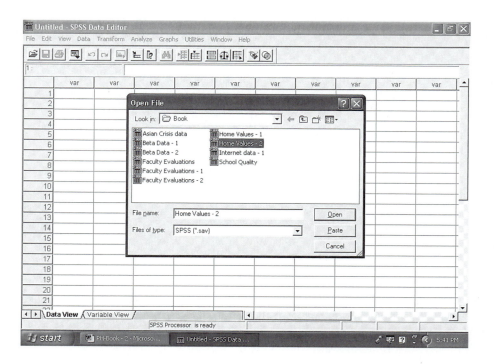

The SPSS "Data" window will appear.

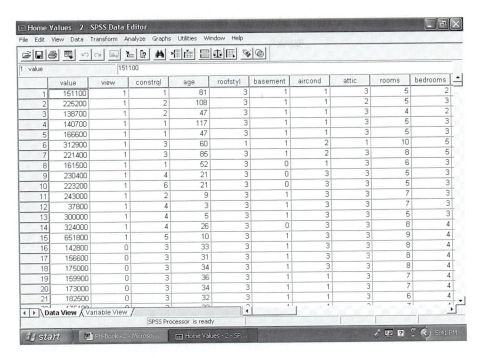

To perform a linear regression, click "Analyze," "Regression," and then "Linear."

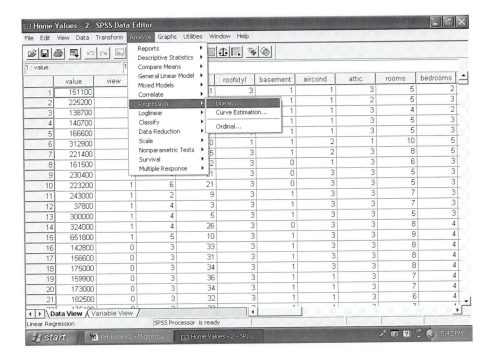

The "Linear Regression" window will appear.

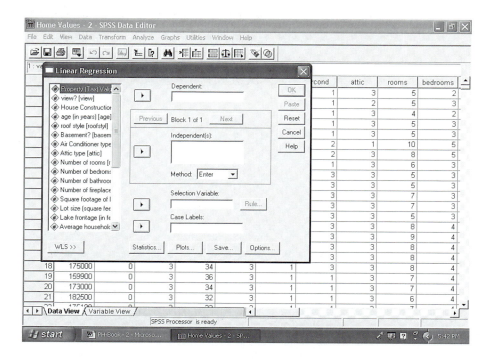

Consider the variable "House Construction Quality [constrql]." "House Construction Quality" rates how well a home is built on a scale from 1 (worst quality) to 6 (best quality). Let's use other variables in the dataset to try to explain or predict this measure of quality. Look at the variables that remain and try to hypothesize not only the variables that would be significant, but also the direction of the effect.

For example, the variable "view?" is a dummy variable where a value of "1" is assigned if the home has a view of Lake Erie (is on Lake Erie) and a value of "0" if the home does not have a view (is not on Lake Erie). You might hypothesize that a lakefront home in the north would have to be of very high quality (very sturdy) to withstand the harsh winter winds and "lake effect" snowstorms. Therefore, you would hypothesize "view?" to be significantly positively related to construction quality.

The age of the home could certainly be significant. Most would hypothesize that newer is better. Time has a negative effect on the quality of almost any physical asset, whether it is cars, planes, or homes.

Four home-specific attributes should be considered. The presence of an attic, a basement, and/or an air conditioner, as well as the home's roofing material, may all contribute to quality.

Finally, consider the size of the home. You might hypothesize that larger, more expensive homes would be built with higher-quality materials. Conversely, smaller homes might be constructed for the primary purpose of affordable living. As such, using the highest-quality building materials is a luxury these owners cannot afford.

Which measure of size will you use? You have several from which to choose. "Lot size" measures the total area of the plot of land on which the home is built. That is, it includes the area of the home and yard. "Homesqft" measures the total square feet of living space (i.e., just the area of the house itself). "Rooms" is simply the total number of rooms in the house. You can likely assume that the more rooms the house has, the bigger it is. The same analogy goes for the variables "Number of bedrooms [bedrooms]," "Number of bathrooms [bathroom]," and "Number of fireplaces [fireplac]." In the next section, we will discuss the reasons why only one of these variables can be used at a time. Let's select the variable "homesqft" to represent size, because it is an industry standard.

To specify the regression, start by highlighting the variable "House Construction Quality [constrql]." Now click the "right arrow" button next to the box titled "Dependent" to specify the dependent variable.

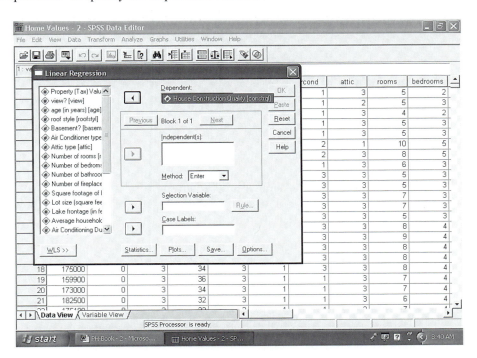

The same procedure will be followed to specify the list of independent variables. You could go one-by-one and highlight each independent variable from the list of variables and click the "right arrow" button next to the box titled "Independent(s)."

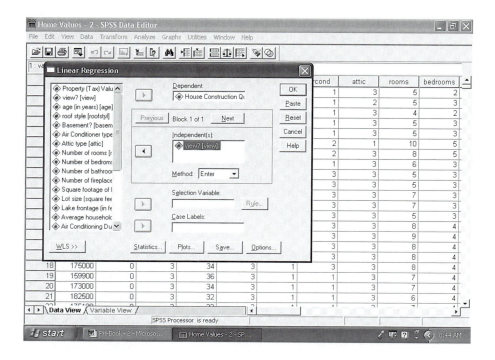

Alternatively, you could highlight all of the independent variables at one time and then click the "right arrow" button next to the "Independent(s)" list just once. To use this method, simply hold down the "Ctrl" key on your keyboard as you left-click with your mouse on each independent variable from the variable list.

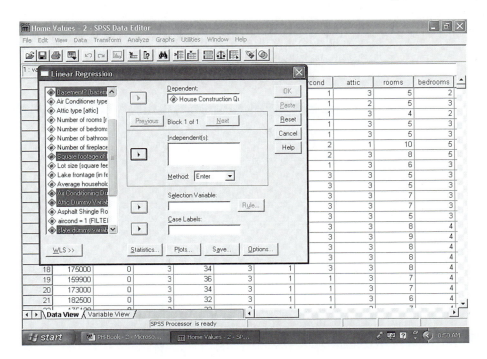

Click the "right arrow" button next to the "Independent(s)" box.

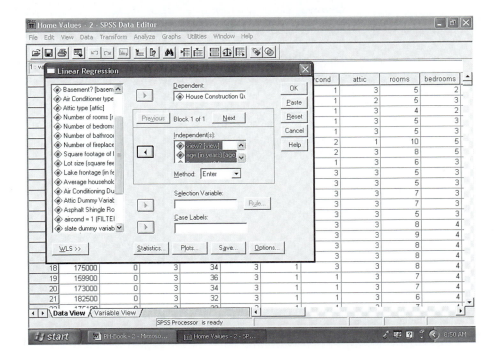

You are now ready to estimate the regression. To do so, simply click "OK." The following SPSS "Output" window will appear. Scroll down and you will see the "Model Summary" and "ANOVA" tables.

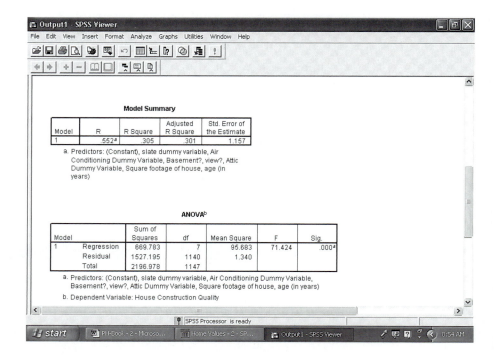

These tables provide information about the overall regression. The single most important number to refer to is the F-statistic. This is a test of the overall model's significance. Because the value of "Sig." is below .01, the model is statistically significant beyond the .01 level.

Scroll down to the table titled "Coefficients." This table examines each individual independent variable to see if it significantly influences the dependent variable, "House Construction Quality [constrql]."

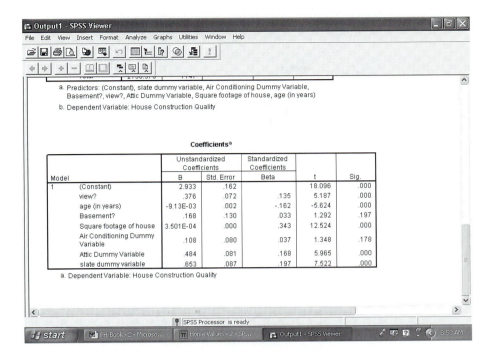

a. Predictors: (Constant), slate dummy variable, Air Conditioning Dummy Variable, Basement?, view?, Attic Dummy Variable, Square footage of house, age (in years)

b. Dependent Variable: House Construction Quality

Coefficients[a]

Model		Unstandardized Coefficients		Standardized Coefficients	t	Sig.
		B	Std. Error	Beta		
1	(Constant)	2.933	.162		18.096	.000
	view?	.376	.072	.135	5.187	.000
	age (in years)	-9.13E-03	.002	-.162	-5.624	.000
	Basement?	.168	.130	.033	1.292	.197
	Square footage of house	3.501E-04	.000	.343	12.524	.000
	Air Conditioning Dummy Variable	.108	.080	.037	1.348	.178
	Attic Dummy Variable	.484	.081	.168	5.965	.000
	slate dummy variable	.653	.087	.197	7.522	.000

a. Dependent Variable: House Construction Quality

Five of the seven independent variables are statistically significant beyond the .01 level, as indicated by their "Sig." values. The only two variables that are not significant are whether or not the home has a basement ("Basement?") and whether or not the home has air-conditioning ("Air Conditioning Dummy Variable"). The finding that high-quality homes may not have air-conditioning is surprising at first glance. Most would consider air-conditioning a must for all but the lowest-quality homes. However, this sample of homes is from northern Ohio, where it rarely gets hot enough to use an air conditioner. Moreover, roughly half of the homes in the sample are located along the shoreline of Lake Erie. These properties have a tremendous breeze that also contributes to the absence of a need for air-conditioning.

Before our model is complete, we must remove the nonsignificant variables and reestimate the equation using only significant relationships. Only then can we get unbiased estimates for our coefficients.

Let's perform the regression analysis again, this time removing the variables "basement" and "ac_dum." To do so, you can either stay in the SPSS "Output" window or go back to the "Data" window. From either window, click "Analyze," "Regression," and then "Linear."

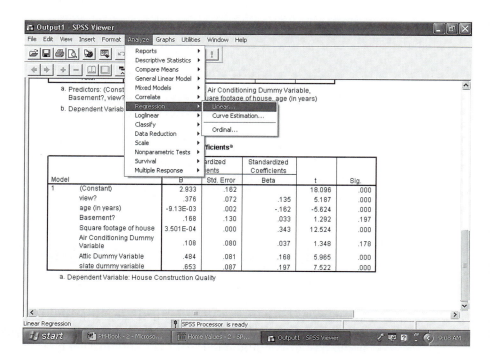

You will see the "Linear Regression" window.

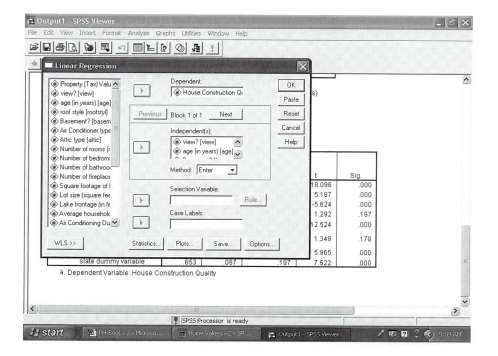

All we need to do is remove the two undesirable independent variables from the "Independent(s)" list. To do this, simply highlight them (one at a time or both together using the "Ctrl" key on your keyboard), then click on the "left arrow" button, which is now pointing back toward the original list of variables.

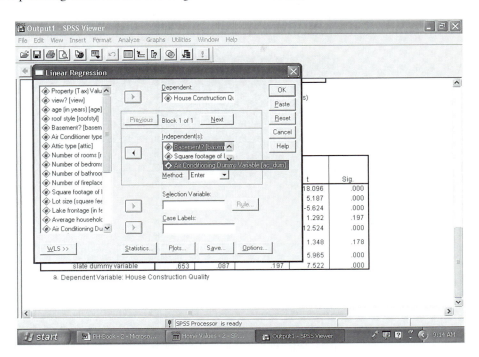

After clicking the "left arrow" button, your screen should look like this.

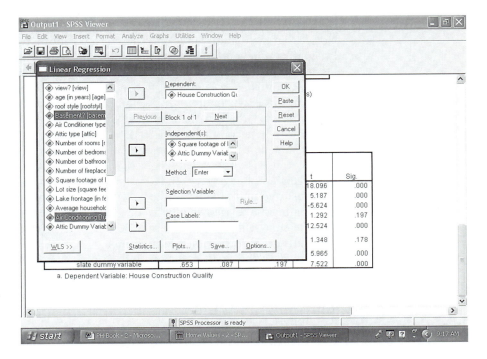

If you want, you can double-check that you have only five independent variables remaining in your analysis. When you are satisfied that your regression is specified the way you intended, click "OK." The SPSS "Output" screen will appear.

After you scroll down to the bottom of the SPSS "Output" screen, you will see the results from your most recent regression analysis.

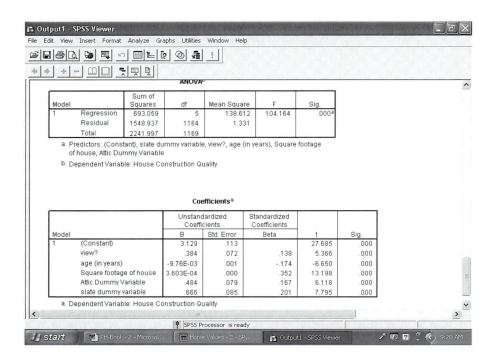

Notice that the overall model's F-statistic is a robust 104.164. This number is statistically significant beyond the .01 level, as indicated by the corresponding "Sig." value.

Under the "Coefficients" table, you will notice that all five remaining independent variables are statistically significant beyond the .01 level as well.

Because this is our final model, we are now prepared to discuss and interpret the beta coefficients. Consider the variable "Square footage of house [homesqft]." The unstandardized beta coefficient is 3.603E-04 in scientific notation, or .0003603 in decimal form. This means that for every additional square foot added to the house, the increase (because the coefficient is positive) in the rating for the variable "constrql" is .0003603. This amount is very small, primarily because an increase in the size of the home by just one unit (1 square foot) is an extremely small increase. Moreover, if we were estimating the relationship between square footage and the price of the home, the beta coefficient would be much larger because the units for price are much smaller than the units for construction quality rating.

Let's discuss the coefficient on the variable "age." The value is –9.76E-03, or –.00976. This means that for each additional year older the house is, it loses (because the coefficient is negative) .00976 in its rating of construction quality. This negative relationship is just as we predicted based on the knowledge that time deteriorates the quality of physical assets.

9.3 TESTING FOR MULTICOLLINEARITY

In our previous example, we explained construction quality using five independent variables. One of the significant variables was the size of the home as measured in square feet. Although six variables ("lotsize," "homesqft," "rooms," "bedroom," "bathroom," and "fireplace") related to size, we only entered one of them into the regression analysis. The reason for this was to avoid violating one of the most important assumptions in regression. This assumption is that no variable can be expressed or represented by a linear combination of the others. If this occurs, your regression is said to suffer from *multicollinearity*.

The problem with multicollinearity is that its presence means that the beta values associated with your independent variables are biased. In other words, you cannot trust your results. If you cannot trust the accuracy of your results, you cannot draw conclusions, and you might as well not even perform the test.

Many people screen for multicollinearity by performing a correlation analysis on the independent variables to be entered into the regression. For example, we would perform a correlation test on the six size-related variables: "lotsize," "homesqft," "rooms," "bedroom," "bathroom," and "fireplace." To perform such a correlation, click "Analyze," "Correlate," and then "Bivariate."

The following SPSS "Output" screen will appear.

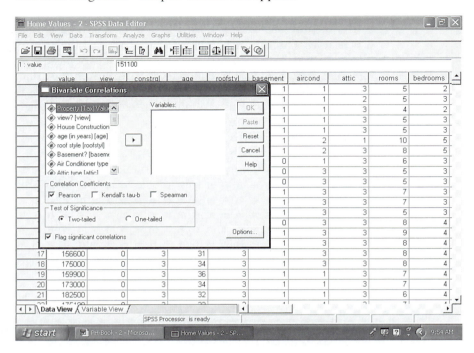

Select the six size-related variables and move them into the box titled "Variables." To do this, highlight all six variables at one time by holding down the "Ctrl" key on your keyboard as you left-click with your mouse on each variable from the variable list. Alternatively, because the six variables are right next to each other, you could also hold down the "Shift" key on your keyboard and press the "arrow down" key until all the variables are highlighted.

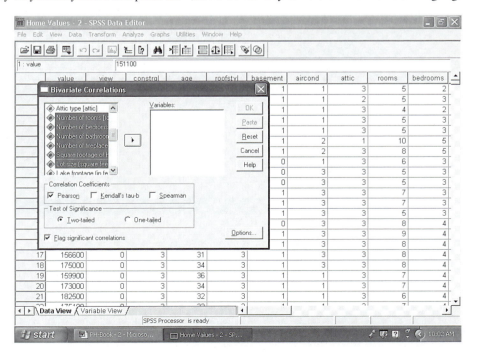

Either way, after you have highlighted all the variables, just click the "right arrow" button next to the "Variables" list.

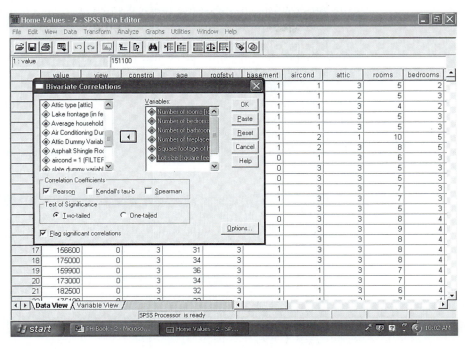

Click "OK" to perform the test. The SPSS "Output" window will appear.

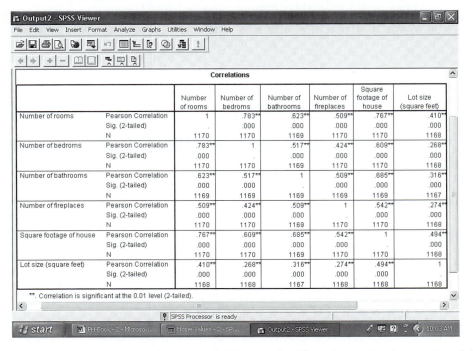

Not surprisingly, all six of these variables are significantly positively correlated. In fact, many of the variables are subsets of each other. For this reason, they should not all be entered into a regression analysis.

One of the most common misconceptions in regression is that a test for correlation is a definitive test for multicollinearity. This is not true. A correlation will identify one-to-one relationships, but it is not powerful enough to determine if *two or more* variables could, together, be used to represent another independent variable. That is, a correlation test can be used to indicate the potential presence of multicollinearity, but it *cannot* allow you to reach the conclusion that multicollinearity is not present.

To test for multicollinearity directly, you must consult VIF (variance inflation factor), tolerance, condition indexes, and variance proportions measures. Fortunately, SPSS will generate these measures for you with just the click of a button.

To perform the test, go back to the "Linear Regression" window. To get there from the main SPSS "Data" window, click "Analyze," "Regression," and then "Linear."

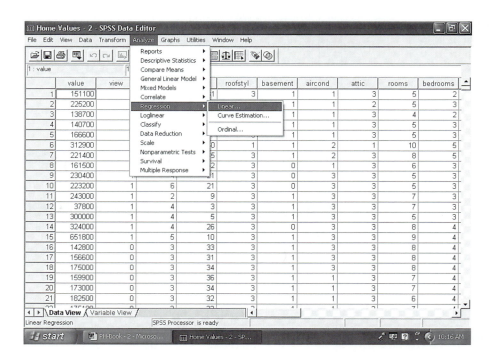

The "Linear Regression" window will appear.

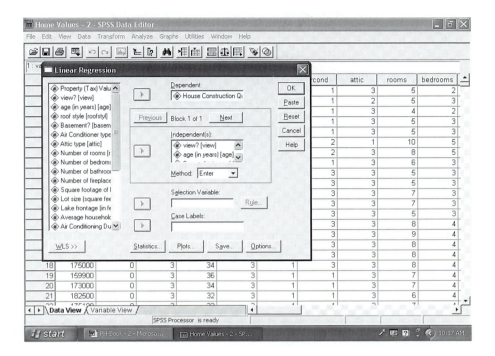

If you have not closed out of SPSS since performing the last regression, the variables will already be specified. If you have closed out, just specify the model again using "House Construction Quality [constrql]" as the dependent variable and "view? [view]," "age (in years) [age]," "Square footage of house [homesqft]," "Attic Dummy Variable [atticdum]," and "slate dummy variable [slat_dum]" as the independent variables.

In the "Linear Regression" window, click on the button marked "Statistics."

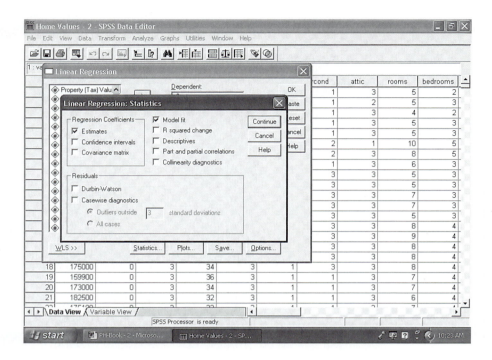

Check the box labeled "Collinearity diagnostics" by left-clicking on it with your mouse.

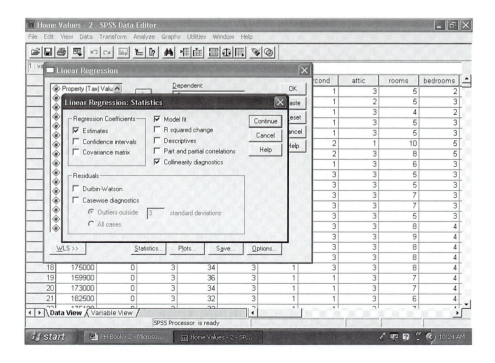

Click "Continue" to get back to the "Linear Regression" window.

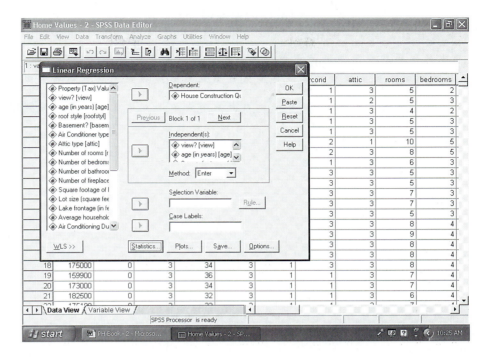

Click "OK" to perform the regression and generate the multicollinearity diagnostic results. The SPSS "Output" window will appear. After scrolling down, you will see the results for the overall model as well as those for the independent variables.

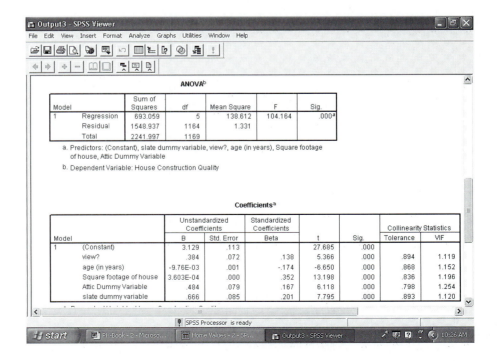

Unlike the first time this model was estimated, the columns headed "Collinearity Statistics" appear in the "Coefficients" table. The two statistics reported are "Tolerance" and "VIF." Tolerance values below .10, or alternatively, VIF values above 10, indicate the presence of multicollinearity. Because the values in this table are all near 1.0, multicollinearity is not an issue.

Scroll down to the last table in the "Output" window.

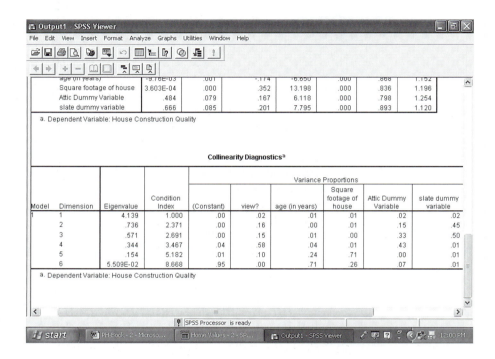

The first step in identifying the presence of multicollinearity is to examine all condition index values above 30 (some statistics books recommend a more restrictive cut-off value of 15). Once you find a row with a condition index value above 30, examine the "Variance Proportions" values. If at least *two* of the variables have a "Variance Proportions" value above .90 (associated with a condition index above 30), your model is plagued with multicollinearity.

In our example, the largest condition index is only 8.668. Thus, there is no need to even consider the "Variance Proportions." Our model does not possess multicollinearity, and therefore, our results can be correctly interpreted without bias.

9.4 PERFORMING A TWO-STAGE LEAST SQUARES REGRESSION

In regression analysis, it is assumed that the explanatory (predictor) variables are truly independent (or exogenous). That is, they are determined outside the model. However, it is often the case that the list of explanatory variables may contain a variable that is determined by the other independent variables inside the model. In other words, if your list of explanatory variables contains a variable that is not truly independent, two-stage least squares (2SLS) regression should be used. Alternatively stated, 2SLS is a variation of regression that must be done when the independent variables are not all independent.

An example will greatly aid in our understanding of why this procedure is needed. In the SPSS file "Home Values - 2," let's create a model to explain home prices. The variable "value" indicates the price of the home. The variables we will create to explain home value will include whether or not the home has a view of Lake Erie ("view"), the age of the home ("age"), the size of the home as measured by square footage ("homesqft"), and how well the home is built ("constrql").

As previously illustrated, "Construction Quality (constrql)" is a function of five independent variables. Three of these variables are also hypothesized to predict home values.

$$value = f\,(\textbf{view, age, homesqft}, constrql)$$
$$constrql = f\,(\textbf{view, age, homesqft}, atticdum, slat\_dum)$$

Therefore, when predicting home value in the first equation, only three of the variables are truly independent (i.e., exogenous, which means determined outside the model). The fourth is endogenous (determined inside the model). If we were to perform a regular regression, we would have biased results. Instead, we need to perform a 2SLS regression.

As the name implies, 2SLS performs the analysis in two stages. The first stage involves estimating the equation exactly the way we did when we specified the model to explain "Construction Quality (constrql)." The second stage involves using the "unstandardized predicted value" from this regression and substituting it in for the variable "constrql" when estimating the second regression to explain "value." Stated another way, we will perform the first regression as follows:

$$constrql = f\,(view, age, homesqft, atticdum, slat\_dum)$$

Using the predicted value "pre_constrql," we will estimate the second regression as follows:

$$value = f\,(view, age, homesqft, \textbf{pre\_constrql})$$

9.4.1 PERFORMING A 2SLS REGRESSION IN SPSS

To illustrate the concept of 2SLS regression, we will consider the dataset "Home Values - 2." To open the "Home Values - 2" file in SPSS, click "File" and then "Open" or simply click on the "Open File" icon. Then select the file "Home Values - 2" by double-clicking on it.

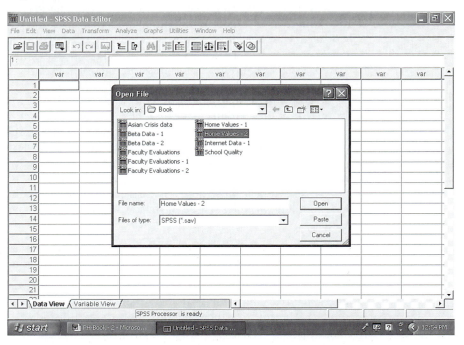

The SPSS "Data" window will appear.

	value	view	constrql	age	roofstyl	basement	aircond	attic	rooms	bedrooms
1	151100	1	1	81	3	1	1	3	5	2
2	225200	1	2	108	3	1	1	2	5	3
3	138700	1	2	47	3	1	1	3	4	2
4	140700	1	1	117	3	1	1	3	5	3
5	166600	1	1	47	3	1	1	3	5	3
6	312900	1	3	60	1	1	2	1	10	5
7	221400	1	3	85	3	1	2	3	8	5
8	161500	1	1	52	3	0	1	3	6	3
9	230400	1	4	21	3	0	3	3	5	3
10	223200	1	6	21	3	0	3	3	5	3
11	243000	1	2	9	3	1	3	3	7	3
12	37800	1	4	3	3	1	3	3	7	3
13	300000	1	4	5	3	1	3	3	5	3
14	324000	1	4	26	3	0	3	3	8	4
15	651800	1	5	10	3	1	3	3	9	4
16	142800	0	3	33	3	1	3	3	8	4
17	156600	0	3	31	3	1	3	3	8	4
18	175000	0	3	34	3	1	3	3	8	4
19	159900	0	3	36	3	1	1	3	7	4
20	173000	0	3	34	3	1	1	3	7	4
21	182500	0	3	32	3	1	1	3	6	4

Let's perform stage 1 by specifying the regression for "Construction Quality [constrql]" exactly as we did before. Click "Analyze," "Regression," and then "Linear."

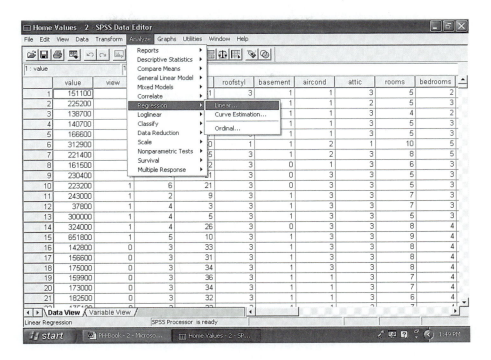

Specify the dependent variable, "House Construction Quality [constrql]," by high-lighting it. Then click on the "right arrow" button next to the "Dependent" box.

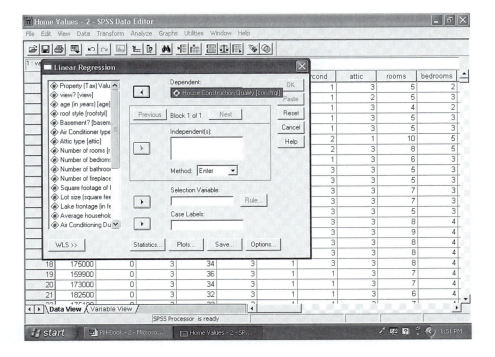

Specify your five independent variables ("view," "age," "homesqft," "atticdum," "slat_dum") by highlighting them and clicking on the "right arrow" button next to the box titled "Independent(s)."

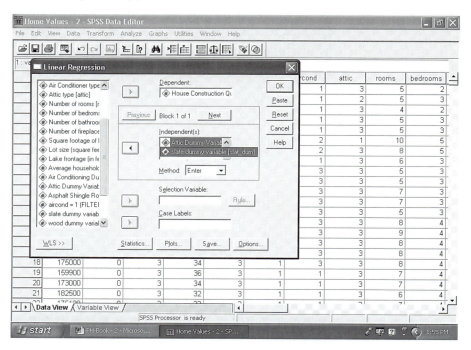

We need to tell SPSS to save the unstandardized predicted value from this equation so we can use it in stage 2. To do this, click the button labeled "Save" at the bottom of the "Linear Regression" screen. A window titled "Linear Regression: Save" will appear.

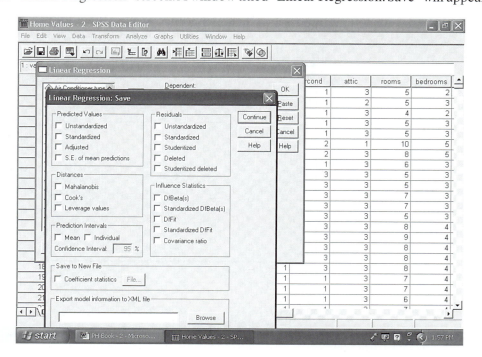

Under the category "Predicted Values," check the box labeled "Unstandardized" by left-clicking on it with your mouse.

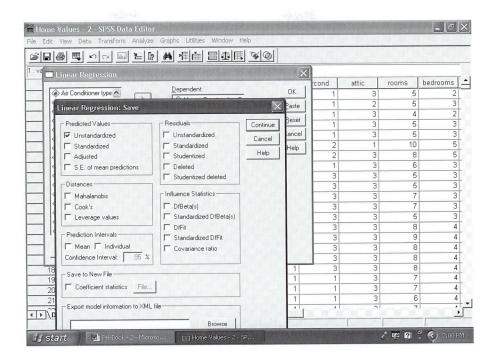

Click "Continue" to return to the "Linear Regression" window.

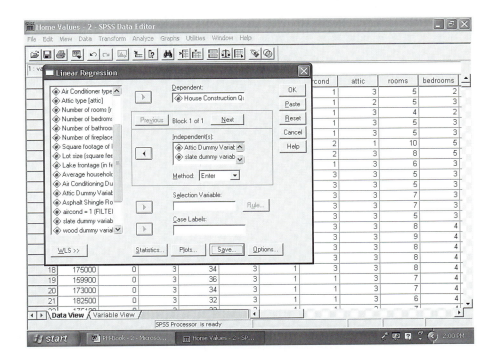

Click "OK" to perform the regression and save the predicted values as a new variable. The SPSS "Output" screen will appear.

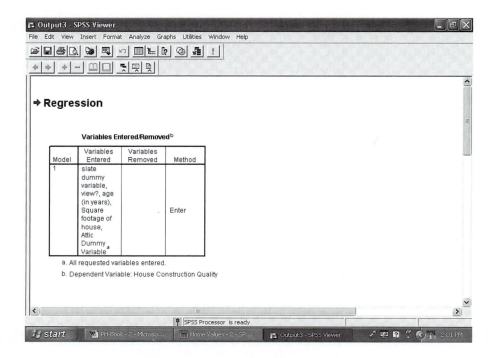

Because we examined this output in great detail earlier in the chapter and because we already know the equation is correctly specified, there is no need to repeat all of that again here. Instead, let's confirm that the variable containing predicted values has been created. To do this, go back to the SPSS "Data" window by clicking "Window" and then "1 Home Values - 2 - SPSS Data Editor."

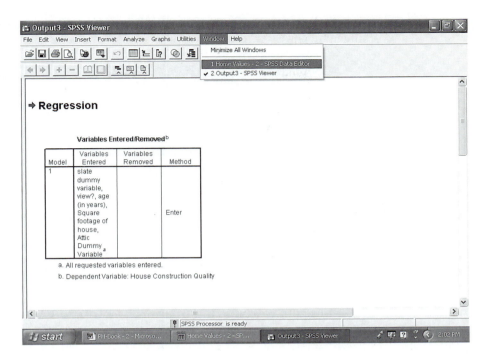

The SPSS "Data" window will appear.

Go to the right by clicking on the arrow bar at the bottom of the screen or by using the arrow keys on your keyboard. The last column of data will be your new variable, automatically titled "pre_1." This is the default name given by SPSS. Of course, you can rename it if you like.

Let's perform stage 2 of the 2SLS regression. Click "Analyze," "Regression," and then "Linear."

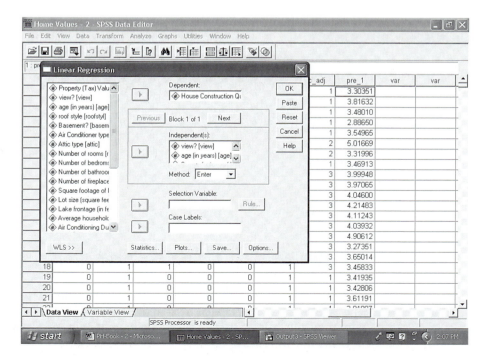

You will see the previously specified "Linear Regression" screen. You can start the screen from scratch by clicking the "Reset" button or change the variables out according to this second model.

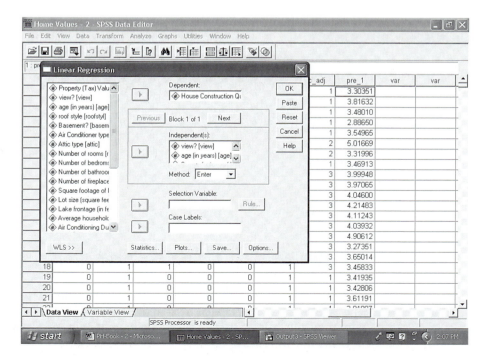

The dependent variable is now "Property (Tax) Value [value]." Specify the variable by switching it out with "constrql."

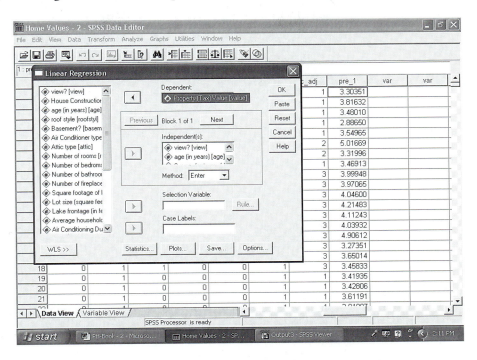

Remove the two unneeded independent variables "atticdum" and "slat_dum" by highlighting them in the "Independent(s)" list and clicking the "left arrow" button next to the box.

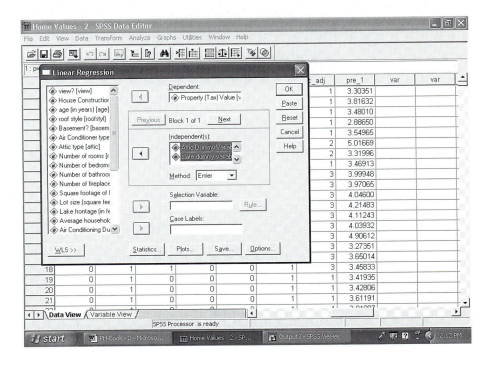

Only three independent variables, "view," "age," and "homesqft," should remain.

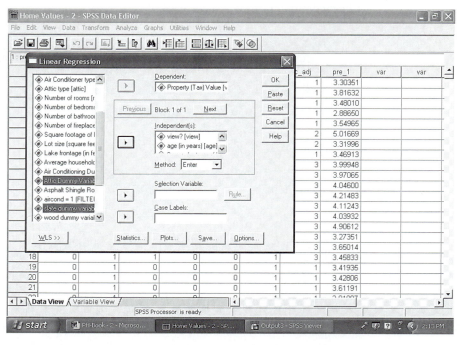

Finally, we need to include the fourth variable, "pre_1." This variable can be found at the very bottom of your list. Highlight it and include it in the "Independent(s)" list.

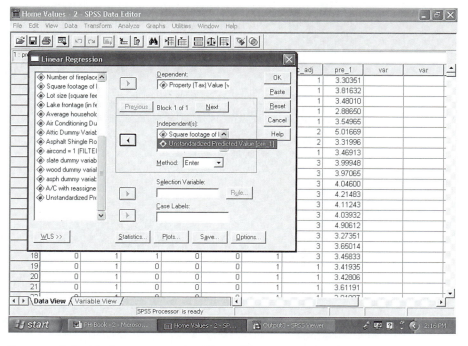

Because I decided not to use the "Reset" button, under the "Save" button, I have specified to SPSS to save my predicted values again. These values are completely unnecessary. Feel free to deselect this option or just ignore the new series.

Click "OK" to perform the regression that completes the second stage of the 2SLS. The SPSS "Output" window will appear. After scrolling down a bit, you will see the results for the overall model.

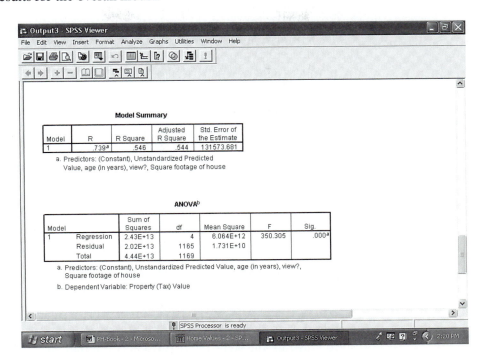

The values associated with the individual explanatory variables are found by scrolling down even further.

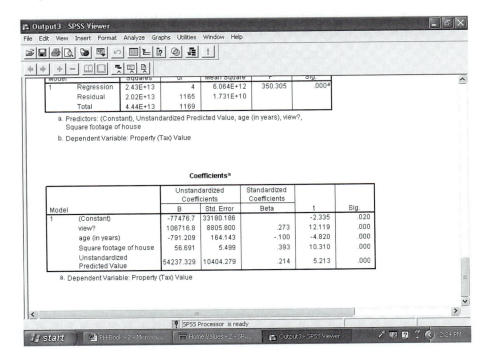

The unstandardized beta coefficients (B) are true estimates. That is, they can be interpreted in the same way that we have previously discussed. For example, for every year older a house gets, its value decreases (because it has a negative coefficient) by $791.21. Similarly, an additional square foot added to the house increases (because it has a positive coefficient) the value of the home by $56.69.

The R-square and standard errors reported here are not the ones that you want. This is because the two stages have been performed separately. Alternatively stated, the R-square and standard errors reported here are associated with the variable "pre_1" instead of the actual value of "constrql." If you want to know the R-square and standard errors associated with "constrql," you have to perform all the estimations at one time.

Older versions of SPSS allowed this option as part of the "Advanced Statistics" module. However, more recently, SPSS developed a more detailed "Regression" module where 2SLS is now performed directly. In sum, you can still perform 2SLS by doing each step separately, as we did here. The only drawback is that if you have a special interest in the details of the output, you will not be able to measure them unless you buy the "Regression" module. Most readers will not need this level of information.

9.4.2 PERFORMING A 2SLS REGRESSION IN EVIEWS

In the previous section, we demonstrated the use of 2SLS regression by performing each stage separately in SPSS. Subscribers to EViews can quickly perform the procedure using just one input window. The benefits of performing a 2SLS regression in EViews are not only the reduced time it takes to perform both steps at once, but also the interpretable summary statistics/output it creates.

To illustrate the steps required to perform the 2SLS regression, we will consider the EViews Workfile titled "homes values - 2." To open this file, click "File," "Open," and then "Workfile."

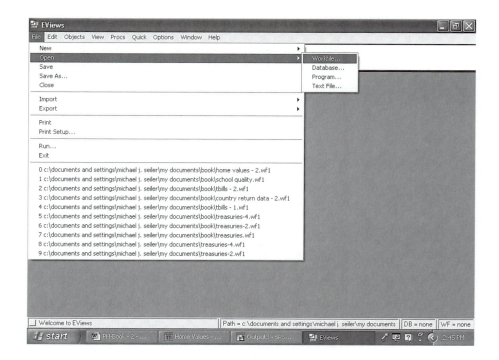

Select the file "home values - 2" by double-clicking on it. Alternatively, you could single-click on it and then click "Open."

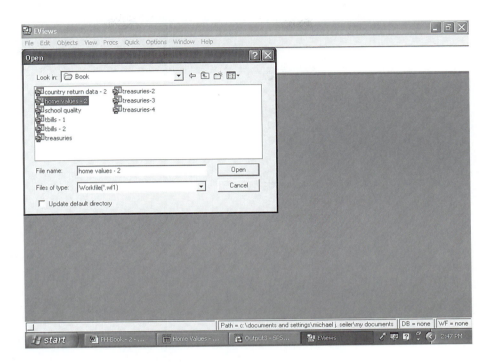

After maximizing your window, your screen should look like this.

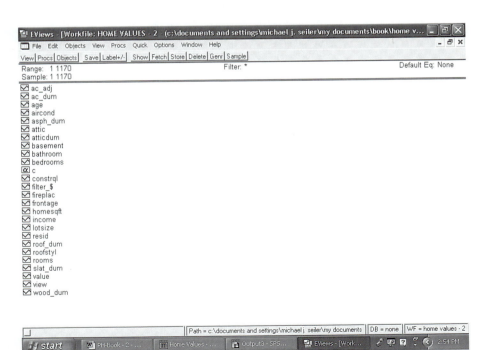

Select the variables that relate to the second stage of the regression. Start by highlighting the dependent variable "value," then continue by highlighting the independent variables "view," "constrql," "age," and "homesqft." You must hold down the "Ctrl" key on your keyboard when you select each subsequent variable.

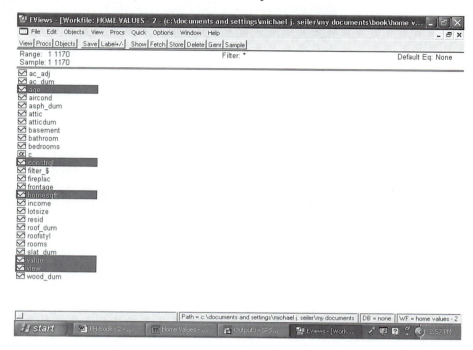

Place your mouse pointer over any part of the highlighted area. Double left-click and a small window will open. Select "Open Equation."

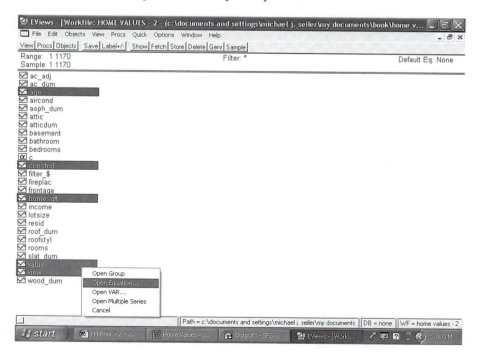

The "Equation Specification" window will appear.

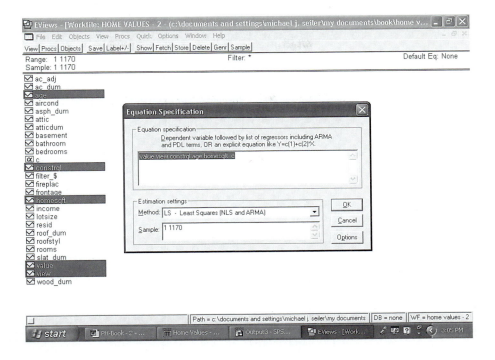

In the "Estimation settings" area, you should see the box titled "Method." Click on the "down arrow" button to view all of the possible methods. Select the method "TSLS - Two Stage Least Squares (TSNLS and ARMA)."

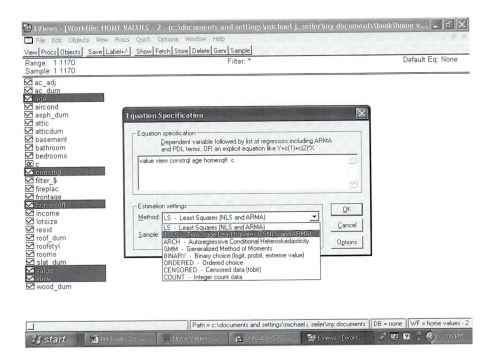

After selecting this method, a variation of the previous "Equation Specification" window will appear.

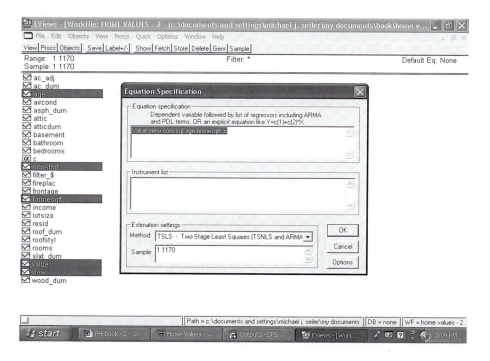

Notice that the originally highlighted variables appear in the top box in the order in which you highlighted them. All that really matters is that the dependent variable "value" is listed first. The remaining variables are all the independent variables. They can be listed in any order. If later you think of an additional variable you wish to add, you can simply type it in manually. Note that the variable "c" is automatically included by EViews. This simply means that your equation will be specified as having a constant.

Let's turn our attention to the "Instrument list." This list includes variables that influence other variables in the model but that are not influenced by those other variables. That is, they can be used to predict other variables in the model. However, the other variables *cannot* be used to predict them.

Under the "Instrument list" box, type in the following five variables: "view," "age," "homesqft," "atticdum," and "slat_dum." These are the five variables that were found to predict "House Construction Quality [constrql]." Your screen should look like this.

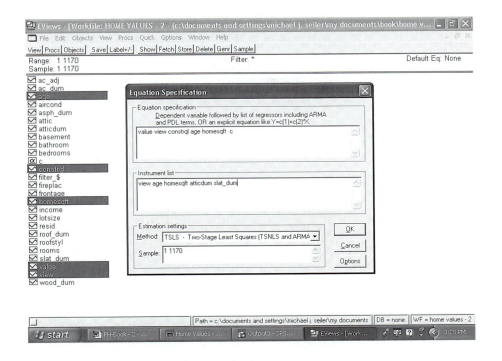

Note that you do not have to include the variable "c" in the "Instrument list" because EViews will do it automatically. If you include the variable "c," it will not change anything. It is like telling a friend not to forget something that they were not going to forget anyway. It is redundant, but does no harm.

When specifying your "Instrument list," one condition must be satisfied. The number of variables in the instrument list must be equal to or greater than the number of variables included in the upper box (the explanatory variables list). You can ignore counting the "constant (c)," because this is included in both equations automatically. Just to clarify, if the variables included in the "Instrument list" are the same as the variables included in the upper box (the explanatory variables list), you are performing a regular (one-stage) regression.

Getting back to the test, once the equation has been specified, click "OK" to perform the test. The output will appear. After maximizing the window, your screen will look like this.

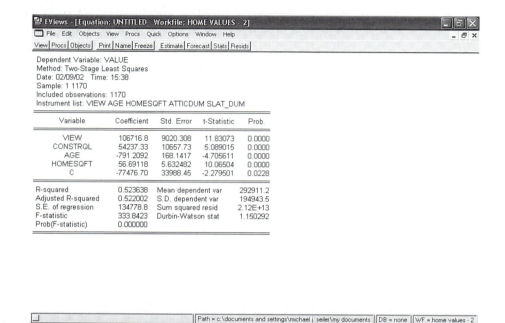

You can verify that the beta coefficients are identical to those generated in SPSS when the two stages were performed separately. The R-square and standard errors are slightly different from the values reported in SPSS. (Again, these differences are due completely to the fact that the two stages have been performed separately in SPSS versus both at one time here in EViews. If we performed the stages separately in EViews, our results would match those from SPSS.) Accordingly, the t-statistics, "Prob." values, F-statistic, and so on will be slightly different. The statistics generated from the simultaneous estimates are completely accurate.

FACTOR ANALYSIS
------⟊⟊⟊------

When performing research, you will often find that the construct you wish to examine is not directly observable. For example, let's try to identify the characteristics that make for an effective finance professor. Could you use just one word to fully describe what makes a good teacher? Most likely, you would find it necessary to point to several attributes: knowledgeable, fair, encourages critical thinking, likes teaching, confident, willing to meet with students, good listener, effective teaching methods, well-defined syllabus, appropriateness in written assignments, interesting course material, clear presentation skills, and so on.

Characteristics such as those just listed are known as variables because each can be directly observed or measured. However, they all relate to an underlying but not directly observable construct(s). Instead of using each of these characteristics as separate independent variables in a regression, factor analysis can be used.

Factor analysis is a statistical technique where many variables can be statistically grouped or reduced down to just a few factors. This dramatic reduction in the number of independent variables allows for much easier interpretation of the results. Moreover, each factor contains variables that are highly correlated with each other but have a low correlation with the variables in the other factors. Therefore, problems, such as multicollinearity, that would otherwise exist can be substantially reduced if not eliminated altogether.

To illustrate the concept of factor analysis, we will refer to the dataset "Faculty Evaluations - 2." "Faculty Evaluations - 2" is a cross-sectional dataset containing the student evaluations of 11 professors in the Department of Finance at a 4-year university in the Midwest. The first 34 questions represent student responses. The remaining seven were added after the survey was administered to measure other characteristics of the class and the professor. Although each variable discussed in this chapter will be explained in the text, additional information on each variable can be found in the Appendix.

10.2 PERFORMING A FACTOR ANALYSIS

To open the "Faculty Evaluations - 2" file in SPSS, click "File" and then "Open" or simply click on the "Open File" icon. Then select the file "Faculty Evaluations - 2" by double-clicking on it.

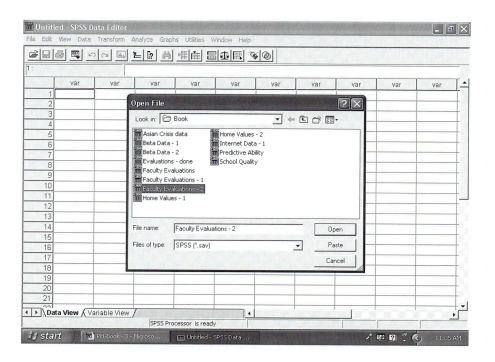

The SPSS "Data" window will appear.

Our goal is to determine the characteristics required to be an effective teacher. As such, we should first agree on our measure of "effectiveness."

Click on the SPSS tab marked "Variable View."

Look down the list of questions and pick the one(s) that truly measure how effective a teacher is in the classroom. My choice is Q34, the "Amount Learned" by the student. After all, shouldn't that be an educator's primary goal?

We are now ready to identify the variables that would contribute to, or explain, student learning. The list of variables I hypothesize to have a significant effect on student learning include Q7–Q15, Q17–Q18, and Q21–Q33. I cannot emphasize enough how important it is to consider each variable carefully. Do not just throw all your variables in and expect SPSS to do the work for you. The rule "garbage in = garbage out" applies here, as it does in all financial research. If you cannot see how a question on this student evaluation of teaching (SET) survey explains teaching effectiveness (student learning), do not include the variable in the analysis.

It is possible to perform a regression analysis with Q34 ("Amount Learned") as the dependent variable and Q7–Q15, Q17–Q18, and Q21–Q33 as the independent variables. However, this model would be wrought with multicollinearity.

Instead, let's perform a factor analysis on the 24 independent variables. To do so, click "Analyze," "Data Reduction," and then "Factor."

The "Factor Analysis" window will appear.

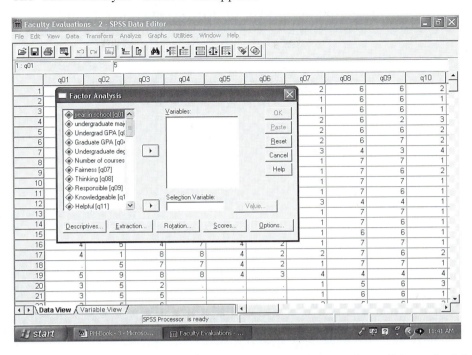

Select the 24 independent variables by highlighting them. Then click on the "right arrow" button in the middle of the screen to move them into the box marked "Variables:". You can do this individually or you can use the "Ctrl" key to select them all at the same time. In either event, when you have included the 24 variables in the analysis, your screen should look like this.

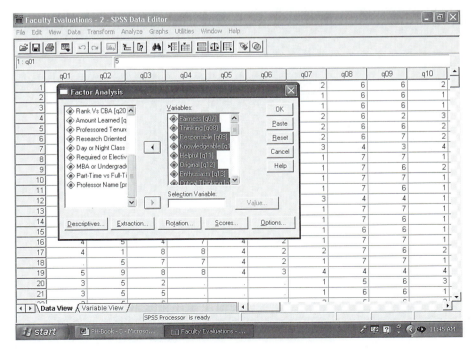

At the bottom of the "Factor Analysis" window, there are five buttons. Click on the one in the middle titled "Rotation." A window named "Factor Analysis: Rotation" will pop up.

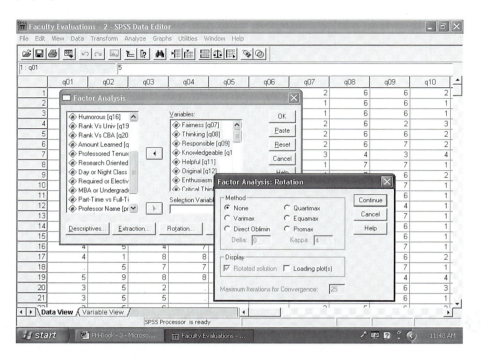

For now, select the method known as "Varimax." The various rotation methods will be explained later in the chapter when such a discussion will be more meaningful to you.

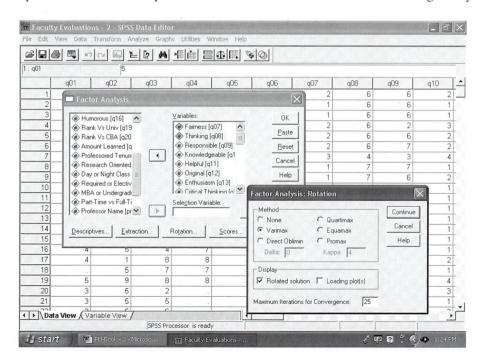

Click "Continue" to get back to the "Factor Analysis" window.

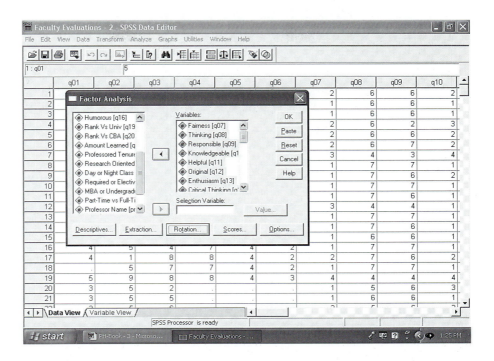

Click on the button marked "Scores." A small window titled "Factor Analysis: Factor Scores" will appear.

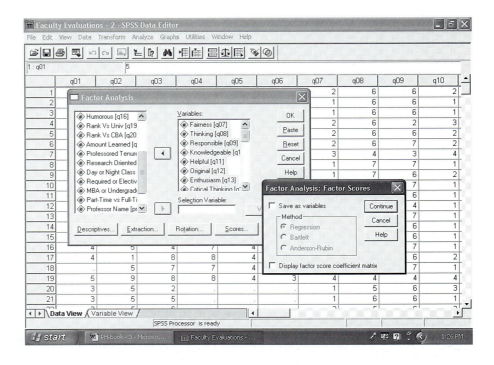

Check the box marked "Save as variables" by left-clicking on it with your mouse.

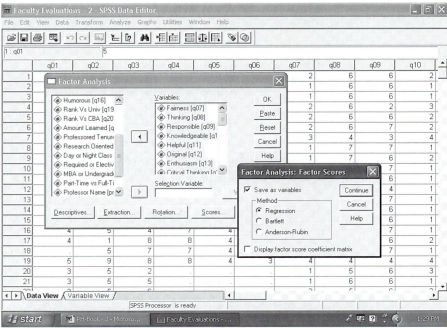

This tells the computer to create a new variable for each factor that emerges from the factor analysis. The reason we want a new variable to be created is because we plan to use the results of our factor analysis to perform a regression.

From the "Factor Analysis: Factor Scores" window, click "Continue."

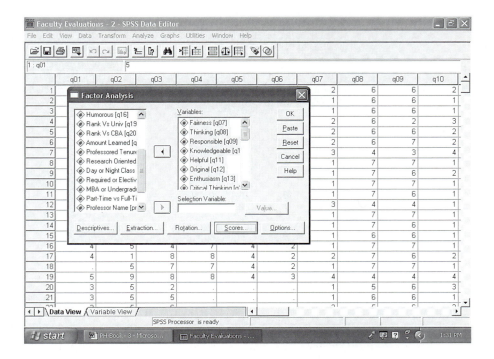

Click "OK" to perform the factor analysis. The following SPSS "Output" window will appear.

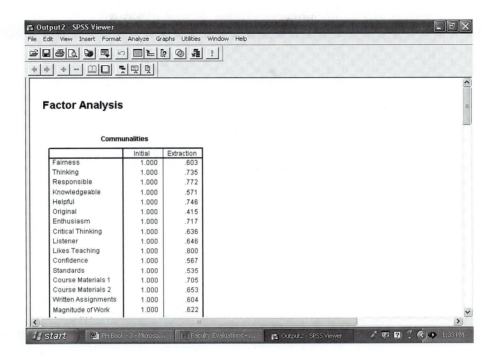

The first table in the "Output" window reports the communality of each variable in the analysis. Communalities report the percentage of variance within each variable that is explained by the resulting factors. For example, the resulting factors explain 60.3% of the variance in the variable Q7 ("Fairness"). The remaining 39.7% of unexplained variance is commonly referred to as the "uniqueness" of the variable.

Scrolling down the "Output" window (and centering for the sake of presentation), we see the "Total Variance Explained" by each resulting factor.

Initial Eigenvalues			Extraction Sums of Squared Loadings			Rotation Sums of Squared Loadings		
Total	% of Variance	Cumulative %	Total	% of Variance	Cumulative %	Total	% of Variance	Cumulative %
12.385	51.606	51.606	12.385	51.606	51.606	8.529	35.540	35.540
2.282	9.510	61.116	2.282	9.510	61.116	4.968	20.698	56.238
1.112	4.634	65.751	1.112	4.634	65.751	2.283	9.513	65.751
.957	3.988	69.739						
.799	3.331	73.070						
.671	2.795	75.865						
.565	2.353	78.218						
.546	2.274	80.492						
.504	2.101	82.593						
.455	1.895	84.488						
.441	1.836	86.324						
.396	1.649	87.973						
.371	1.544	89.517						
.333	1.388	90.905						
.315	1.313	92.218						
.298	1.241	93.459						
.275	1.146	94.605						
.256	1.066	95.671						
.225	.939	96.610						
.219	.912	97.521						
.179	.747	98.268						

Each row in this table references the first, second, and third factor that emerged, and so on. Because 24 variables are included in the analysis, it is mathematically possible to have 24 factors. Of course, if this were the case, it would be as if no factor analysis had been done at all.

The factors are reported in the order of greatest amount of variance explained to the least amount of variance explained. Only factors with an Eigenvalue greater than 1.0 will be considered in the solution. In this example, we see that three factors have emerged. Moreover, the three resulting factors account for 65.751% of the variance.

As a quick aside, the Eigenvalue cutoff of 1.0 is not based on a solid statistical formula for significance. Instead, it is a rule of thumb and an option that can easily be changed in SPSS. However, because there is no reason to select a different number, we will leave this default setting alone.

The next table in the "Output" window is the "Component Matrix."

Component Matrix[a]	Component		
	1	2	3
Fairness	.745	-.117	-.186
Thinking	-.850	-2.37E-03	.115
Responsible	-.857	-8.60E-03	.192
Knowledgeable	.718	.106	-.211
Helpful	.817	-.116	-.256
Original	-.618	8.346E-02	.158
Enthusiasm	.834	-3.27E-03	-.149
Critical Thinking	.794	-1.49E-02	-.079
Listener	-.755	3.069E-02	.275
Likes Teaching	.876	1.903E-02	-.180
Confidence	-.707	-.130	.224
Standards	4.419E-02	.727	-.066
Course Materials 1	.711	-.113	.432
Course Materials 2	.724	-1.79E-02	.357
Written Assignments	.697	-2.14E-02	.343
Magnitude of Work	-.108	.781	3.E-03
Courses' Value	.737	3.709E-02	.395
Course Content	-5.76E-02	.697	-.101
Syllabus	.770	4.208E-02	.155
Challenging	.180	.754	.102
Teaching Methods	.893	-7.16E-03	4.E-02

This matrix represents the unrotated solution. The unrotated solution identifies the relationship between the individual variables and the resulting factors on which they load. For example, recall that in the "Communalities" table, the value for the variable Q7, "Fairness," was .603. This means that 60.3% of the variance in this variable is explained by all three resulting factors. This (unrotated) "Component Matrix" furthers our understanding by providing the breakdown of that 60.3%. Specifically, it tells us how much of the variance is explained by factor 1, factor 2, and factor 3 separately.

In the (unrotated) "Component Matrix" table, the variable Q7, "Fairness," associates the values .745, −.117, and −.186 with factors 1 through 3, respectively. These numbers represent the correlation between the variable and each factor. Therefore, the square of each number represents the proportion of variance explained by each factor. Moreover, the sum of these squares represents the total proportion of variance explained by all the factors. The calculation is as follows:

$$(.745)^2 + (-.117)^2 + (-.186)^2 = .555025 + .013689 + .034596 = .60331 = 60.3\%$$

The problem with an unrotated solution is that the factors are often difficult to interpret. That is, a given variable might load highly on more than one factor. As such, it will be difficult for a researcher to determine in which factor, or grouping, the variable belongs.

To reduce/prevent a single variable from loading too highly on more than one factor, a procedure known as *rotation* is often used in factor analysis. Rotation does not affect the communality of each variable, nor does it change the total variance explained by the model. It does, however, affect the percentage of variance explained by each factor. On the plus side, rotation allows variables a greater opportunity to load highly on just one factor while having near-zero or nonsignificant loadings on all other factors. In this way, the researcher is much more certain which variables belong to which factors. It also makes it easier to name the resulting factors.

The two primary methods used to rotate the factors are *orthogonal rotation* and *oblique rotation*. (Although SPSS lists five methods, the other three are just variations of the two primary methods.) In orthogonal rotation (or "varimax" in SPSS), the axes about which the rotation occurs are maintained at right angles. This method minimizes the number of factors on which a single variable has a high loading. Moreover, orthogonal rotation results in factors that are not correlated with each other. This is a desirable attribute when the resulting factors will be used in a subsequent analysis, such as regression.

The goal of oblique rotation (or "direct oblimin" in SPSS) is also to allow for greater ease in interpreting the factors. However, in an oblique rotation, the axes about which the factors are rotated are not maintained at right angles. Moreover, the resulting factors can be correlated.

Now that we have exhausted a side discussion on the two rotation methods, let me alleviate your anxiety by saying that empirically, the results from the two methods are extremely similar in almost all cases. For one thing, the communalities for each variable are not affected by the rotation method. Also, the percentage of variance explained by the overall model is completely unaffected by the rotation method.

The only potential differences caused by the various rotation methods relate to the number of factors that emerge and the resulting factor loadings. In my experience, it would be rare for the number of factors to be different based on the rotation method. Moreover, very few variables move from one factor to another when changing rotation methods. That is, the variables in the analysis almost always load on the same factors independent of which rotation method is used.

Earlier we decided to use the "varimax" rotation method. The results associated with this method are reported in the next table, "Rotated Component Matrix." To view this matrix, simply scroll down to the next table in the SPSS "Output" window.

Output2 - SPSS Viewer
File Edit View Insert Format Analyze Graphs Utilities Window Help

Rotated Component Matrix[a]

	Component 1	Component 2	Component 3
Fairness	.714	.284	-.108
Thinking	-.756	-.404	-1.14E-02
Responsible	-.808	-.346	-1.85E-02
Knowledgeable	.704	.249	.115
Helpful	.814	.270	-.105
Original	-.595	-.233	7.608E-02
Enthusiasm	.763	.367	5.988E-03
Critical Thinking	.690	.400	-6.75E-03
Listener	-.773	-.218	2.083E-02
Likes Teaching	.815	.367	2.900E-02
Confidence	-.703	-.232	-.139
Standards	6.435E-02	-2.52E-02	.728
Course Materials 1	.325	.766	-.111
Course Materials 2	.379	.713	-1.50E-02
Written Assignments	.365	.686	-1.86E-02
Magnitude of Work	-.100	-5.81E-02	.780
Courses' Value	.366	.752	3.973E-02
Course Content	2.684E-03	-.113	.698
Syllabus	.533	.577	4.755E-02
Challenging	4.105E-02	.239	.754
Teaching Methods	.702	.554	6.751E-04
Course Objectives	.638	.589	-4.35E-03
Class Organization	.698	.564	4.226E-02
Course Expectations	.515	.612	9.233E-02

start   PH-Book - 3 - Microso...   Faculty Evaluations - ...   Output2 - SPSS Viewer   2:33 PM

The values in this table are known as "factor loadings." The greater the absolute value of the factor loading, the more important the variable is in representing the factor. By rule of thumb, factor loadings are typically required to be greater than .50.

Rotated Component Matrix[a]			
	Component		
	1	*2*	*3*
Fairness	.714	.284	−.108
Thinking	−.756	−.404	−1.14E-02
Responsible	−.808	−.346	−1.85E-02
Knowledgeable	.704	.249	.115
Helpful	.814	.270	−.105
Original	−.595	−.233	7.608E-02
Enthusiasm	.763	.367	5.988E-03
Critical Thinking	.690	.400	−6.75E-03
Listener	−.773	−.218	2.083E-02
Likes Teaching	.815	.367	2.900E-02
Confidence	−.703	−.232	−.139
Standards	6.435E-02	−2.52E-02	.728
Course Materials 1	.325	.766	−.111
Course Materials 2	.379	.713	−1.50E-02
Written Assignments	.365	.686	−1.86E-02
Magnitude of Work	−.100	−5.81E-02	.780
Courses' Value	.366	.752	3.973E-02
Course Content	2.684E-03	−.113	.698
Syllabus	.533	.577	4.755E-02
Challenging	4.105E-02	.239	.754
Teaching Methods	.702	.554	6.751E-04
Course Objectives	.638	.589	−4.35E-03
Class Organization	.698	.564	4.226E-02
Course Expectations	.515	.612	9.233E-02

Extraction Method: Principal Component Analysis.

Rotation Method: Varimax with Kaiser Normalization.

[a]Rotation converged in 4 iterations.

To aid our understanding, I have highlighted the factor loadings that I feel best associate each variable with the appropriate factor. This part of the analysis relies more on the "art" of research and less on the "science."

Let's consider the first 11 variables in the table (Q7–Q15 and Q17–Q18). The attributes the students are rating are titled "Fairness," "Thinking," "Responsible," "Knowledgeable," "Helpful," "Original," "Enthusiasm," "Critical Thinking," "Listener," "Likes Teaching," and "Confidence." These variables describe the professor. It is no wonder that these variables load on the same factor. Let's think of this factor as "Professor Characteristics."

Looking at the column associated with factor 2, we see high loadings for Q22–Q24 ("Course Materials 1," "Course Materials 2," and "Written Assignments") and Q26 ("Courses' Value"), among others that we will discuss momentarily. These variables seem to have a common theme; they are all related to the course itself. Let's think of this factor as representing "Course Characteristics."

The last column in the table represents factor loadings for the third factor. The significant variables are Q21 ("Standards"), Q25 ("Magnitude of Work"), Q27 ("Course Content"), and Q29 ("Challenging"). These four variables relate to the workload required in the course. For this reason, I will name this factor "Workload." Feel free to come up with more descriptive titles on your own.

Many times when performing a factor analysis, you will observe a variable that loads highly on more than one factor (even after rotating the solution). This is not a problem. However, you should identify the appropriate factor that the variable will represent. Nineteen of the variables clearly load onto just one factor. The other five are Q28 ("Syllabus"), Q30 ("Teaching Methods"), Q31 ("Course Objectives"), Q32 ("Class Organization"), and Q33 ("Course Expectations"). All five remaining variables load on both factor 1 and factor 2 but not factor 3. As such, all we have to do is select between factors 1 and 2. Let's consider each variable separately.

Q28 is the variable "Syllabus." A syllabus is a class document written by the professor. Its purpose is to state what will be covered in the course, how many tests there will be, how grades will be determined, what chapters will be covered and when, and so forth. Therefore, I would definitely consider this variable to belong to factor 2, "Course Characteristics."

Q30 ("Teaching Methods") should be an easy sell. Clearly this relates to the professor and the effectiveness of his or her teaching style. As such, it belongs in factor 1.

As the titles indicate, Q31 ("Course Objectives"), Q32 ("Class Organization"), and Q33 ("Course Expectations") seem to relate to the course itself. Therefore, I would definitely consider these variables to belong to factor 2, "Course Characteristics." Note that for two of these variables, Q31 and Q32, the factor loadings were actually slightly higher under the other factor. Do not let your results drive your theory. Your theory should come first. This is an important lesson, especially for people who are new to research.

10.3 USING FACTOR SCORES IN A REGRESSION

When the factor analysis was set up, we specified to SPSS that we wanted to save the resulting factors as new variables. Go to the SPSS "Data" window. Click on the "Data View" tab and scroll to the right of your dataset.

Faculty Evaluations - 2 - SPSS Data Editor

File   Edit   View   Data   Transform   Analyze   Graphs   Utilities   Window   Help

1 : q01   5

	research	time	req_elec	mba_und	fullpart	profname	fac1_1	fac2_1	fac3_1	var
1	1	1	2	1	1	9	-.49762	-.14503	-.02238	
2	1	1	2	1	1	9	-.40721	-.41629	-.13490	
3	1	1	2	1	1	9	-.30312	-.85495	.03747	
4	1	1	2	1	1	9	.94735	-1.47710	-1.16524	
5	1	1	2	1	1	9	-.25247	-.63209	-.10496	
6	1	1	2	1	1	9	-.52395	-.09258	-.73681	
7	1	1	2	1	1	9	1.07073	-.08673	-.05336	
8	1	1	2	1	1	9	-.47605	-1.21220	-.72969	
9	1	1	2	1	1	9	-1.27627	.83634	.16936	
10	1	1	2	1	1	9	-.38503	-1.08477	-.52326	
11	1	1	2	1	1	9	-.27500	-.17112	.34261	
12	1	1	2	1	1	9	.			
13	1	1	2	1	1	9	-1.29906	-.11693	.25342	
14	1	1	2	1	1	9	-.84908	-.80867	-.14762	
15	1	1	2	1	1	9			.	
16	1	1	2	1	1	9	-1.18297	-.29577	-.38397	
17	1	1	2	1	1	9				
18	1	1	2	1	1	9	-.62497	.08394	-.20689	
19	1	1	2	1	1	9	.80325	.26816	1.72853	
20	1	1	2	2	1	9	-.70310	.76041	.92022	
21	1	1	2	2	1	9	-.16056	-.48628	1.92372	

Data View   Variable View

SPSS Processor is ready

start   PH-Book - 3 - Microso...   Faculty Evaluations - ...   3:42 PM

You will notice that three new variables have been automatically created. SPSS provides generic titles to the new variables: "fac1_1," "fac2_1," and "fac3_1." You can rename the variables to better reflect your results if you like. The titles "fac1_1," "fac2_1," and "fac3_1" relate to our longer titles, "Professor Characteristics," "Course Characteristics," and "Workload," respectively. Remember that titles can only be up to eight characters long.

Now that the factor analysis has been performed, we can estimate our regression. Recall that our goal is to explain teaching effectiveness. The dependent variable, "teaching effectiveness," is being measured, or proxied, by Q34 ("How much the student learned in the class"). The independent variables include the 24 variables on which we performed a factor analysis. However, now that the factor analysis has been performed, we do not need a regression with 24 independent variables. Instead, we can simply use the three factors that emerged.

To estimate the regression, click "Analyze," "Regression," and then "Linear."

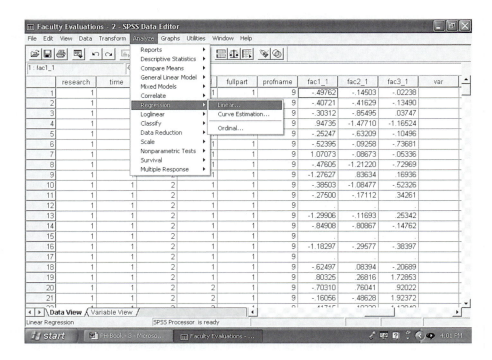

The SPSS "Linear Regression" window will appear.

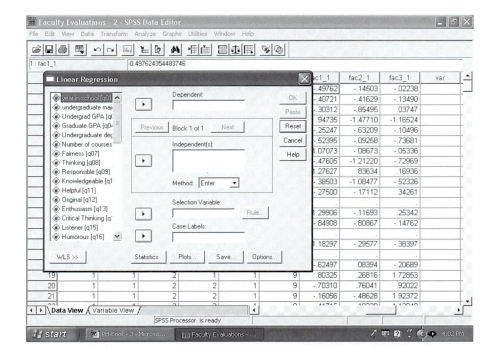

In the left-most box, you will see the list of available variables. Go down the list until you see the variable "Amount Learned [q34]." Highlight this variable by single-clicking on it.

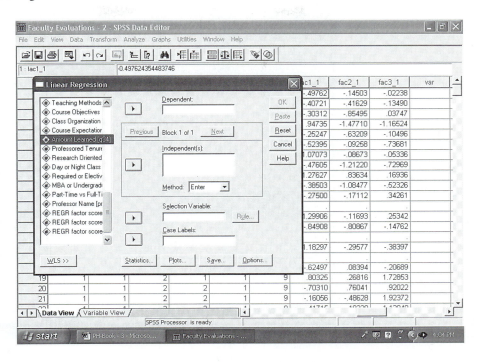

Select it as the dependent variable by clicking on the "right arrow" button next to the box titled "Dependent."

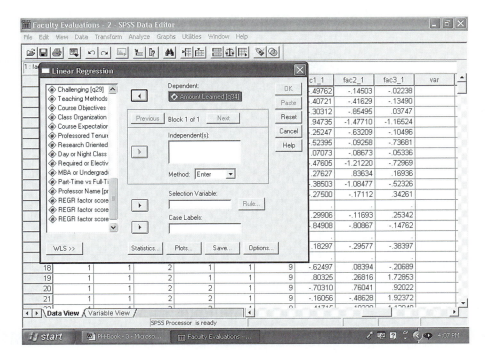

Select the three newly created factors. Go to the very bottom of the variable list and highlight "REGR factor score 1 for analysis 1 [fac1_1]," "REGR factor score 2 for analysis 1 [fac2_1]," and "REGR factor score 3 for analysis 1 [fac3_1]."

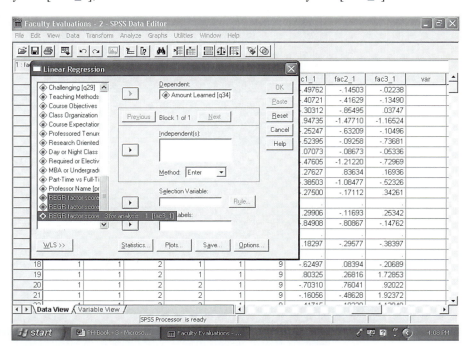

Designate these three factors as the independent variables to be used in the regression by clicking the "arrow" button next to the box titled "Independent(s)." After doing so, your SPSS window should look like this.

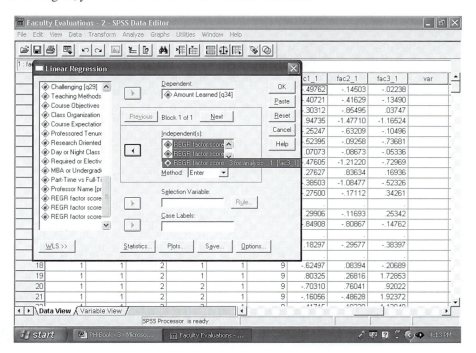

Click the "OK" button to estimate the regression. You should now see the following SPSS "Output" screen.

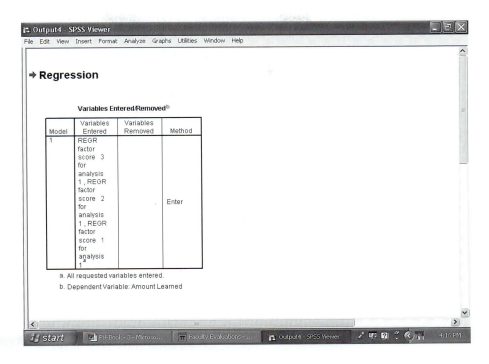

Scroll down the window until you reach the "Model Summary" and the "ANOVA" tables.

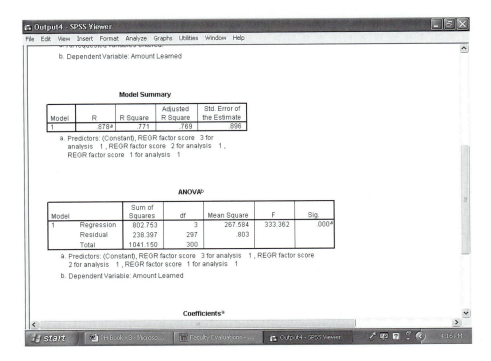

The "Model Summary" and "ANOVA" tables report the results for the overall model. As indicated by the F-statistic and the corresponding "Sig." value, the overall model is significant and quite robust.

If we scroll down further, we can see the results for the individual factors.

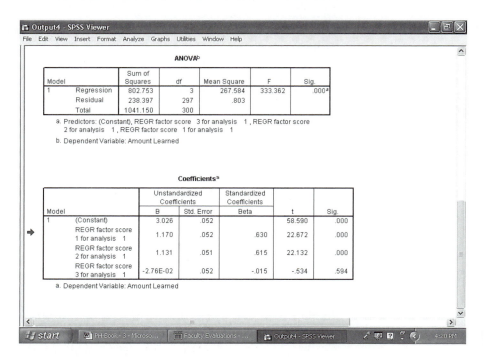

Under the "Coefficients" table, we see that the first two factors are statistically significant, whereas the third factor is not significant. Based on the titles we gave our factors, we would interpret these results to say that "professor" and "course" characteristics significantly affect the amount students learn in the classroom. However, the "workload" required in the course is not significantly related to how much students learn.

10.4 USING A SUMMATED SCALE IN A REGRESSION

As you know, the three new factors were created automatically by SPSS. As such, they do not reflect our slight reclassification of the five questions that loaded highly onto more than one factor. For this reason, there is a difference between the regression results we just obtained and the results we would have obtained had our exact factor specifications been used in the regression analysis. Fortunately, a technique known as creating a *summated scale* enables us to reflect our preferences in a regression.

Creating a summated scale is a very straightforward procedure. First, we must identify which variables load onto which factors. This has already been done (in our previous discussion). We must then create one new variable for each different factor. Instead of calculating complicated factor scores as we did before, all we have to do is take the average value of the variables in each factor. This average value will be calculated for each respondent (student) in the sample. Finally, we will estimate a regression using the three (summated scale) independent variables and the dependent variable (Q34). The results are interpreted just as they would be in any regression. Let's do an example.

Recall that the three factors are composed of the following variables: "Professor Characteristics" (Q7–Q15, Q17–Q18, Q30), "Course Characteristics" (Q22–Q24, Q26, Q28, Q31–Q33), and "Workload" (Q21, Q25, Q27, Q29). To calculate a summated-scale-based variable for factor 1, in the SPSS "Data" window, click "Transform" and then "Compute."

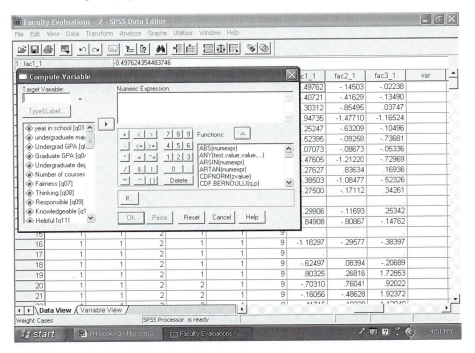

The following "Compute Variable" window will appear.

In the box labeled "Target Variable:" type the name "summfac1." This is short for "summated scale factor 1."

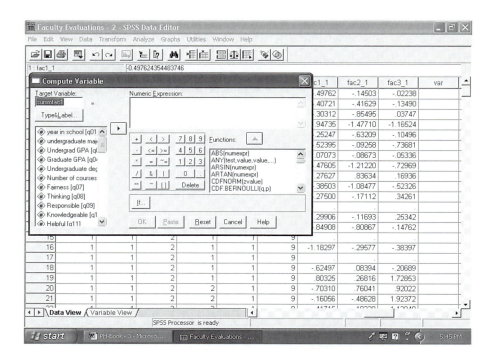

Underneath this box is a button titled "Type&Label." Click the button to open the window "Compute Variable: Type and Label."

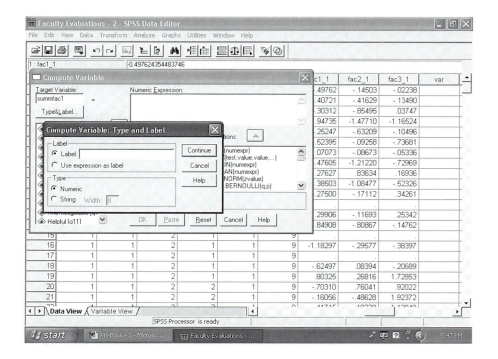

Type the label "summated scale factor 1."

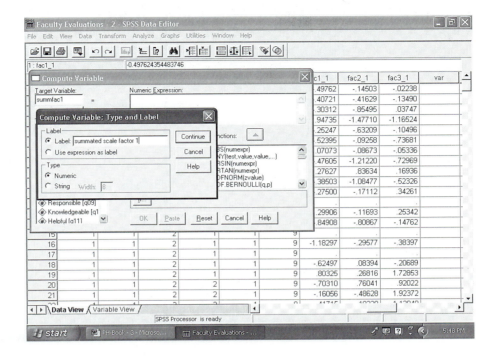

Click "Continue" to return to the "Compute Variable" screen.

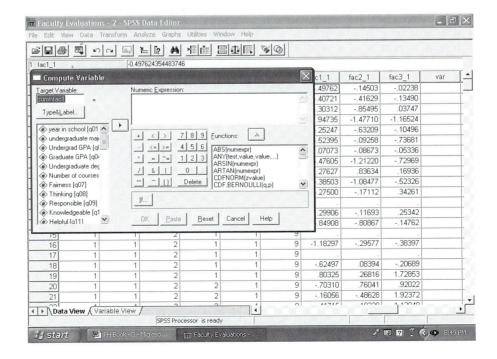

We need to tell SPSS to compute the average value of each variable for each respondent. This formula will be placed in the box titled "Numeric Expression." If you do not already know the SPSS command for calculating the mean, you can find it by scrolling through the "Functions" box.

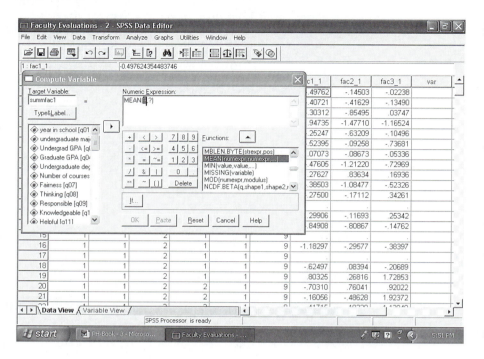

After the command "MEAN," include the names of each variable in factor 1.

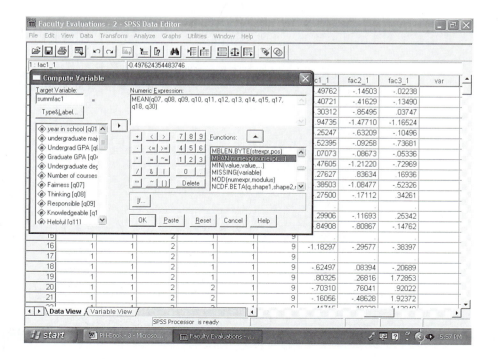

Click "OK" to complete the new variable. You can see your newly created variable in the farthest-right column in the SPSS "Data" window.

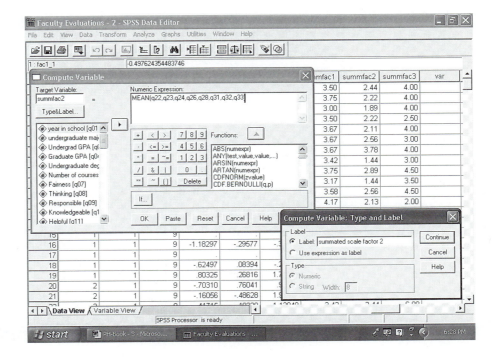

Now do the same for the second factor. Because the procedure has just been shown in great detail, for the sake of brevity, all three screens will be shown here at once.

Your SPSS "Data" window should appear as follows.

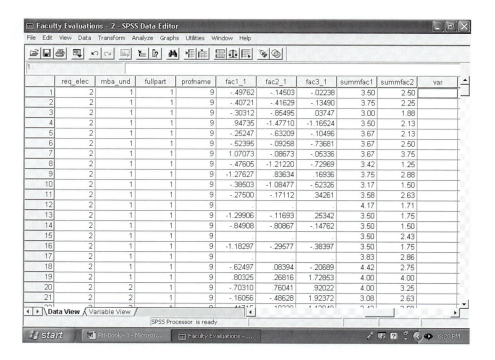

Finally, complete the summated scale variable for the third factor. The "Compute Variable" window should be completed as shown here.

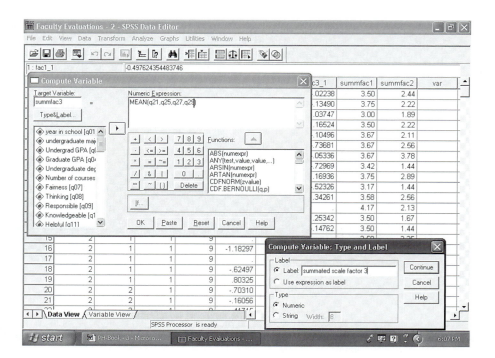

Your SPSS "Data" window should now look like this.

With our newly created independent variables ready, we can now estimate the regression. From the SPSS "Data" window, click "Analyze," "Regression," and then "Linear."

The "Linear Regression" window will pop up.

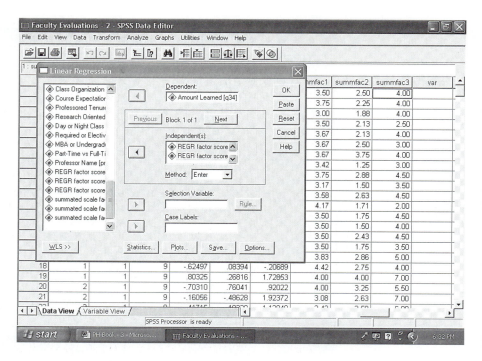

SPSS still remembers your last regression. You can either click the "Reset" button and respecify the model from scratch or you can swap out the three previous factors with the newly created summated scale factors. To do the latter, highlight the three previously used independent variables.

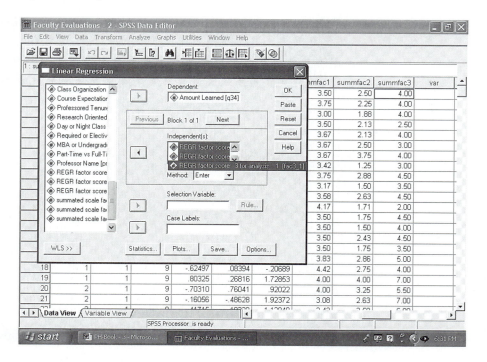

Now click the "arrow" button next to the "Independent(s)" box to remove the three factors.

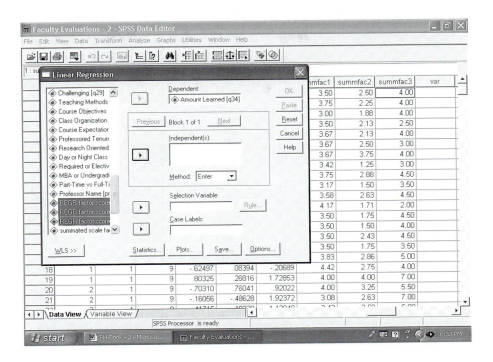

At the bottom of the variable list are the three newly created summated scale factors. Highlight these three factors.

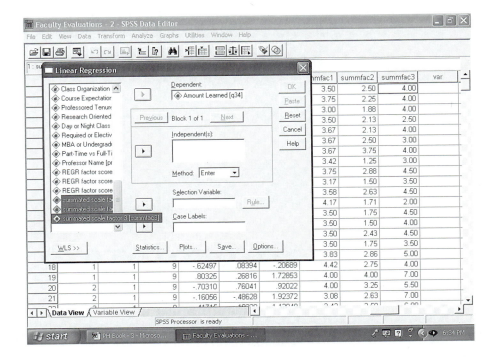

Click the "arrow" button next to the box marked "Independent(s)" to include the three new factors in the regression.

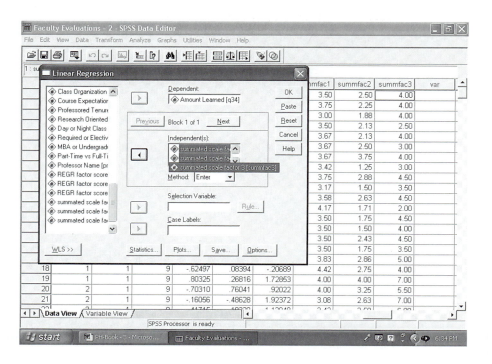

Click on the "OK" button to perform the regression. After scrolling down a few rows, the following SPSS "Output" window can be seen.

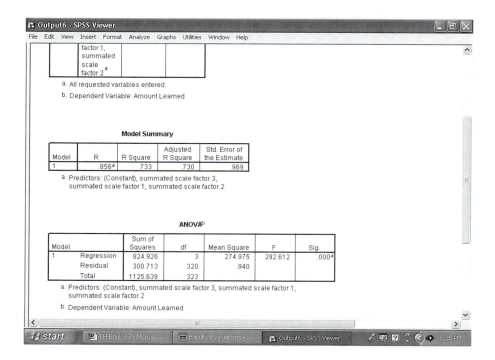

The "Model Summary" and "ANOVA" tables report that the overall regression model is statistically significant and quite robust as indicated by the "Sig." value.

Scrolling down to the bottom of the table, we see that t-statistics for the first two factors are again statistically significant, whereas the third factor is not significant.

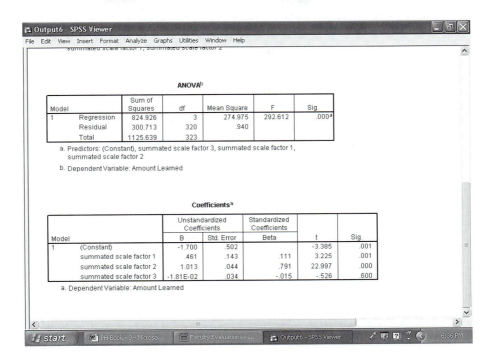

The results from the two methods are extremely similar in our example. In general, the greater the extent to which the variables load onto just one factor, the less likely it is that the researcher will have to choose which variables belong to which factors, and the more similar the results will be.

To complete this section, save the SPSS "Data" file under the name "Faculty Evaluations - 3." That way, if you ever want to go back to this model, you will not have to repeat all of these steps.

11

CALCULATING
A STOCK'S BETA

11.1 PURPOSE OF CALCULATING A STOCK'S BETA

Total risk is equal to systematic risk plus unsystematic risk. In a diversified portfolio (all rational investors will be diversified), unsystematic risk will be diversified away. Therefore, all that remains is systematic risk, or risk that cannot be removed through diversification. Because systematic risk is all that remains, it is the measure of risk used by investors to establish the required rate of return on a stock. *Beta* is the measure of this systematic (or nondiversifiable) risk.

Mathematically, beta is equal to the covariance between a stock and the market divided by the variance on the market. You are probably not interested in the formula for beta. Instead, you are interested in how to calculate beta.

A stock with a beta above 1.0 indicates that the stock is more risky than average. Conversely, a stock with a beta value below 1.0 indicates that the stock has a risk level below the market average.

To demonstrate the calculation of beta, we will consider the dataset "Beta Data - 2." This time series dataset contains the monthly yield on 3-month Treasury Bills, the value of the S&P 500 Index, and stock prices (adjusted for stock splits) for both Microsoft and Netegrity from January 1998 through December 2001. It also contains the returns and excess returns for the S&P 500, Microsoft, and Netegrity.

11.2 CALCULATING BETA

To open the "Beta Data - 2" file in SPSS, click "File" and then "Open" or simply click on the "Open File" icon. Then select the file "Beta Data - 2" by double-clicking on it.

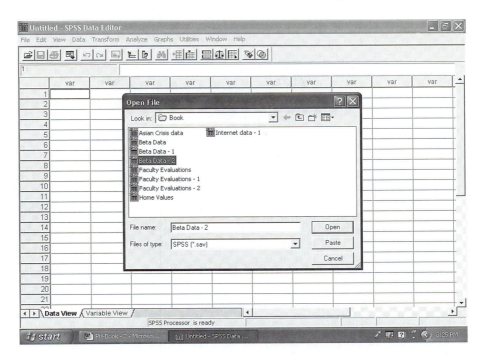

You should see the SPSS "Data" screen.

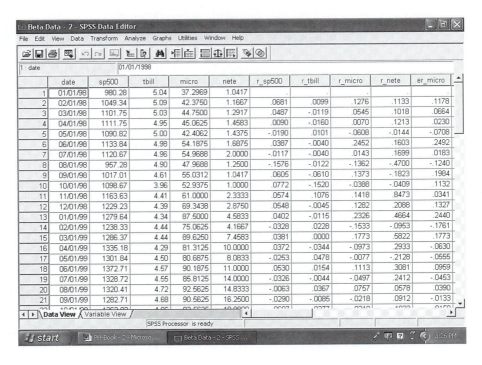

Beta is calculated by regressing the excess returns on a stock (the one for which you are calculating beta) against the excess returns on the market (the market portfolio is approximated by the S&P 500 Index).

In Chapter 2, the calculation of excess return was explained in great detail. For this example, we will simply use the variables that are already in the dataset.

Let's calculate beta for Microsoft. To estimate this regression, click "Analyze," "Regression," and then "Linear."

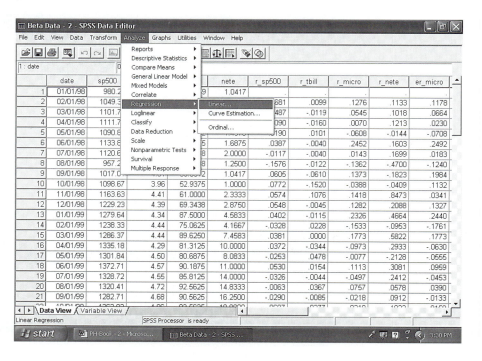

The "Linear Regression" screen will appear.

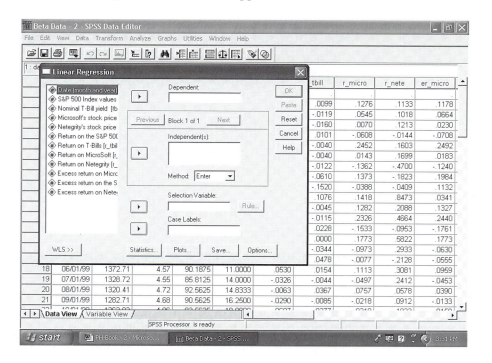

The dependent variable is the excess return on Microsoft, "er_micro." To convey this to SPSS, highlight the variable "Excess Return on Microsoft [er_micro]" from the list of variables.

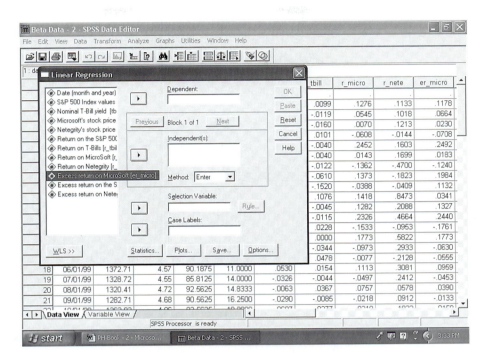

Click on the "right arrow" button next to the box titled "Dependent."

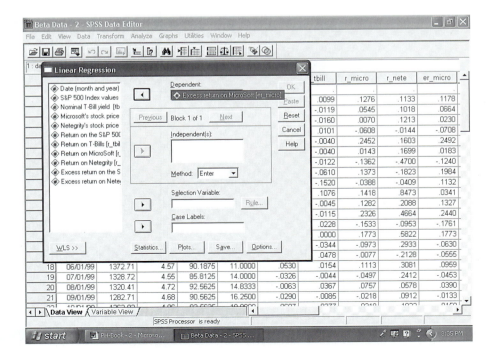

The only independent variable we need is the excess return on the S&P 500. To select this series, highlight "Excess return on the S&P 500 Index [er_sp500]" from the list of variables.

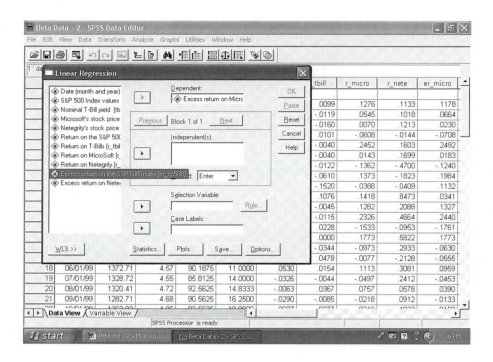

Click on the "right arrow" button next to the box titled "Independent(s)."

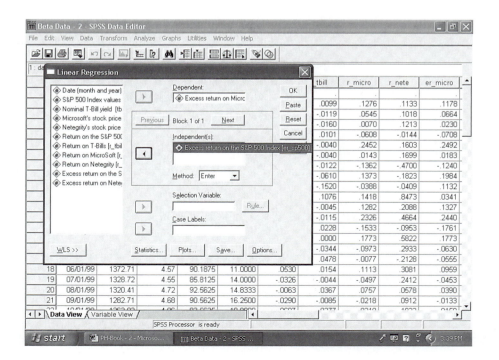

Click "OK" to perform the test. The SPSS "Output" screen will appear. Scroll down to the bottom of the "Output" window to get to the beta value for Microsoft.

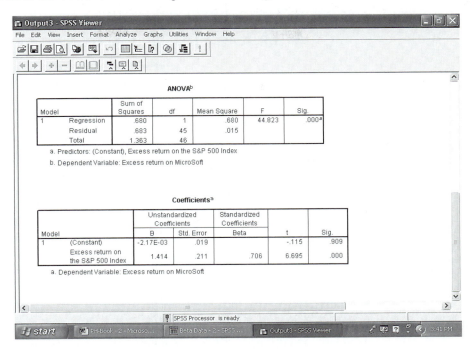

In the last table, "Coefficients," find the *unstandardized* beta coefficient that is associated with your only independent variable, "Excess return on the S&P 500 Index [er_sp500]." The value in our example is 1.414. This is the beta of Microsoft.

11.3 INTERPRETING BETA

As we just established, 1.414 is the unstandardized beta coefficient. This beta coefficient is interpreted the same way we would interpret any beta coefficient resulting from a regression. Beta is a measure of sensitivity. Specifically, it measures how much a one-unit change in the excess return on the S&P 500 (the independent variable) should change the excess return on Microsoft (the dependent variable).

For example, if the excess return on the market increases by 1%, we would expect, on average, the excess return on Microsoft to increase by 1.414%. If the excess return on the market increases by 2%, we would expect, on average, the excess return on Microsoft to increase by 2.828% (2 × 1.414%). Conversely, if the excess return on the market were expected to decrease by 5%, we would expect, on average, the excess return on Microsoft to decrease by 7.070% (5 × 1.414%).

The beta of the market (the average stock on the market) is always equal to 1.0. We know this because the calculation involves regressing the excess returns on the S&P 500 against the excess returns on the S&P 500. Any time you estimate a simple regression where the dependent variable and the independent variable are the same, the beta will equal 1.0.

Because the beta on the average stock is equal to 1.0, a beta value above 1.0 indicates that a stock is more risky than average. Conversely, a beta value below 1.0 indicates a stock with a risk below the market average.

12

PREDICTIVE ABILITY

12.1 PURPOSE OF MEASURING PREDICTIVE ABILITY

One of the longest-standing debates in finance is whether or not fund managers have the ability to predict the performance of individual stocks or mutual funds. Instead of debating the issue further, this chapter shows you how to form your own opinion on this issue. We will examine a technique known as the information coefficient (IC) method that will enable you to measure the predictive ability of an analyst to select the best-performing mutual funds. This analysis could also be performed for individual stocks or any other asset.

To measure an analyst's predictive abilities, we will consider the dataset "Predictive Ability." This file contains cross-sectional data relating to 247 mutual funds. For each of the funds, the returns for 1998 and 1999 are given, as well as the resulting fund ranking. Finally, the predicted mutual fund rankings, associated with five industry analysts, are also listed.

12.2 MEASURING PREDICTIVE ABILITY USING ORDINAL RANKINGS

To open the "Predictive Ability" file in SPSS, click "File" and then "Open" or simply click on the "Open File" icon. Then select the file "Predictive Ability" by double-clicking on it.

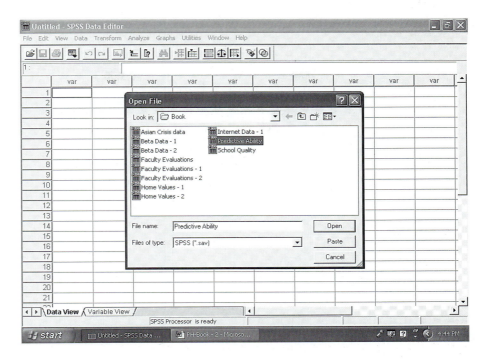

You should see the SPSS "Data" screen.

This sample includes 247 small capitalization growth mutual funds. The annual returns for the years 1998 and 1999 are provided for each fund. Assume today's date is January 1, 1999. Each of five analysts will attempt to predict the order (or rank), from best to worst, in which the funds will perform in 1999.

The analysts' predicted rankings are provided in the columns "analyst1," "analyst2," "analyst3," "analyst4," and "analyst5." The predictive ability of each analyst can be determined in two ways. The first is to perform a regression. To estimate the regression, select "Analyze," "Regression," and then "Linear."

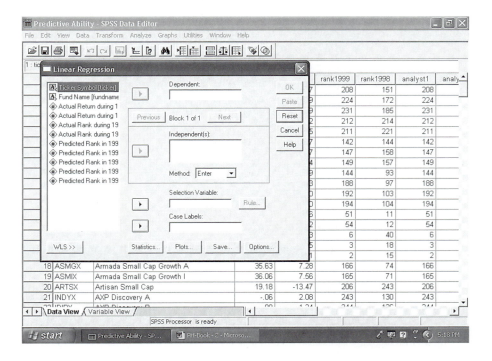

The "Linear Regression" window will appear.

For the dependent variable, select "Actual Rank during 1999 [rank1999]." Under the box titled "Independent(s)," select the variable "Predicted Rank in 1999 by Analyst 1 [analyst1]."

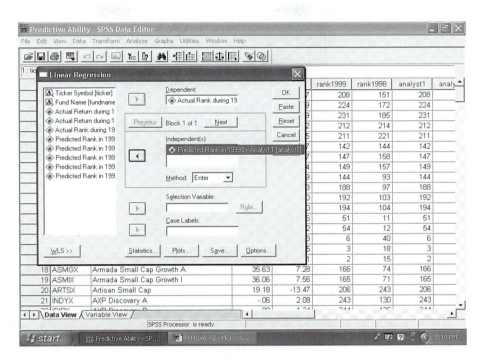

Click "OK" to perform the regression. The SPSS "Output" window will appear.

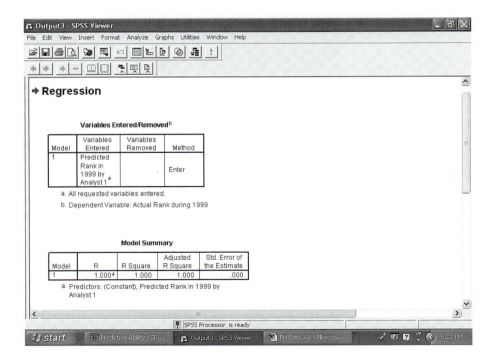

Notice that the R-square value is 1.000. Scroll down to the next two output tables in SPSS. They will appear as follows.

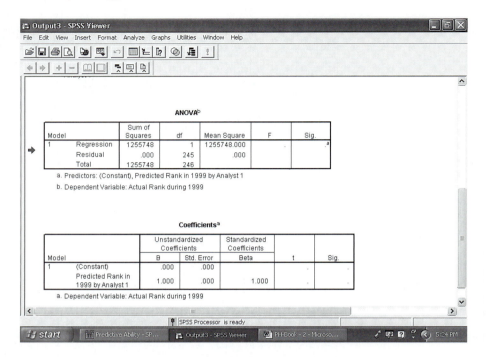

The beta value for the regression is also 1.000. In this situation, analyst 1 has perfect predictive ability. Although this would never happen in reality, I wanted to show you the extreme case of an analyst successfully predicting with 100% accuracy the ranking of all 247 funds. In other words, we have just established the upper boundary for predictive ability. Let's perform the same analysis for analyst 2. To estimate the regression, select "Analyze," "Regression," and then "Linear."

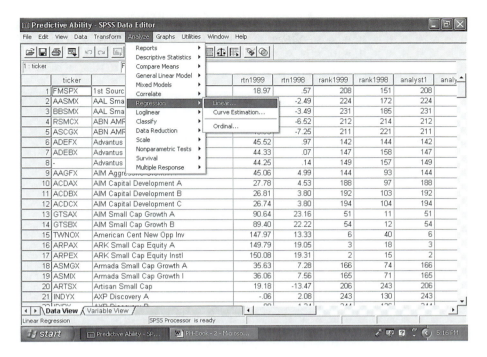

The "Linear Regression" window will appear.

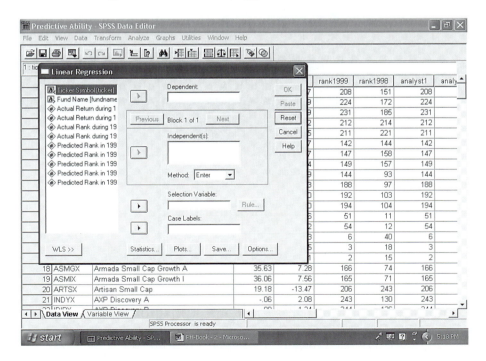

For the dependent variable, select "Actual Rank during 1999 [rank1999]." Under the box titled "Independent(s)," select the variable "Predicted Rank in 1999 by Analyst 2 [analyst2]."

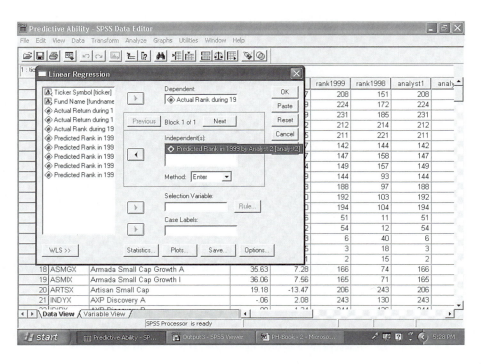

Click "OK" to perform the regression. The SPSS "Output" window will appear.

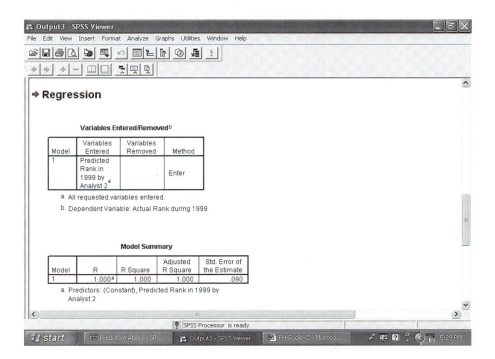

Again, we see an R-square value of 1.000. If you scroll down to the next two SPSS "Output" tables, you will see a beta value of –1.000.

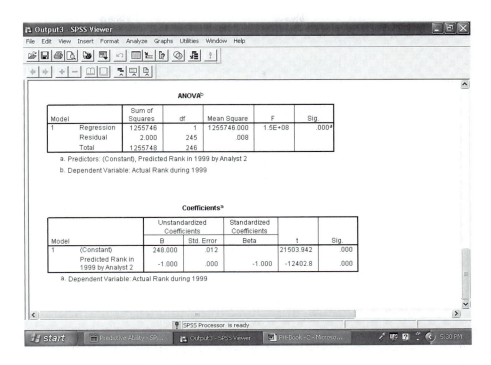

This means that analyst 2 could not have done a worse job of selecting mutual funds. Stated another way, the mutual fund that analyst 2 said would perform the best actually did the worst. The fund that analyst 2 said would rank second ranked second from the last. This horrific predictive ability sets the boundary for the lowest ability that can be observed. We have now established that all predictive ability (or IC) values will be equal to or between plus and minus 1.0. A value of 1.0 indicates perfectly positive predictive ability. A value of −1.0 indicates perfectly negative predictive ability. In the middle, a value of 0.0 indicates what would be expected if the analyst selected funds by randomly drawing fund names out of a hat or throwing darts at a board.

Let's measure the predictive ability of analyst 3. For the sake of brevity, only the output will be shown here. However, as a reminder, when performing the regression, place "Actual Rank during 1999 [rank1999]" in the "Dependent" box. Under the box titled "Independent(s)," select the variable "Predicted Rank in 1999 by Analyst 3 [analyst3]." The SPSS "Output" tables will appear as follows.

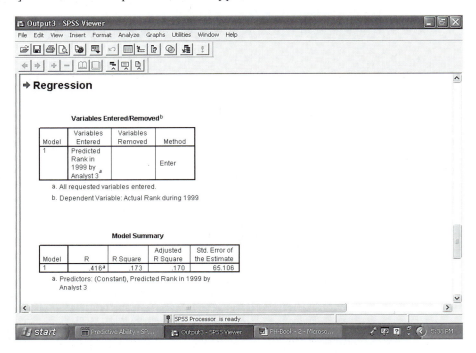

The final two tables can be viewed by scrolling down the window.

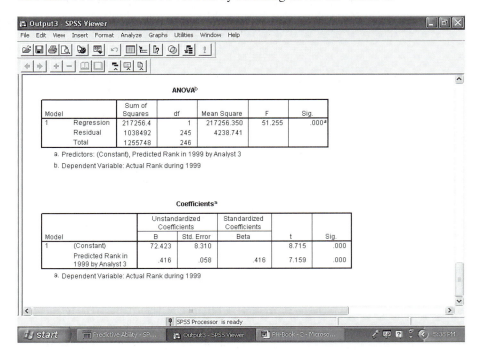

Notice that the beta value, .416, is associated with a statistically significant t-statistic (7.159). We know this because the "Sig." value is below .05. Another way to interpret the beta value is that it is the same as the correlation coefficient. Moreover, the beta value is the same as the number reported for the model's overall R value.

Let's get back to what this significant beta value means. When determining the significance of beta, regression compares the beta value to zero. Therefore, we would interpret the beta value of .416 to be statistically significantly different from zero. In our example, a beta of zero would indicate that an analyst has no predictive power whatsoever. Alternatively stated, it is the value we would expect to see if the analyst randomly assigned the predictive ranking to each fund. This is what we would expect if we pulled the fund names out of a hat and ranked them in the order in which we pulled them.

That being said, because the predictive ability beta associated with analyst 3 is significantly different from zero, we would say that the analyst is doing better than we would if we were to draw mutual fund names out of a hat (or throw darts at a board).

To measure the predictive ability of the remaining two analysts, analysts 4 and 5, the same procedure would be run. For the sake of brevity, only the results for the beta value and the corresponding t-statistics are reported. The beta value for analyst 4 is –.104, and the associated t-statistic is –1.63 ("Sig." = .104). The negative value means that analyst 4 did worse than what we would expect to do if we were to throw darts at a board. However, because the t-statistic is not statistically significant, we would interpret the result as meaning that the analyst did not significantly differ from a person with no predictive ability.

The beta value for analyst 5 is .127. The associated t-statistic is 2.004 ("Sig." = .046). Therefore, analyst 5 does show significant ability to rank mutual funds at the 95% level of confidence (because the "Sig." value is below .05).

In practical terms, because analysts 1, 3, and 5 demonstrated significant predictive ability, they can expect to keep their jobs. Analysts 2 and 4, on the other hand, should update their resumes and start looking for alternative places of employment.

Instead of performing regressions to demonstrate predictive ability, it is possible to perform the same analysis using a simple correlation coefficient. In fact, this method may be preferred because all five predictive assessments can be performed at once.

To perform the calculations all at the same time, select "Analyze," "Correlate," and then "Bivariate."

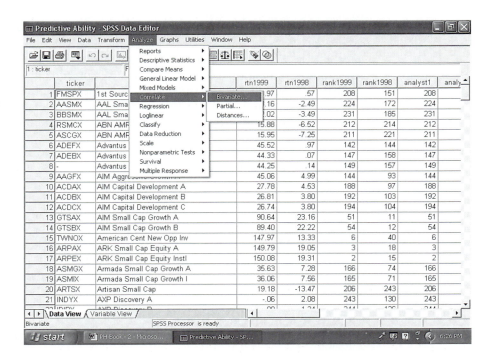

The following "Bivariate Correlations" window will appear.

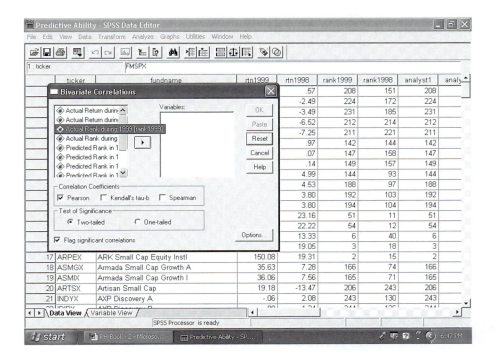

Select all six variables: "Actual Rank during 1999 [rank1999]," "Predicted Rank in 1999 by Analyst 1 [analyst1]," "Predicted Rank in 1999 by Analyst 2 [analyst2]," "Predicted Rank in 1999 by Analyst 3 [analyst3]," "Predicted Rank in 1999 by Analyst 4 [analyst4]," and "Predicted Rank in 1999 by Analyst 5 [analyst5]."

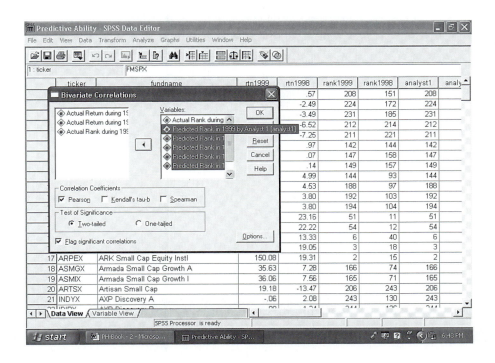

Click "OK" to perform the test. The results from the correlation analysis are as follows.

Correlations

		Actual Rank during 1999	Predicted Rank in 1999 by Analyst 1	Predicted Rank in 1999 by Analyst 2	Predicted Rank in 1999 by Analyst 3	Predicted Rank in 1999 by Analyst 4	Predicted Rank in 1999 by Analyst 5
Actual Rank during 1999	Pearson Correlation	1	1.000**	-1.000**	.416**	-.104	.127*
	Sig. (2-tailed)	—	—	.000	.000	.104	.046
	N	247	247	247	247	247	247
Predicted Rank in 1999 by Analyst 1	Pearson Correlation	1.000**	1	-1.000**	.416**	-.104	.127*
	Sig. (2-tailed)	—	—	.000	.000	.104	.046
	N	247	247	247	247	247	247
Predicted Rank in 1999 by Analyst 2	Pearson Correlation	-1.000**	-1.000**	1	-.416**	.104	-.127*
	Sig. (2-tailed)	.000	.000	—	.000	.105	.046
	N	247	247	247	247	247	247
Predicted Rank in 1999 by Analyst 3	Pearson Correlation	.416**	.416**	-.416**	1	.014	.112
	Sig. (2-tailed)	.000	.000	.000	—	.821	.080
	N	247	247	247	247	247	247
Predicted Rank in 1999 by Analyst 4	Pearson Correlation	-.104	-.104	.104	.014	1	.416*
	Sig. (2-tailed)	.104	.104	.105	.821	—	.000
	N	247	247	247	247	247	247
Predicted Rank in 1999 by Analyst 5	Pearson Correlation	.127*	.127	-.127*	.112	.416**	1
	Sig. (2-tailed)	.046	.046	.046	.080	.000	—
	N	247	247	247	247	247	247

As you can see, the beta values reported in the regressions are the same as the Pearson Correlation Coefficients reported in the correlation analysis. Moreover, the associated t-statistics and "Sig." values are the same as well.

12.3 MEASURING PREDICTIVE ABILITY USING RAW RETURNS

Mathematically speaking, when measuring an analyst's ability to pick stocks or mutual funds, it is more accurate to use raw returns. However, in practice, the results should be extremely similar. The use of ranking data, as opposed to raw data, will cause a "smoothing" of the results. That is, the use of ranking data will tend to pull in extremely high and low values. The result will be a measure that makes the analyst appear more able to predict performance. Again, however, the difference is negligible.

To perform the test for predictive ability using raw returns, the same procedure should be followed as detailed in the previous section. Empirically, it has been found that analysts have a modest ability to differentiate between attractive and unattractive stocks. The correlation coefficient has been found to range between .05 and .20 for analysts as a group.

13

EVENT STUDIES

13.1   PURPOSE OF AN EVENT STUDY

It is generally understood that stock prices reflect relevant information that is known about a firm's future. As such, when new relevant information reaches the market, the price of the stock should change accordingly. If the market is perfectly efficient, we should see the stock price change instantaneously to reflect this newly learned information. However, this is not always the case. Instead, it is often observed that the new information is leaked out several weeks before the official public announcement by the firm. Conversely, it might take more than one period for the market to fully interpret the news.

In order to measure how a firm's stock price reacts to new information, an *event study* methodology is used. For example, you might want to determine the impact of a merger announcement on the price of a firm's stock. Other common firm-specific events that can be examined include stock splits, earnings announcements, a bond rating upgrade (or downgrade), and the adverse (or favorable) ruling in a major court decision.

The impact of market-wide events on a firm can be measured as well. Examples of market-wide events include the Federal Reserve raising (or lowering) interest rates, changes in accounting regulations, and newly released macroeconomic data such as new home sales, consumer sentiment, gross domestic product (GDP), retail sales, the CPI, and the unemployment rate.

13.2   BACKGROUND

An event study requires eight steps:

1. Identify the event date (the date on which the event occurred).
2. Define the event window.
3. Define the estimation period.
4. Select the sample of firms.
5. Calculate "normal" (nonevent) returns (the returns that would have occurred in the absence of the event).
6. Calculate abnormal returns (ARs) (the actual returns that occurred because of the event minus the returns that would have occurred without the event, that is, nonevent returns).
7. Calculate cumulative abnormal returns (CARs) (the aggregation of the ARs).
8. Determine the statistical significance of the ARs and CARs.

13.2.1   IDENTIFY THE EVENT DATE

The first step is to identify the event date. Although this sounds easy, it does require some thought. The event date is defined as the time when the market first learns of the relevant new information (the event). For example, when a company experiences a change in its bond rating, should you consult the Moody's wire service to identify the exact date? Does the Wall Street Journal Index publish all rating changes? Should you get the change from another third-party data provider? Studies have shown that discrepancies and reporting delays exist among providers. The less accurate you are in identifying the event date, the less powerful the test, and therefore, the less able you are to accurately measure the impact of the event on the firm.

Event studies can be performed using any data frequency (e.g., monthly, daily, intraday). However, daily data are the most common for several reasons. First, monthly observations are far too infrequent to isolate the event from the period before and after the event. It is like trying to watch a slight-of-hand card trick with the naked eye as opposed to having a slow-motion camera where you can see the trick done frame by frame. Second, in theory, intraday data should allow you to better understand the market's reaction to an event if the event can be associated with an exact time of day. However, this is rarely the case. In addition, if you are unable to pinpoint the exact event time, using intraday data can weaken the power of your test.

13.2.2 DEFINE THE EVENT WINDOW

Once you have identified the date on which the event occurred, the next step is to define the number of trading periods (usually days) preceding and following that date to include in the event window. Researchers have not established a recommended number of days. In general, the more unnecessary days you have in the event window, the less powerful the test. That is, the more certain you are about the event date, the smaller the event window can be, and the more powerful will be your measurement of the significance of the event on the firm's stock price.

As an example, when examining stock returns surrounding a merger announcement, studies have found that the price of the target firm significantly increases in value well before there is any public information available to justify the change in price. This phenomenon, known as *leakage*, describes an environment where someone involved with the merger (e.g., lawyers, board members, analysts, etc.) leaked the news to someone who ultimately purchased shares of stock in the target firm. The price of the target firm significantly increases in value well before there is any public information available to justify the price increase. This has been found to occur up to a month in advance of the public announcement of a merger. In our example, you should include enough days in the event window to pick up the effects of leakage. If you do not, you will not be measuring the full effect of the event on the stock price of the firm.

Again, researchers have not reached consensus on the optimal number of trading days to include in the event window. For extremely certain events with little to no chance of leakage (such as the sudden death of a CEO), as few as plus and minus 10 trading days can be used (–10 through +10, where zero is defined as the event date). For less certain event dates and for events with substantially long periods of suspected leakage, a window of –30 through +30 can be used. In sum, the event window should cover the entire effect of the event but at the same time be as short as possible.

13.2.3 DEFINE THE ESTIMATION PERIOD

The estimation period is the period of time over which no event has occurred. It is used to establish how the returns on the stock should behave in the absence of the event. There are three main choices concerning the estimation period: before the event window, during the event window, and after the event window.

The most common method is to define the estimation period as the period of time before the event window. For example, if the event window is −10 through +10, the estimation period might occur from −60 through −11. If the event window is −30 through +30, the estimation period might occur from −120 through −31. The theory behind making sure that the estimation period and event window do not overlap is that you want an unbiased estimate of how the firm's stock price behaves when the event is not present. If the two overlap, you have what is known as *contamination.*

It might sound very strange to have an estimation period concurrent with the event window, but in some circumstances there is no other choice. For example, consider IPOs. If you want to test if new stock issues over- or underperform in the first few days of trading, it is not possible to have an estimation period before the event window.

It is possible to define the estimation period as the period after the event window. The only reason for doing this is if the event was so dramatic that it changed the fundamental relationship between the behavior of the stock and the market. For example, if the event window is −20 through +20, the estimation period might range from +21 through +100 or +21 through +180.

Estimation periods for daily data longer than 1 year (roughly 250 trading days) are rare. Studies using weekly data typically use a year of returns (52 weekly returns). Finally, for monthly data, it is necessary to go back much further. Because regression is most often used during the estimation period, 30 observations are generally viewed as the minimum required to obtain reliable results. To be on the safe side, studies using monthly data might consider the inclusion of 60 observations (5 years worth of returns).

In closing, the number of periods in the estimation period is not standard for all studies. In general, you want to make the interval wide enough to capture the relationship between the stock and the market, but not so wide that the estimated relationship no longer applies to the firm today.

The following graphical representation should help readers understand the typical event study time frame.

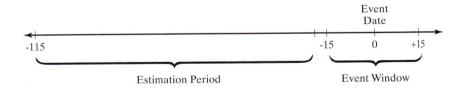

13.2.4 SELECT THE SAMPLE OF FIRMS

No matter what event is being studied, you must define the screening criteria you will use to select your final sample. For example, are you interested in firms listed only on the New York Stock Exchange (NYSE) or belonging to a certain industry? How many trading day observations will you require a firm to have in order to avoid the problems of nonsynchronous (infrequent) trading?

One screening criterion should be the exclusion of firms that experienced more than one major event over either the estimation period or the event window. You want to kick these firms out of the sample because of contagion effects (i.e., not being able to distinguish between two effects because both occurred around the same period of time). Which event is driving the returns on the stock? Because more than one event is occurring, you cannot be sure.

13.2.5 CALCULATE NORMAL (OR NONEVENT) RETURNS

The next step is to determine what the returns on the sample of stocks would be in the absence of the event. These are called *normal returns*. Normal returns can be calculated by four different methods: mean return, market return, proxy (or control) portfolio return, and risk-adjusted return.

13.2.5.1 Mean Return

The mean return approach assumes that the mean of the stock's return over the event window is expected to be the same as the mean over the estimation period. That is, ARs are defined as the difference between actual return and expected return, where the expected return for each of the days in the event window is equal to the mean return on the stock over the estimation period. This approach is extremely simple. Surprisingly, under certain conditions, the assumption has been found to do a fairly decent job of determining normal returns. The consensus in the field is that it is not as good as more advanced methods, but at the same time, it is not much worse.

When will this simple method cause problems? Serious problems will arise in the case where the firms in the sample have event dates that are very close together, which is known as *event clustering*. Event clustering is usually associated with market-wide events such as the Federal Reserve raising (or lowering) interest rates and changes in accounting regulations. Event clustering can occur when examining firm-specific events such as earnings announcements and rulings in a major court decision, but it is less likely.

A second situation where the mean return method is a problem is when the market is trending up (a bull market) or down (a bear market). In this case, the method will produce upwardly and downwardly biased estimates, respectively, of the firm's expected return over the event window. These biases would be in the reverse direction if the estimation period were taken after the event window.

In sum, the mean return method for generating expected returns for a stock over the event window works OK when the firms have event dates that are spread far apart and when the returns on the stocks in the sample are relatively stable (not steadily going up or down). When in doubt, use a more advanced method to generate expected returns.

13.2.5.2 Market Return

The market return approach assumes that the mean of the stock's return over the event window is expected to be the same as the mean of the market's return over the event window. As such, there is no estimation period either before or after the event window. Therefore, ARs are defined as the difference between actual return and expected return, where the expected return for each of the days in the event window is equal to the return on the market each day. The "market" is almost always defined as the return on the S&P 500.

Not requiring a separate estimation period is particularly attractive in situations where no previous stock price data can be obtained, such as when examining IPOs. In addition to not requiring an estimation period, this method of obtaining expected returns is nice because it does not require any assumed linkage between the past and the future. That is, models that use past data to generate expected returns implicitly assume that relationships that held in the past will hold in the future. This can often be a bad assumption.

The market return approach has been found to perform as well as more advanced methods unless event clustering is present. That is, if the event dates for the firms in the sample occur around the same calendar date, the results could be biased.

13.2.5.3 Proxy (or Control) Portfolio Return

The proxy (or control) portfolio return can be conducted in several different ways. My method is to explain that this approach is just like the market return approach, except that instead of using the market (S&P 500) as the expected return on each stock, an industry return is used. It is widely known in financial research that "industry" and "firm size" significantly affect a stock's risk and return. Obtaining an industry return series is extremely easy to do. In fact, numerous Web sites provide these data for free. However, obtaining an industry return series that also controls for firm size is difficult to find. You would have to calculate such a series yourself. For this reason, it is enough to simply control for industry.

The other theoretical justification behind using the industry as a benchmark instead of the entire market is that the industry better controls for the risk of your sample firm. Everyone knows that there is a risk-return tradeoff. That is, the higher the risk, the higher the expected return should be. Assume that one of your sample firms is from the high-tech sector. This firm certainly has a higher level of risk than the overall market. Therefore, it does not make sense to assume that the return on your sample high-tech firm would be the same as the return on the market. However, the risk of your sample firm likely is the same as the risk of the industry in which it operates. Therefore, using the return from the industry is a reasonable estimate of what the returns on your sample firm would be if no event had occurred.

As a casual observation, if you watch the financial news networks, at the end of each day they report which industries have done well and which have done poorly. Different industries appear on the up and down list each day. Therefore, it does not make sense to assume that all industries are the same as the market as a whole.

In sum, with the proxy (or control) portfolio return approach, all you have to identify is the industry in which your sample firm belongs. Then, apply the industry return as the expected return for that stock. Alternatively stated, ARs are defined as the difference between actual return and expected return, where the expected return for each of the days in the event window is equal to the return on the industry in which each firm belongs. Like the market return method, this approach has the advantage of not requiring an estimation period. On the downside, it does not handle event clustering well.

13.2.5.4 Risk-Adjusted Return

The risk-adjusted return approach is the most commonly used method to generate expected returns over the event window. With this method, ARs are defined as the difference between the actual return and the expected return, where the expected return for each of the days in the event window is predicted using a regression.

Researchers have debated how many independent variables should be used to forecast expected returns in the regression. Studies have found that one independent variable (the single-index market model) works as well as models that contain numerous independent variables. As the name implies, the single-index market model uses only the returns on the S&P 500 as the relevant benchmark.

The second minor consideration is whether regular (nominal) returns or excess returns on the stock and the S&P 500 should be used. Those in favor of excess returns state that the use of excess returns is consistent with the concepts behind the Capital Asset Pricing Model (CAPM). In practice, however, most studies use regular (nominal) returns. Therefore, to obtain the predicted returns on a stock in your sample, you should regress the return on the stock against the return on the market. Alternatively stated, you first obtain the predicted values for each day in the event window by regressing the return on your sample stock against the return on the S&P 500. Then subtract the predicted value for each day from your actual return for each day in the event window to get the AR.

13.2.6 CALCULATE ARS

No matter which of the four methods you use to define normal returns over the event window, calculating ARs is done the same way. You simply take the actual return from the sample stock and subtract your predicted normal return for each day in the event window.

13.2.7 CALCULATE CARS

The CARs are simply the sum of the ARs. For example, if the event window is defined as 10 days before through 10 days after the event (-10 through $+10$), the CAR on day -10 is the same as the AR on day -10. The CAR on day -9 is equal to the sum of AR (-10) and AR (-9). The CAR on day -8 is equal to the sum of AR (-10), AR (-9), and AR (-8). Finally, the CAR on day -7 is equal to the sum of AR (-10), AR (-9), AR (-8), and AR (-7). This will be the pattern for all 21 days in the event window.

13.2.8 DETERMINE THE STATISTICAL SIGNIFICANCE OF THE ARS AND CARS

The purpose of statistics is to determine the significance level of an event. For this reason, determining the statistical significance of the ARs and CARs is the last step. Instead of introducing lengthy formulas here, they will be presented throughout the example.

13.3 PERFORMING AN EVENT STUDY

Firms often hold special meetings where only a few large institutional investors and analysts are invited. The claim has been made that during these meetings, private information is revealed for the first time. This quasi-public release of price-relevant information leads to a discussion as to whether this constitutes a violation of insider trading laws, as only those who attend receive the pertinent information. If private information is released during these meetings, then those in attendance will have an unfair or asymmetric information advantage over all other investors. As such, they could use the information to their advantage and earn an abnormal rate of return. We will use an event study to determine if these special investor meetings are associated with the release of relevant and previously private information.

13.3.1 IDENTIFYING THE EVENT DATE

Fortunately, these special meeting dates are readily available via a firm's Web site and annual reports, as well as through several financial reporting agencies. These sources will provide the exact date of the meeting, but they do not report the exact starting and stopping times. Therefore, when choosing the frequency of the data to analyze, the use of intraday data is not possible. Instead, the use of daily data is the clear preference.

13.3.2 DEFINING THE EVENT WINDOW

Because the event date can be identified with a high degree of certainty, an excessively large event window is not necessary. At the same time, it is important to include several days before the event to determine if leakage occurred and several days after the event to determine if the meeting attendants waited a few days before trading in the market.

As discussed earlier, the selection of the exact window size is more of an art than a science. Based on our very certain event date, we will use a relatively narrow 31-day event window. That is, we will consider 15 days before through 15 days after the event (–15 through +15).

13.3.3 DEFINING THE ESTIMATION PERIOD

As with the event window, researchers have not reached consensus on the appropriate length of the estimation period. We will select a 100-day estimation period. Moreover, as in most event studies, this estimation period will occur over the interval preceding the event. Therefore, the estimation period will run from 115 days before the event through 16 days before the event (–115 through –16). Alternatively stated, it will precisely precede the event window. Again, the timeline can be represented as follows.

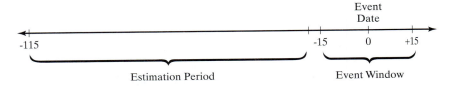

13.3.4 SELECTING THE SAMPLE OF FIRMS

The initial sample will consist of all firms that held special investor meetings from January 1, 1999, to the present. The reason for going back to 1999 is because we want to consider meetings that occurred over both bull and bear markets. (A follow-up examination could measure behavior during bull versus bear markets by splitting the sample.) Any firm that experienced another major corporate event (such as those discussed earlier) over the estimation period or event window was excluded from the sample to avoid the contagion effect. Finally, for the sake of keeping this example simple and manageable, we will examine only 40 firms. These 40 firms have been selected at random from the initial larger sample. The list of firms, their ticker symbols, and the date of their special meeting are provided in the following table.

Number	Firm Name	Ticker	Meeting Date
1	Ackerley Group	AK	January 24, 2002
2	Airgas	ARG	November 19, 2001
3	Allergan	AGN	January 22, 2002
4	Amerada Hess	AHC	December 12, 2001
5	AmerUS Group	AMH	November 13, 2001
6	Anixter International	AXE	February 8, 2002
7	Applied Biosystems Group	ABI	January 10, 2002
8	Bank One	ONE	July 26, 2001
9	Baxter International	BAX	March 24, 2000
10	Beckman Coulter	BEC	July 31, 2001
11	Blyth	BTH	January 8, 2002
12	Catalina Marketing	POS	March 5, 2002
13	Celera Genomics Group	CRA	January 10, 2002
14	Compaq Computer Corporation	CPQ	January 25, 2002
15	Corning	GLW	February 1, 2002
16	Covance	CVD	January 9, 2002
17	Dow Chemical	DOW	May 1, 2001
18	Gucci Group	GUC	March 18, 1999
19	Honeywell International	HON	January 29, 2002
20	Infonet Services	IN	June 26, 2000
21	Kerr-McGee	KMG	December 5, 2001
22	La-Z-Boy	LZB	April 20, 2001
23	Morgan Stanley Dean Witter	MWD	October 25, 2000
24	NCR	NCR	July 24, 2001
25	Office Depot	ODP	January 8, 2001
26	Pacific Century Financial	BOH	April 23, 2001
27	Rite Aid	RAD	November 10, 1999
28	Royal Caribbean Cruises	RCL	November 20, 2001
29	Scotts	SMG	November 30, 2001
30	Shaw Group	SGR	April 20, 2001
31	Smart & Final	SMF	November 30, 2001
32	Sprint PCS Group	PCS	November 3, 2000
33	Teledyne Technologies	TDY	February 5, 2002
34	Texas Instruments	TXN	March 2, 2000
35	TransCanada Pipelines	TRP	November 5, 2001
36	Transoceanic Sedco Forex	RIG	December 6, 1999
37	United Technologies	UTX	February 14, 2002
38	Unumprovident	UNM	May 17, 2001
39	Waste Management	WMI	June 14, 2001
40	Wendy's International	WEN	July 27, 2001

13.3.5 CALCULATING NORMAL (OR NONEVENT) RETURNS

We will use the most popular method to establish normal returns. That is, we will use the single-index market model (the risk-adjusted return method) to determine what the returns on each company would have been had no event occurred. The proxy for the return on the market will be the return on the S&P 500. This is also quite standard.

13.3.6 CALCULATING ARS, CARS, AND THEIR SIGNIFICANCE

A number of different methods can be used to determine ARs. The methods range from simply being different ways of doing the same thing to methods designed to handle violations in event study assumptions. In fact, it is possible to write an entire book, if not many books, on the topic of event study methodologies. However, the purpose here is to present a very common method that can and should be used in most circumstances. The method presented here is commonly referred to as a Standardized Abnormal Return (SAR) test (which assumes cross-sectional independence).

13.3.6.1 Setting up the Event Study in Excel

The first step in performing the standardized abnormal return test is to create an Excel spreadsheet. In cells "A3" through "A5," type "time (relative to the event date)."

In cells "B4" and "B5," enter "Firm Return." In "C4" and "C5," enter "S&P 500 Return." In cells "D2" through "D5," enter "estimation period Firm Residuals." Enter "event window Market Residuals" in cells "E2" through "E5." Finally, enter "Maximum Likelihood estimate of the variance used in SAR" in cells "F1" through "F5." Center all titles for aesthetic purposes.

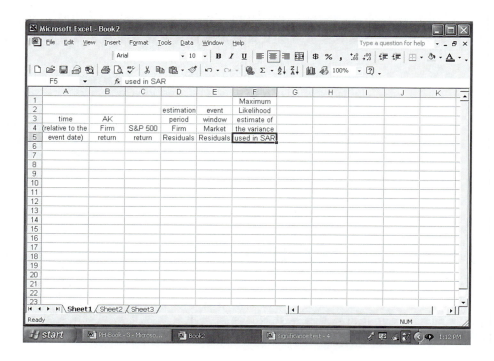

Enter the numbers "–115" in cell "A6" and "–114" in cell "A7." Then highlight both cells.

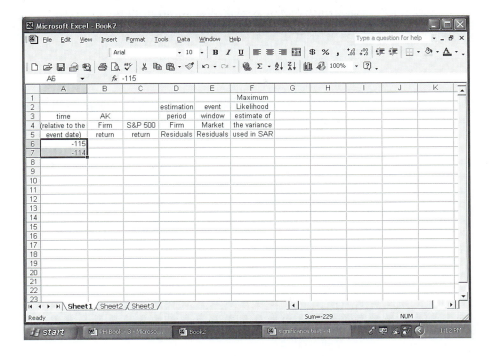

Right-click and hold down your mouse button in the lower-right-hand corner of cell "A7" and drag down to cell "A136."

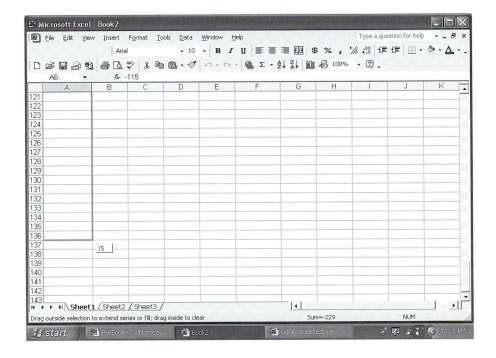

You will know to stop at "A136" because the number "15" will appear in the yellow box next to your mouse pointer. We want to extend this series because we want to place the return of each firm and the market in the right place in our Excel sheet. Because we need returns ranging from –115 before to +15 after the event date (recall that the estimation period will be from –115 through –16; the event window will go from –15 through +15), this is the range for the series we created. When you are done, your Excel sheet should look like this.

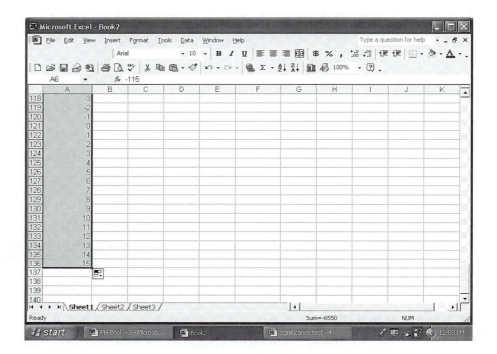

We are now ready to insert the returns on both the individual stock and the market for each of the days in our sample. Let's begin with the first stock: Ackerley Group (AK). Because most readers will not have direct access to return data, let's download price data. We can then convert it to a return. When calculating a return, it is important to control for stock splits and dividends. Fortunately, the Web site chart.yahoo.com/t does this for you. Go to this site and type in the ticker symbol "AK."

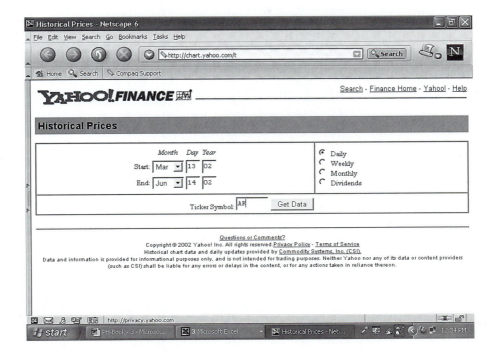

Do not worry about selecting the exact starting and stopping dates for which you need stock prices. Instead, go back roughly 6 months before the meeting date and stop about 1 month after. Remember, the number of trading days is not the same as the number of calendar days. If you take the time to calculate the exact number of days, you will waste valuable research time.

The special meeting date for Ackerley Group was January 24, 2002. Therefore, let's select the starting month as June. Leave the day as "13" for the sake of speed, but remember to change the year to 2001. The ending date can be set to March. Again, do not worry about the day in March; we will trim off the dates we do not need later. Your screen should look like this.

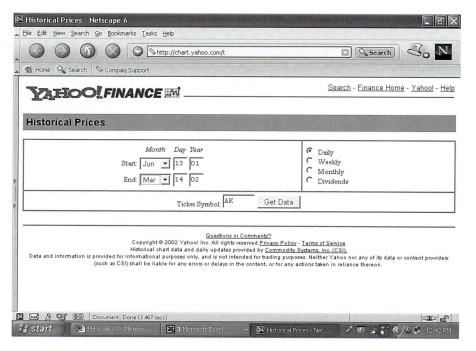

Click on the "Get Data" button.

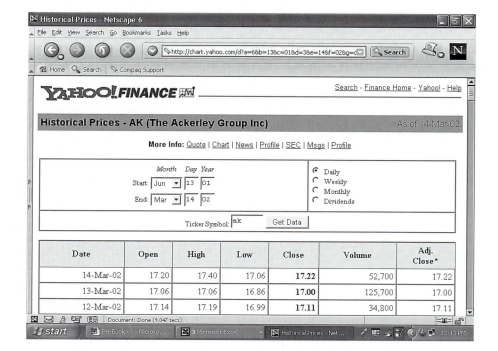

Scroll to the very bottom of the window.

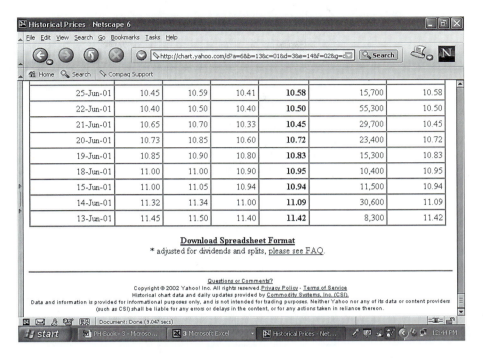

Click "Download Spreadsheet Format."

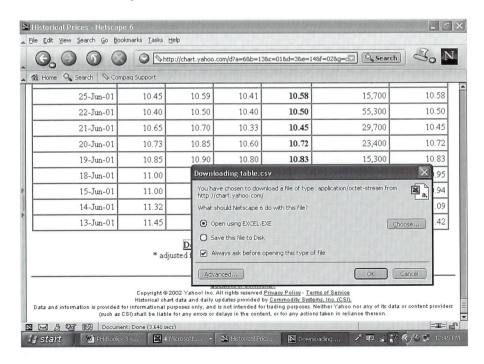

Do not select the "Open using EXCEL.EXE" option. If you do, the following Excel file will open.

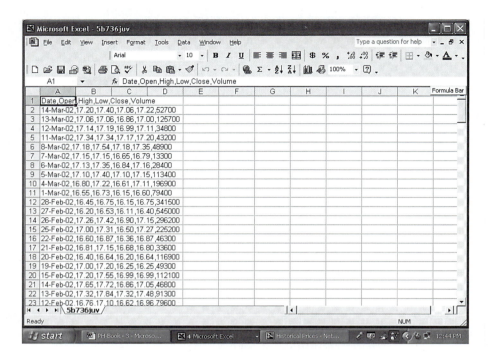

All the information is entered into column "A." As such, it is not in a user-friendly format. To fix this, select "Save this file to Disk." The following screen will appear.

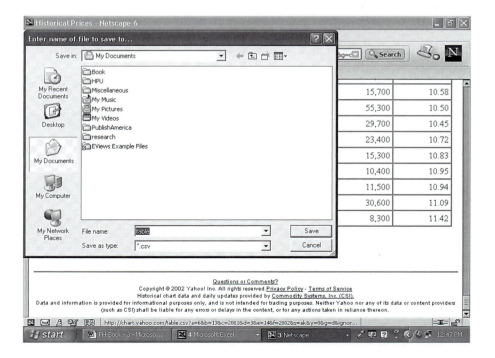

Title the file "AK" and click "Save." In a new Excel Workbook, click "Open."

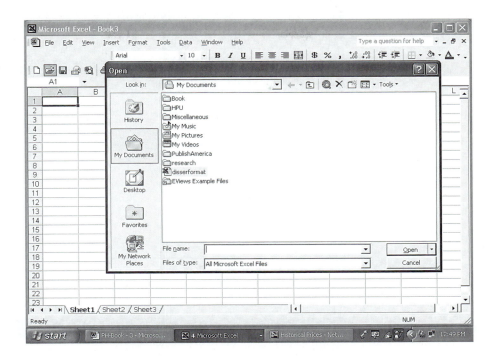

Because the file is not an Excel file, you will have to go under the box marked "Files of type:" and click on "All Files."

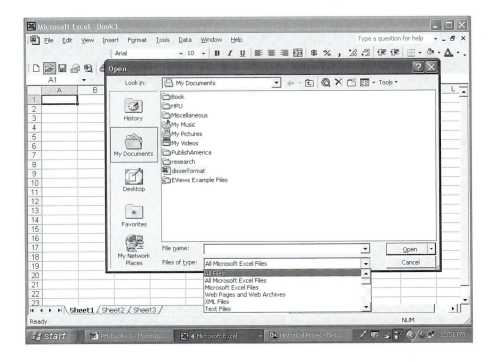

Double-click on the file "AK."

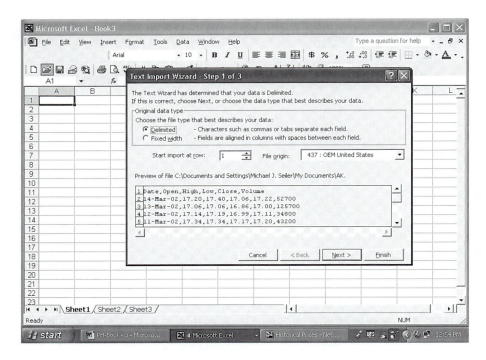

Click "Next." Under the category "Delimiters," check the box titled "Comma." You should see that the data are now separated.

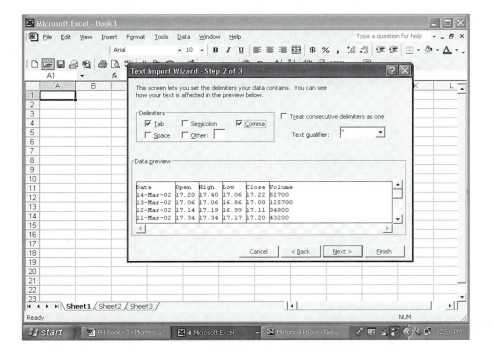

Click "Finish." Your Excel sheet should look like this.

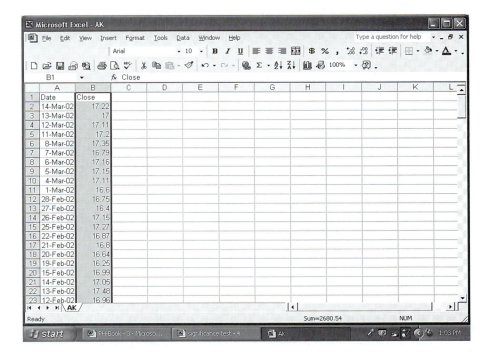

The only column we care about is "Close." This represents the closing stock price (which incorporates both stock splits and dividends). For this reason, I like to delete the unnecessary data. Keep only the date and closing prices.

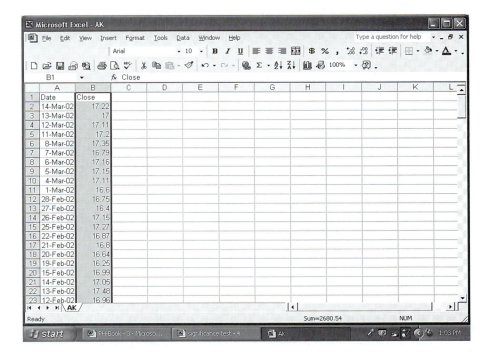

Notice that the downloaded data starts with the most recent price and goes backward in time. We want the series to go forward in time. Therefore, we need to flip the series. To do this, highlight both series.

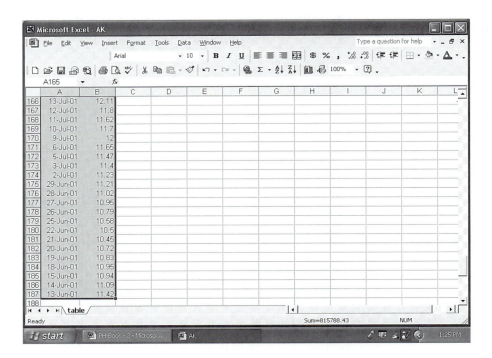

Then click on the icon representing the command "Sort Ascending."

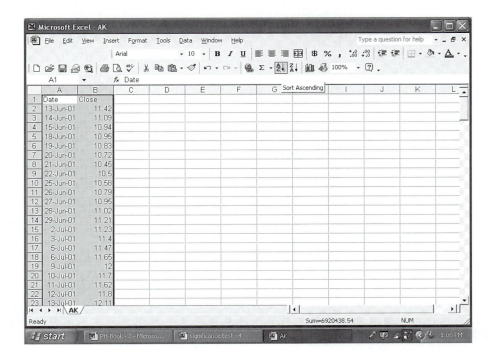

The next step is to calculate a return. In Chapter 2 we established that this can be done by taking the natural log (LN) of the present day's close divided by the previous day's close. That is,

$$Return = \text{LN}(P_t / P_{t-1}) \tag{13.1}$$

Do this for all cells in column "C." After using the "Copy" command, you should have returns for all days in the sample (except the first).

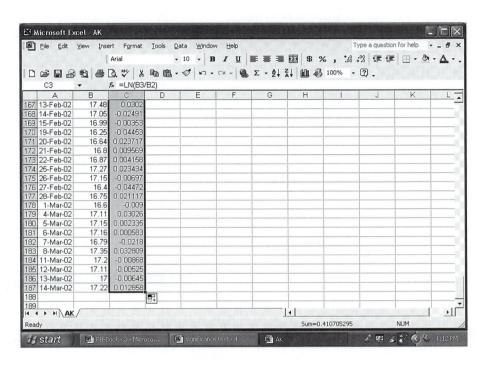

Now all we need to do is get the returns lined up correctly relative to the event date. To do so, first locate the row corresponding to the event date, January 24, 2002. This is row 153.

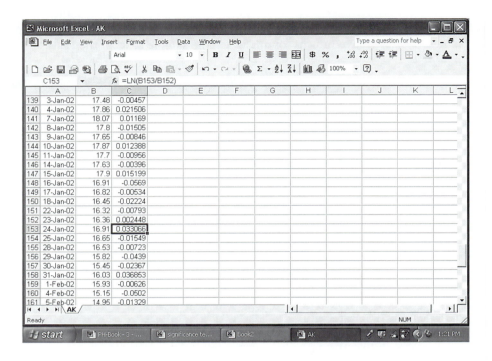

Because we are looking for returns –115 days before the event date, we simply need to subtract 115 from 153. As a result, we need to copy data starting in cell "C38." To determine the stopping date, we need to go 15 days after the event date: 153 + 15 = 168. In sum, we should copy the range from cell "C38" through "C168."

Highlight this range and click "Copy."

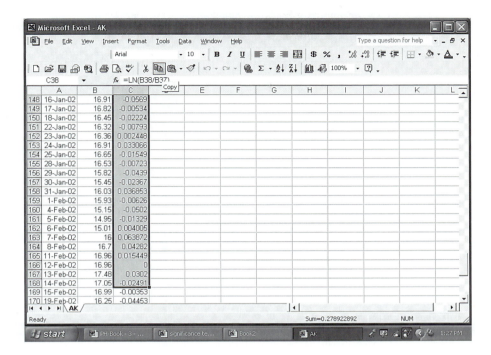

Go to cell "B6" in your Excel other worksheet and click "Edit" and then "Paste Special."

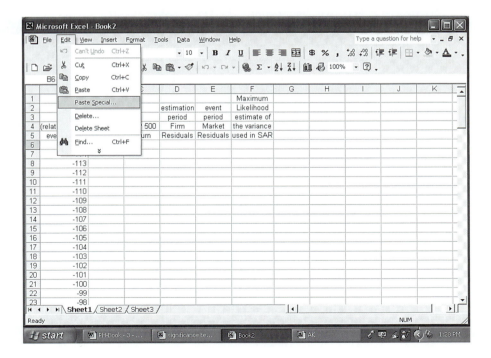

You will see the following screen.

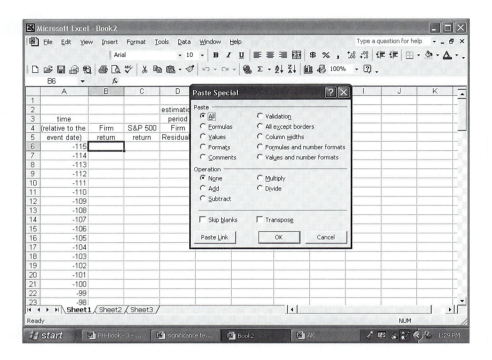

In the "Paste Special" window, select "Values." Click "OK."

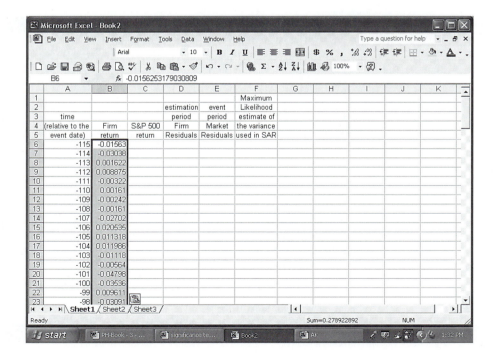

If you scroll down, you will see that the series stops in cell "B136" (which corresponds to time +15).

Before we go any further, let's save our newly created event study worksheet. Let's call it "event study - 1."

Now that the return series for the first firm in our sample has been correctly lined up relative to the event date, the same thing needs to be done for the S&P 500. Because the steps for including the S&P 500 returns are the same as they are for an individual firm, I will not show all the steps over again. However, to save time, you should consider the following. When you download the S&P 500 Index values, do not just select the range from 6 months before to 1 month after the event date for the Ackerley Group. Instead, as your starting date, use a date that is 6 months prior to the earliest event date in the entire sample. In this case, the earliest event date of all the firms is March 18, 1999. For your ending date, select a date 1 month after the latest event date for all the firms in the sample. In our example, the last event date is March 5, 2002.

The reason for doing this is so you will only have to download the S&P 500 data once. Otherwise, you will have to do it 40 times (once for each firm in your sample). This shortcut will reduce your time on the Internet by roughly 50%.

Let's jump to the step where you have already downloaded the S&P 500 Index and calculated its return. After identifying the event date as January 24, 2002, you will see that this value is in row 853.

Therefore, you will need to copy and paste values from cells "C738" through "C868." When you are done, your "event study - 1" file will look like this.

This process should be repeated for all 40 firms. To start, the titles presented in cells "B1" through "F5" should be copied because they are needed for each stock in the sample. Leave a space between each set of titles for aesthetic purposes. After copying the titles, go back and insert the ticker symbol over the title "Firm return." For the first stock, this will be in cell "B3." For the second stock, it will be in cell "H3," and so forth. This identification step is done to reduce the likelihood of making a mistake.

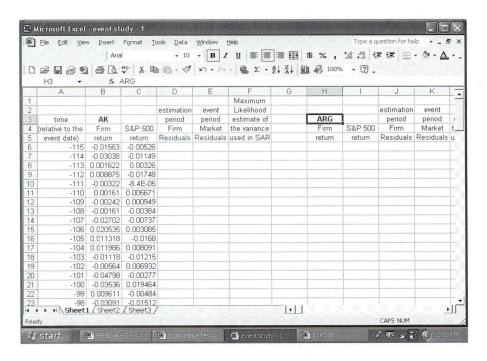

Although copying the titles will take very little time, downloading and aligning the returns for all 40 stocks and aligning the returns on the S&P 500 will take several hours. When you are done, your spreadsheet should look like this.

Notice that the panes have been frozen. This is helpful when maneuvering around large spreadsheets.

13.3.6.2 Performing Intermediate Calculations

A number of intermediate calculations must be performed before event window ARs can be measured. Ultimately, we are going to compute a SAR for each firm and for each day in the event window. In order to do that, we will need the following formula.

$$SAR_{jt} = \frac{AR_{jt}}{\sqrt{s^2_{AR_{jt}}}} \tag{13.2}$$

where

$$SAR_{jt} = \text{SAR for firm } j \text{ at time } t$$

$$AR_{jt} = \text{AR for firm } j \text{ at time } t$$

$$\sqrt{s^2_{AR_{jt}}} = s_{AR_{jt}} = \text{square root of the variance of the AR for firm } j \text{ at time } t$$
$$= \text{standard deviation of the AR for firm } j \text{ at time } t$$

The calculation of AR is relatively straightforward. Unfortunately, the formula for standard deviation is quite lengthy. For now, let's focus strictly on the formula for the variance (which is just the part inside the radical). The formula for variance is given by the following equation.

$$s^2_{AR_{jt}} = \left(\frac{\sum_{t=-115}^{-16} \left(AR_{jt(est.period)} - \overline{AR}_{j(est.period)} \right)^2}{D_j - 2} \right) * \left(1 + \frac{1}{D_j} + \frac{\left(R_{mt(event.window)} - \overline{R}_{m(est.period)} \right)^2}{\sum_{t=-115}^{-16} \left(R_{mt(est.period)} - \overline{R}_{m(est.period)} \right)^2} \right) \tag{13.3}$$

where

$$s^2_{AR_{jt}} = \text{variance of the AR for firm } j \text{ at time } t$$

$$AR_{jt(est.period)} = \text{AR for firm } j \text{ at time } t \text{ over the estimation period}$$

$$\overline{AR}_{j(est.period)} = \text{mean AR for firm } j \text{ over the estimation period}$$

$$D_j = \text{number of observed trading day returns for firm } j \text{ over the estimation period}$$

$$R_{mt(event.window)} = \text{return on the market (S\&P 500) at time } t \text{ over the event window}$$

$$R_{mt(est.period)} = \text{return on the market (S\&P 500) at time } t \text{ over the estimation period}$$

$$\overline{R}_{m(est.period)} = \text{mean return on the market (S\&P 500) over the estimation period}$$

Although this formula appears menacing at first, if we take it step by step, it really is not that bad. Let's go to the Excel file we are in the process of creating titled "event study - 1." In cells "A139" through "A143," type in the titles "**Estimation Period Statistics:**," "Alpha," "Beta," "Variance in the Firm Residuals," and "Variance in the Market Residuals," respectively. Your spreadsheet should look like this.

Our first intermediate goal is to measure the relationship between the return on the stock and the return on the market in the absence of an event. The way to do this is to perform a regression between the two series (over just the estimation period). Instead of actually performing a regression, Excel offers two different functions that effectively do the same thing. The difference is that the functions are more efficient.

Our first step in determining the relationship between the stock and the overall market in the absence of an event is to calculate the alpha (or regression intercept) between the market return and the return on our first stock, "AK." Go to cell "D140" and type in the formula:

$$=INTERCEPT(B6:B105,C6:C105)$$

Then press "Enter."

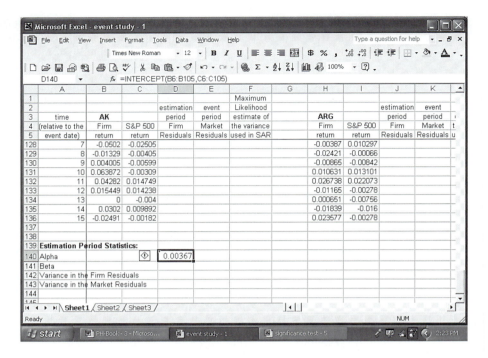

Similarly, in cell "D141" type in the formula:

$$=SLOPE(B6:B105,C6:C105)$$

Then press "Enter."

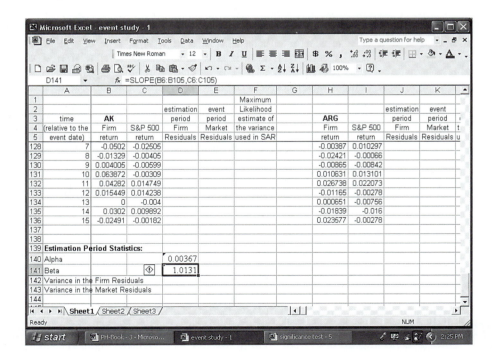

We are now ready to calculate what is called the *estimation period firm residual*. In words, the formula for the estimation period firm residual is the actual return on the stock minus the expected return on the stock given the relationship between the stock and the market (which we just measured). The estimation period firm residual is calculated for all days in the estimation period. We will start at time –115 in cell "D6." In Excel, the formula is written as:

$$=B6-\$D\$140-\$D\$141*C6$$

	A	B	C	D	E	F	G	H	I	J	K
1						Maximum					
2				estimation	event	Likelihood				estimation	event
3	time	AK		period	period	estimate of		ARG		period	period
4	(relative to the	Firm	S&P 500	Firm	Market	the variance		Firm	S&P 500	Firm	Market
5	event date)	return	return	Residuals	Residuals	used in SAR		return	return	Residuals	Residuals
6	-115	-0.01563	-0.00526	-0.01397				-0.02457	0.003855		
7	-114	-0.03038	-0.01149					0.039986	0.005095		
8	-113	0.001622	0.00326					0.008567	0.012907		
9	-112	0.008875	-0.01748					0.03447	-0.0106		
10	-111	-0.00322	-8.4E-05					0.011834	0.005442		
11	-110	0.00161	0.005671					-0.01642	-0.00944		
12	-109	-0.00242	0.000949					-0.00092	-0.00839		
13	-108	-0.00161	-0.00384					0.024558	0.001163		
14	-107	-0.02702	-0.00737					0	-0.01141		
15	-106	0.020535	0.003085					-0.0027	-0.01766		
16	-105	0.011318	-0.0168					-0.00905	-0.00453		
17	-104	0.011986	0.008091					0.007246	-0.0049		
18	-103	-0.01118	-0.01215					-0.05281	0.003428		
19	-102	-0.00564	0.006932					0.052814	0.008671		
20	-101	-0.04798	-0.00277					-0.00452	0.0113		
21	-100	-0.03536	0.019464					-0.05497	-0.00949		
22	-99	0.009611	-0.00484					0.004778	-0.00552		
23	-98	-0.03091	-0.01512					0	-0.00151		

The dollar signs are placed in front of "D140" and "D141" in the formula because we need to copy this formula all the way down to row 105. Let's do that now. With cell "D6" selected, left-click and drag down from the lower-right-hand corner until you reach cell "D105." Release the left mouse button. Your screen should appear as follows.

We have just computed the terms $AR_{jt(est.period)}$ in Equation 13.3. We are now ready to perform the calculation to complete the first half of the variance formula shown in Equation 13.3. That is, we are now ready to calculate the following in Excel:

$$\frac{\sum_{t=-115}^{-16} \left(AR_{jt(est.period)} - \overline{AR}_{j\,(est.period)} \right)^2}{D_j - 2}$$

The numerator can be represented in Excel by typing:

DEVSQ(D6:D105)

The denominator can be written as:

COUNT(B6:B105)-2

In cell "D142," combine the two by typing in the formula:

=DEVSQ(D6:D105)/(COUNT(B6:B105)-2)

	A	B	C	D	E	F	G	H	I	J	K
1						Maximum					
2				estimation	event	Likelihood				estimation	event
3	time	**AK**		period	period	estimate of		**ARG**		period	period
4	(relative to the	Firm	S&P 500	Firm	Market	the variance		Firm	S&P 500	Firm	Market
5	event date)	return	return	Residuals	Residuals	used in SAR		return	return	Residuals	Residuals
128	7	-0.0502	-0.02505					-0.00387	0.010297		
129	8	-0.01329	-0.00405					-0.02421	-0.00066		
130	9	0.004005	-0.00599					-0.00865	-0.00842		
131	10	0.063872	-0.00309					0.010631	0.013101		
132	11	0.04282	0.014749					0.026738	0.022073		
133	12	0.015449	0.014238					-0.01165	-0.00278		
134	13	0	-0.004					0.000651	-0.00756		
135	14	0.0302	0.009892					-0.01839	-0.016		
136	15	-0.02491	-0.00182					0.023577	-0.00278		
137											
138											
139	**Estimation Period Statistics:**										
140	Alpha			0.00367							
141	Beta			1.0131							
142	Variance in the Firm Residuals			0.00168							
143	Variance in the Market Residuals										
144											

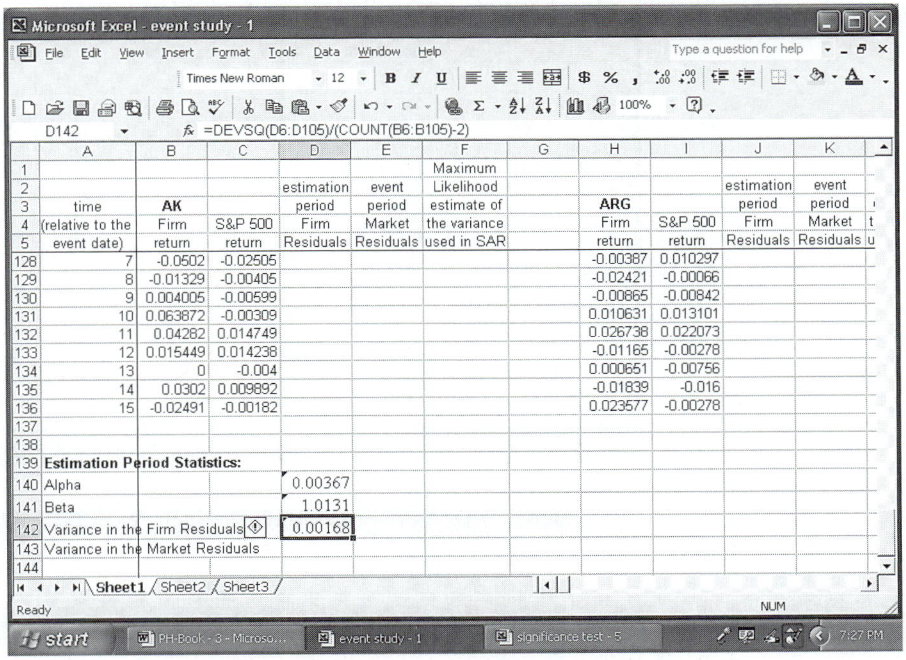

We will now begin to program the right half of Equation 13.3. Specifically, let's represent the term $\left(R_{mt(event.window)} - \overline{R}_{m\,(est.period)}\right)^2$ in Excel. This term is also known as the *event window market residual.* The Excel formula will be carried out in the cell range "E106" through "E136." For cell "E106," the equation is written as:

=(C106-AVERAGE($C$6:$C$105))^2

Again, the dollar signs will be used so that Excel compares each market return over the event window to the same estimation period mean return on the market.

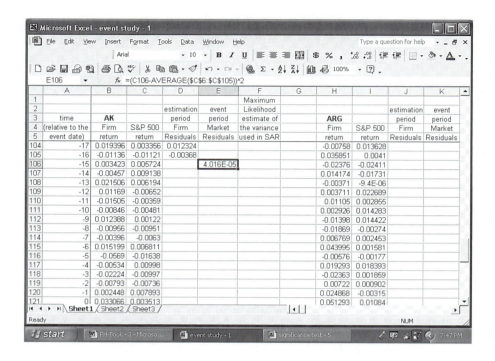

Copy this formula down the column to cell "E136."

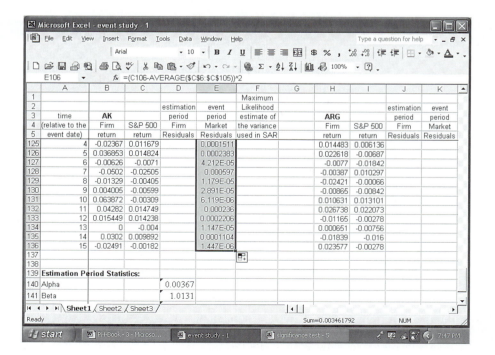

Let's program the term $\sum_{t=-115}^{-16} \left(R_{mt(est.period)} - \overline{R}_{m(est.period)} \right)^2$. In words, this term is called the *variance in the market residuals over the estimation period*. We will place this formula in cell "D143." In Excel, the formula is written as:

$$=DEVSQ(C6:C105)$$

We are now ready to complete the entire variance formula. That is, we are ready to solve for the Maximum Likelihood Estimate of the variance. The calculations will be placed in cells "F106" through "F136." Based an Excel's representation of Equation 13.3, the formula can be written as:

$$=\$D\$142*(1+(1/COUNT(\$B\$6:\$B\$105))+(E106/\$D\$143))$$

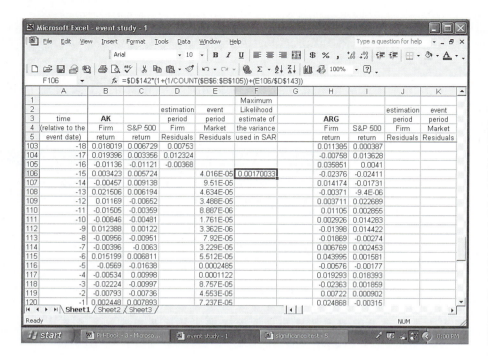

Copy this formula down to cell "F136."

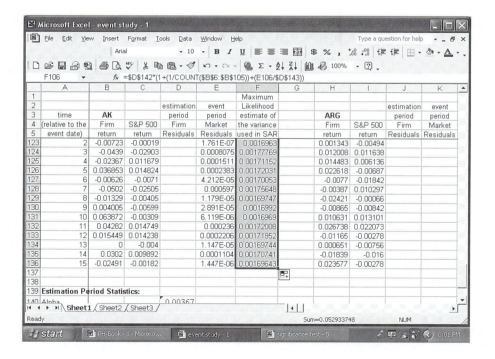

We have just completed the Maximum Likelihood Estimate for the variance of the first firm over all 31 days in the event window. As you may have inferred from the variable $s^2_{AR_{jt}}$, this calculation must be done for all firms. To explain, the subscript t indicates that the calculation must be done for more than one point in time. Specifically, it must be done for all days in the event window. The subscript j means it must be done for all firms. Don't worry; if you can do it once, you can do it 40 times.

Perform the calculations for all 40 firms. When you are done, your spreadsheet should look like this.

	A	HW	HX	HY	HZ	IA	IB	IC	ID	IE	IF
1					Maximum						Maximum
2			estimation	event	Likelihood				estimation	event	Likelihood
3	time		period	period	estimate of		**WEN**		period	period	estimate of
4	(relative to the	S&P 500	Firm	Market	he variance		Firm	S&P 500	Firm	Market	he variance
5	event date)	return	Residuals	Residuals	ised in SAR		return	return	Residuals	Residuals	ised in SAR
124	3	0.003428		1.28E-05	0.000624		0.005615	0.010028		0.000105	0.000323
125	4	0.008671		7.78E-05	0.000625		0.020688	-0.00184		2.59E-06	0.000322
126	5	0.0113		0.000131	0.000627		0.000731	-0.0124		0.000148	0.000324
127	6	-0.00949		8.74E-05	0.000626		-0.0077	-0.02378		0.000555	0.00033
128	7	-0.00552		2.89E-05	0.000623		-0.00443	0.006855		5.02E-05	0.000322
129	8	-0.00151		1.86E-06	0.000623		-0.01453	-0.0145		0.000204	0.000325
130	9	-0.00469		2.06E-06	0.000624		-0.00414	-0.00113		8.21E-07	0.000322
131	10	0.012416		0.000158	0.000627		0.004511	0.023415		0.000559	0.00033
132	11	-0.00149		1.79E-06	0.000623		-0.00038	0.006222		4.16E-05	0.000322
133	12	0.010028		0.000104	0.000626		0.017851	-0.01094		0.000115	0.000323
134	13	-0.00184		2.85E-06	0.000623		0.017538	0.009922		0.000103	0.000323
135	14	-0.0124		0.00015	0.000627		0.011523	-0.00556		2.84E-05	0.000322
136	15	-0.02378		0.000558	0.000638		-0.00503	0.006035		3.92E-05	0.000322
137											
138											
139	**Estimation Pe**										
140	Alpha		0.00032						0.00046		

Save this file. Then save it again under the title "event study - 2."

13.3.6.3 Calculating Total SAR

Now that the preliminary calculations are out of the way, we are ready to compute ARs for each stock over all days in the event window. You may have noticed that we are running out of columns (width) in the Excel spreadsheet. Therefore, we will have to perform the remaining calculations below instead of to the right of our existing calculations. As such, begin by repeating the title "time (relative to the event date)" in cells "A149" through "A151." Then copy the time series that runs from −15 through +15. This will fill cells "A152" through "A182."

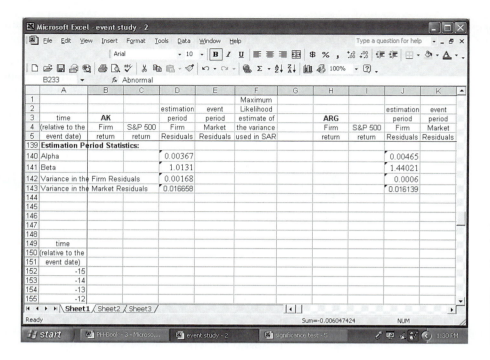

Now create the title "**Abnormal Returns**" in cells "B149" through "B150."

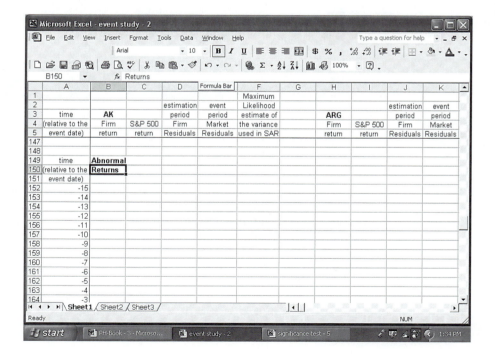

Below the title, in cells "B151" through "AO151," type in the ticker symbols for each stock.

Let's insert the AR formula below each title. The formula for calculating AR is given by Equation 13.4.

$$AR_{jt(event.window)} = R_{jt(event.window)} - \alpha_{j(est.period)} - \beta_{j(est.period)} \times R_{mt(event.window)} \quad \textbf{(13.4)}$$

where

$AR_{jt(event.window)}$ = AR on stock j for each day in the event window
$R_{jt(event.window)}$ = return on stock j for each day in the event window
$\alpha_{j(est.period)}$ = intercept term for stock j measured over the estimation period
$\beta_{j(est.period)}$ = slope term for stock j measured over the estimation period
$R_{mt(event.window)}$ = return on the market for each day in the event window

The alpha and beta have already been calculated in cells "D140" and "D141," respectively. The returns for the first stock and the corresponding returns on the market for each day in the event window are in cells "B106" through "C136." Therefore, all we have to do is bring these numbers together. Let's do this in cell "B152."

In Excel, Equation 13.4 can be represented by the following:

$$=B106-\$D\$140-\$D\$141*C106$$

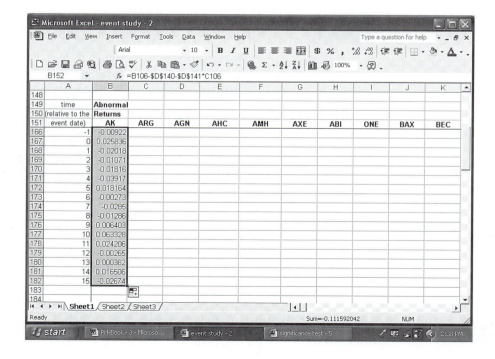

Copy this formula down to cell "B182." For the sake of presentation, I will periodically refreeze the panes.

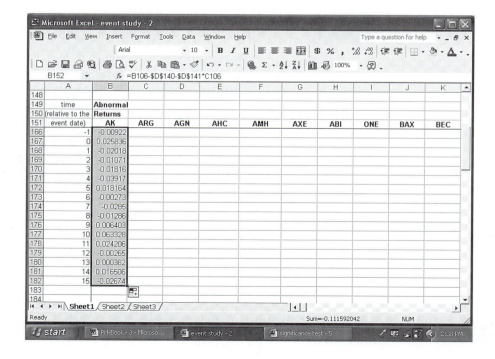

As previously mentioned, the ARs must be computed for all firms in the sample. Therefore, repeat the AR calculations from cells "C152" through "AO182." When you are done, your spreadsheet should look like this.

The next step is to standardize the ARs. Recall from Equation 13.2 that the formula for the SAR is equal to:

$$SAR_{jt} = \frac{AR_{jt}}{\sqrt{s^2_{AR_{jt}}}}$$

In words, the SAR is equal to the AR divided by (or standardized by) the standard deviation of the risk. As you can tell by the subscripts j and t, the SAR must be calculated for all firms (j) over all days in the event window (t).

We just finished calculating the ARs. Moreover, in a previous calculation, we found the variance, $s^2_{AR_{jt}}$. Therefore, all we have to do now is divide the ARs by the square root of the variance. Let's do this for the first stock, the Ackerley Group (AK). In cells "AQ148" through "AQ150," type in the title "**Standardized Abnormal Returns**." Now repeat the ticker symbols in cells "AQ151" through "CD151." As always, this is done to help keep our place in the calculations.

The ARs for the Ackerley Group are found in cells "B152" through "B182." The variance for each day in the event window is provided in cells "F106" through "F136." Therefore, in cell "AQ152," where the SAR is reported, type in the following Excel formula:

$$=B152/SQRT(F106)$$

Copy this formula all the way down to cell "AQ182."

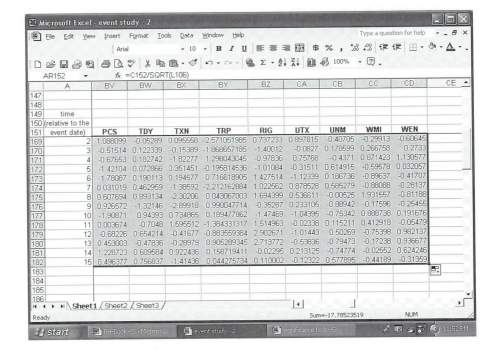

Do this for all 40 firms in the sample. These calculations will be placed in cells "AR152" through "CD182." When you are done, your Excel spreadsheet should look like this.

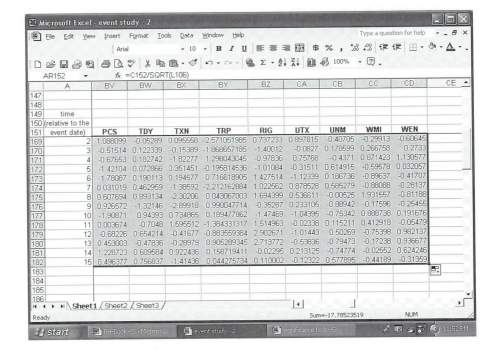

We have now calculated the SARs for all the firms in the sample and for each day in the event window. The next step is to aggregate the SARs for each separate day and determine if the results are significant. To set up the calculations, place the following labels in cells "CF150" through "CH151": "**(Total SAR) TSAR**," "**TSAR Z-statistic**," and "**TSAR p-value**."

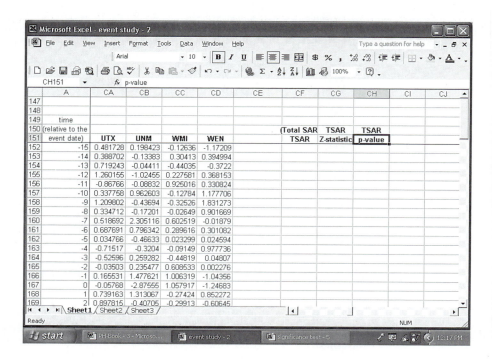

In cell "CF152," we want to add up all the SARs for day –15. To do this, type in the Excel formula:

$$=SUM(AQ152:CD152)$$

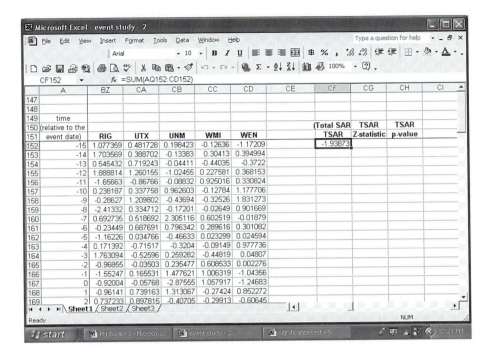

Copy this formula down through cell "CF182."

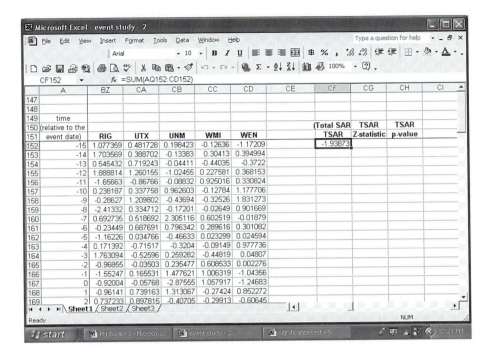

We are now ready to determine if the total SAR (TSAR) results are significant for each day in the event window. The formula for the Z-statistic on the TSAR is given by Equation 13.5.

$$Z-statistic_t = \frac{TSAR_t}{\sqrt{\sum_{j=1}^{N} \frac{D_j - 2}{D_j - 4}}} \qquad (13.5)$$

where

$$Z-statistic_t = Z-\text{statistic for each day in the event window}$$
$$TSAR_t = \text{TSAR for each day in the event window}$$
$$D_j = \text{number of observed trading day returns for firm } j \text{ over the estimation period}$$
$$N = \text{number of firms in the sample}$$

Based on the subscripts, you can infer that the denominator will be the same for all days in the sample. (We know this because there is no subscript t, which denotes time, in the denominator.) However, we do need to perform a calculation for each firm.

For ease of copying the formula, let's place the first calculation in cell "D146." In cell "A145," type in the title "**Other:** (intermediate calculations to get the Z-statistics on TSAR)." Below this, in cell "A146," enter the title "Q_j." Q_j commonly denotes the term under the radical in Equation 13.5. Alternatively stated, it is equal to the variance of the TSAR. Mathematically, it is equal to

$$Q_j = \sum_{j=1}^{N} \frac{D_j - 2}{D_j - 4}$$

Of course, by taking the square root of the variance, we are simply finding the standard deviation. After you have typed in the two titles, your spreadsheet should look like this.

In cell "D146," we will perform the calculation of Q_j for the first firm in the sample. The formula is written in Excel as:

$$=(COUNT(B6:B105)-2)/(COUNT(B6:B105)-4)$$

The Q_j calculation for the second firm should be placed in cell "J146." The Excel formula should be written as:

$$=(COUNT(H6:H105)-2)/(COUNT(H6:H105)-4)$$

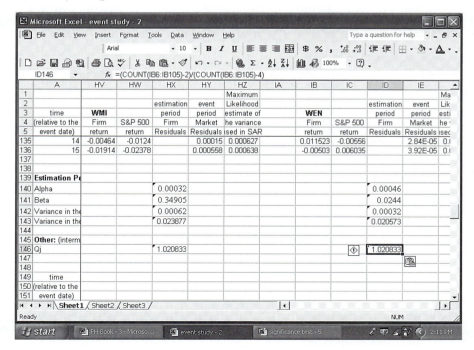

You also could have used the "Copy" and "Paste" functions in Excel. Perform this calculation for all the firms in the sample using the pattern just presented. When you are finished, your spreadsheet should look like this.

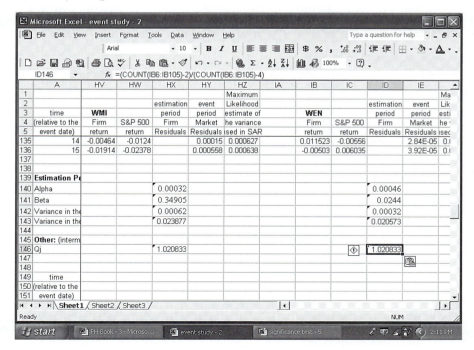

Using Equation 13.5, we are now ready to compute the Z-statistics for each day in the event window. In cell "CG152," type in the following equation:

$$=CF152/SQRT(SUM(\$D\$146:\$ID\$146))$$

First screenshot: Microsoft Excel - event study - 2, formula bar: =CF152/SQRT(SUM($D$146:$ID$146))

	A	BZ	CA	CB	CC	CD	CE	CF	CG	CH	CI
144											
145	Other: (interm										
146	Qj					1.020833					
147											
148											
149	time										
150	(relative to the							(Total SAR	TSAR	TSAR	
151	event date)	RIG	UTX	UNM	WMI	WEN		TSAR	Z-statistic	p-value	
152	-15	1.077359	0.481728	0.198423	-0.12636	-1.17209		-1.93873	-0.3034		
153	-14	1.703569	0.388702	-0.13383	0.30413	0.394994		-2.10991			
154	-13	0.545432	0.719243	-0.04411	-0.44035	-0.3722		-5.43103			
155	-12	1.888814	1.260155	-1.02455	0.227581	0.368153		-5.02412			
156	-11	-1.65663	-0.86766	-0.08832	0.925016	0.330824		-6.64882			
157	-10	0.238187	0.337758	0.962603	-0.12784	1.177706		4.353193			
158	-9	-0.28627	1.209802	-0.43694	-0.32526	1.831273		0.494836			
159	-8	-2.41332	0.334712	-0.17201	-0.02649	0.901669		0.976908			
160	-7	0.692735	0.518692	2.305116	0.602519	-0.01879		9.968858			
161	-6	-0.23449	0.687691	0.796342	0.289616	0.301082		0.054659			
162	-5	-1.16226	0.034766	-0.46633	0.023299	0.024594		-7.43963			
163	-4	0.171392	-0.71517	-0.3204	-0.09149	0.977736		-1.81653			
164	-3	1.763094	-0.52596	0.259282	-0.44819	0.04807		12.79793			
165	-2	-0.96855	-0.03503	0.235477	0.608533	0.002276		-3.61782			
166	-1	-1.55247	0.165531	1.477621	1.006319	-1.04356		-1.67114			

Copy this formula all the way to cell "CG182."

Second screenshot: Microsoft Excel - event study - 2, formula bar: =CF152/SQRT(SUM($D$146:$ID$146))

	A	BZ	CA	CB	CC	CD	CE	CF	CG	CH	CI
144											
145	Other: (interm										
146	Qj					1.020833					
147											
148											
149	time										
150	(relative to the							(Total SAR	TSAR	TSAR	
151	event date)	RIG	UTX	UNM	WMI	WEN		TSAR	Z-statistic	p-value	
170	3	-1.40012	-0.0827	0.178599	0.266758	0.2733		-0.64072	-0.10027		
171	4	-0.97836	0.75768	-0.4371	0.871423	1.130577		-5.37586	-0.84128		
172	5	-1.01084	-0.31511	0.614915	-0.59578	0.032057		8.936683	1.398521		
173	6	1.427514	-1.12339	0.186736	-0.89637	-0.41707		6.365558	0.99616		
174	7	1.022562	0.878528	0.585279	-0.88088	-0.28137		2.767608	0.433109		
175	8	1.694399	0.536611	-0.00525	1.931557	-0.81188		-7.62614	-1.19343		
176	9	-0.35287	0.233105	-0.88942	-0.17596	-0.25455		-17.0293	-2.66495		
177	10	-1.47469	-1.04395	-0.75342	0.888738	0.191676		-1.71875	-0.26897		
178	11	1.514963	-0.02338	0.115211	0.412918	-0.05479		0.155601	0.02435		
179	12	2.902671	-1.01443	0.50269	-0.75398	0.982137		3.68063	0.57599		
180	13	2.713772	-0.53836	-0.79473	-0.17238	0.936677		2.948882	0.461477		
181	14	-0.02295	0.213125	-0.74774	-0.02552	0.624246		2.982186	0.466689		
182	15	0.110002	-0.12322	0.577895	-0.44189	-0.31359		0.560097	0.087651		
183											
184											

Sum=-3.20261689

The Z-statistic follows a standard normal distribution, which means it has a mean of zero and a standard deviation of 1.0. As such, we can use a canned function within Excel to determine the level of significance for each TSAR. To measure this level, write the Excel formula as:

$$=2*(1-NORMSDIST(ABS(CG152)))$$

This formula should be entered into cell "CH152."

	A	BZ	CA	CB	CC	CD	CE	CF	CG	CH	CI
144											
145	Other: (interm										
146	Qj					1.020833					
147											
148											
149	time										
150	(relative to the							(Total SAR	TSAR	TSAR	
151	event date)	RIG	UTX	UNM	WMI	WEN		TSAR	Z-statistic	p-value	
152	-15	1.077359	0.481728	0.198423	-0.12636	-1.17209		-1.93873	-0.3034	0.761588	
153	-14	1.703569	0.388702	-0.13383	0.30413	0.394994		-2.10991	-0.33018		
154	-13	0.545432	0.719243	-0.04411	-0.44035	-0.3722		-5.43103	-0.84991		
155	-12	1.888814	1.260155	-1.02455	0.227581	0.368153		-5.02412	-0.78624		
156	-11	-1.65663	-0.86766	-0.08832	0.925016	0.330824		-6.64882	-1.04049		
157	-10	0.238187	0.337758	0.962603	-0.12784	1.177706		4.353193	0.681241		
158	-9	-0.28627	1.209802	-0.43694	-0.32526	1.831273		0.494836	0.077438		
159	-8	-2.41332	0.334712	-0.17201	-0.02649	0.901669		0.976908	0.152878		
160	-7	0.692735	0.518692	2.305116	0.602519	-0.01879		9.968858	1.560048		
161	-6	-0.23449	0.687691	0.796342	0.289616	0.301082		0.054659	0.008554		
162	-5	-1.16226	0.034766	-0.46633	0.023299	0.024594		-7.43963	-1.16424		
163	-4	0.171392	-0.71517	-0.3204	-0.09149	0.977736		-1.81653	-0.28427		
164	-3	1.763094	-0.52596	0.259282	-0.44819	0.04807		12.79793	2.002775		
165	-2	-0.96855	-0.03503	0.235477	0.608533	0.002276		-3.61782	-0.56616		
166	-1	-1.55247	0.165531	1.477621	1.006319	-1.04356		-1.67114	-0.26152		

Copy this formula down column "CH" until you reach cell "CH182."

In previous chapters, the "p-value" has been explained through definition and example. As a quick reminder, if the p-value is below .05, the results are significant at the 95% level. If the p-value is below .01, the results are significant at the 99% level. Based on the results, we see that two days, –3 and 0, are significant at 95% and one day, +9, is significant at the 99% confidence level.

We have just reached a major milestone in our calculations. That is, all of our efforts up to this point have now culminated in a result that can be directly interpreted. These results allow us to answer our primary research question: "Do special investor meetings convey new and relevant information to the public markets?"

Based on the fact that the event date (day 0) is statistically significant, we can answer the question as follows: "Yes. We are 95% confident that special investor meetings convey new and relevant information to the public markets."

13.3.6.4 Calculating the Cumulative TSAR

The formula for the cumulative TSAR is very straightforward. The test statistic that is used to measure the level of significance of the results is a bit more involved. Both formulas are provided here.

$$CumulativeTSAR_{T_1,T_2} = \sum_{t=T_1}^{T_2} TSAR_t \qquad (13.6)$$

where

$Cumulative\ TSAR_{T_1,T_2}$ = cumulative TSAR for each day in the event window
$TSAR_t$ = TSAR for each day in the event window
T_1 = earliest date in the event window (–15)
T_2 = later date in the event window (ranges from –15 through +15)

$$Z_t = \left(\frac{1}{\sqrt{N}}\right)\left(\frac{\left(\sum\limits_{T_1}^{T_2} SAR_{jt}\right)}{\sqrt{(T_2 - T_1 + 1)\left(\dfrac{D_j - 2}{D_j - 4}\right)}}\right) \qquad \textbf{(13.7)}$$

where

Z_t = the Cumulative TSAR Z-statistic for each day in the event window
N = number of firms in the sample (40)
SAR_{jt} = SAR for firm j for each day in the event window
T_1 = earliest date in the event window (–15)
T_2 = later date in the event window (ranges from –15 through +15)
D_j = number of observed trading day returns for firm j over the estimation period

Let's begin by focusing on the Z-statistic. Specifically, let's work in the denominator on the part under the radical. These calculations will be denoted by Q_{jt}. As the subscripts imply, there will be a different calculation for each of the 40 firms in the sample and for each of the 31 days in the event window.

Begin in cell "CK150" by typing "**Qjt: (intermediate calculations to get the Z-statistics on Cumulative TSAR)**."

In cells "CK151" through "DX151," place the ticker symbols of all 40 firms. These can be "Cut" and "Pasted" from another section of the spreadsheet.

We are now ready to write the Excel formula for Q_{jt}. It can be represented by the following expression:

$$=(\$A152-(-15)+1)*(COUNT(\$B\$6:\$B\$105)-2)/(COUNT(\$B\$6:\$B\$105)-4)$$

For the second stock, the formula should read:

$$=(\$A152-(-15)+1)*(COUNT(\$H\$6:\$H\$105)-2)/(COUNT(\$H\$6:\$H\$105)-4)$$

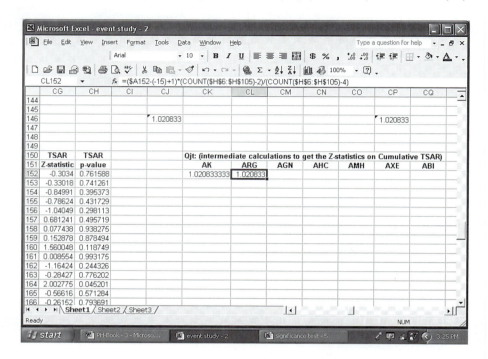

Perform this calculation for all 40 stocks in the sample. That is, complete row 152 for columns "CM" through "DX."

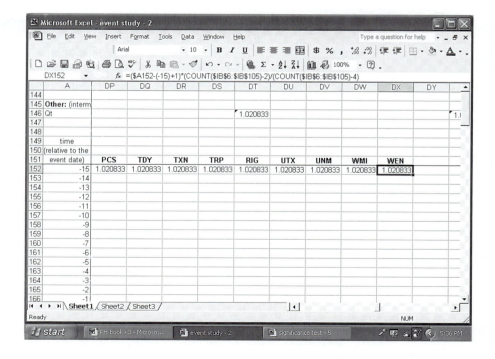

Copy the formulas in row 152 down through row 182 for all firms.

Now that we have calculated the terms under the radical in the denominator of the second term in Equation 13.7, let's continue by computing the entire term. Mathematically, we need to program the following:

$$\left(\frac{\left(\sum_{T_1}^{T_2} SAR_{jt} \right)}{\sqrt{\left(T_2 - T_1 + 1\right)\left(\dfrac{D_j - 2}{D_j - 4}\right)}} \right)$$

In terms of notation, it is often referred to as Z_{jt}. Again, you can infer from the subscripts that we will perform a calculation for each firm and for each day in the event window. To begin, type in the title "**Zjt: (intermediate calculations to get the Z-statistics on Cumulative TSAR)**" in cell "DZ150." Then "Copy" and "Paste" the ticker symbols for each of the 40 firms in cells "DZ151" through "FM151."

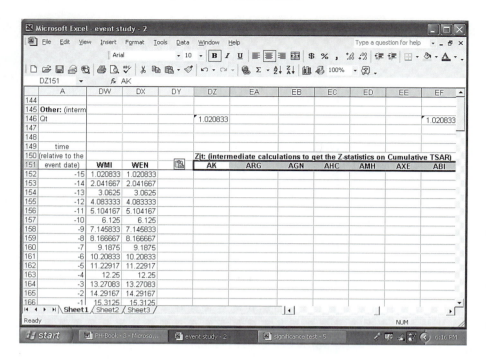

The Excel formula for Z_{jt} can be written as:

$$=\text{SUM(\$AQ\$152:AQ152)/SQRT(CK152)}$$

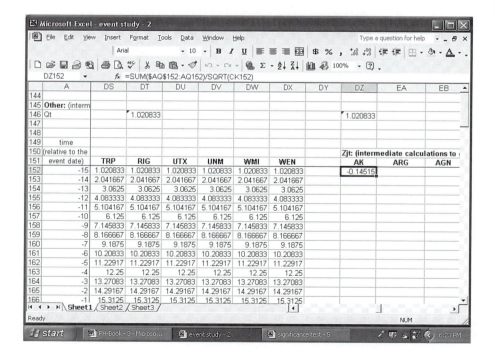

Copy this formula down through column "DZ" until you reach cell "DZ182."

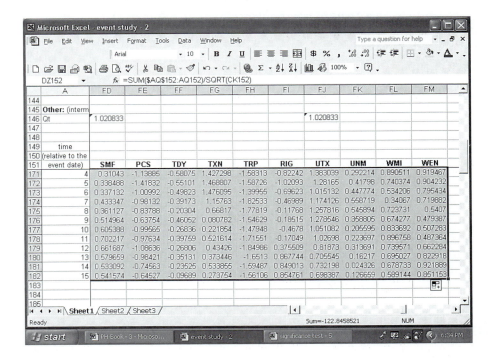

Now do the same for all firms in the sample. When you are done, the spreadsheet should look like this.

Only three columns are left to program. The titles of these columns are "**Cumulative TSAR**," "**Cumulative TSAR Z-statistic**," and "**Cumulative TSAR p-value**." These titles should be placed in cells "FO149" through "FQ151."

The formula for the cumulative TSAR was previously given in Equation 13.6. Again, it is written as:

$$CumulativeTSAR_{T_1,T_2} = \sum_{t=T_1}^{T_2} TSAR_t$$

In Excel, it can be expressed as:

=SUM($CF$152:CF152)

This formula should be entered into cell "FO152." Now copy this formula down to cell "FO182."

Calculating the associated Z-statistic will now be very easy because we already found the value of Z_{it} (the second term in Equation 13.7). To complete the formula, we just have to divide by the square root of N, which is the number of firms in the sample (40).

$$=SUM(DZ152:FM152)/SQRT(40)$$

Place this formula in cell "FP152."

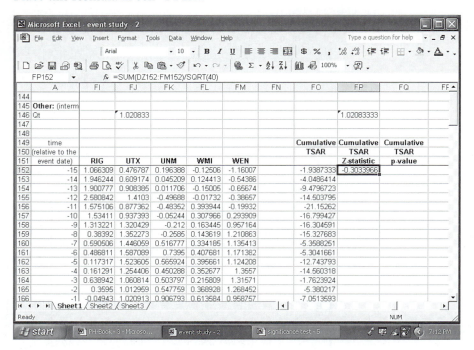

Copy this formula down to cell "FP182."

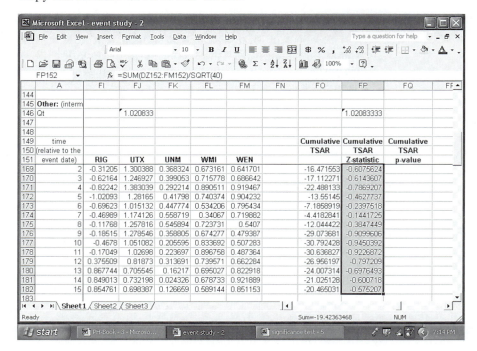

Instead of looking up the Z-values in a statistics table, a convenient step is to compute the p-values. Because this is a standard normal distribution, we can calculate the p-value by using the Excel function "NORMSDIST." The complete Excel formula is given by:

$$=2*(1-NORMSDIST(ABS(FP152)))$$

Type this formula into cell "FQ152."

Complete the spreadsheet by copying the formula down through cell "FQ182."

Because none of the p-values are below .05, the results are *not* statistically significant. This finding is not surprising given that only 3 of the 31 event window days were associated with significant TSARs.

In closing, based on the significant TSAR for day 0, we would say that special investor meetings do convey significant levels of new relevant information. Moreover, based on the nonsignificant cumulative TSARs, we would conclude that excessive leakage did not occur.

14

UNIT ROOT TEST

14.1 PURPOSE OF A UNIT ROOT TEST

The purpose of a unit root test is to determine if a series is difference "stationary." *Stationarity* means that a series is stable over time. More formally, stationarity means that the mean and autocovariances of the series do not depend on time.

Consider the S&P 500 Index as an example. In the 1970s, the S&P 500 Index was started with an initial value of 100. From that point, it drifts up or down depending on how the 500 stocks within the index perform. When the stock market does well, the index increases. In bad years, the index decreases. Over time, stock prices tend to increase at a historical average rate of roughly 10% per year. Therefore, the S&P 500 Index has an upward trend. That is, its mean is a function of time. In the early years, the mean was near 100. In more recent years, the value of the index is in the thousands. Therefore, a stock index is a classic example of a nonstationary series.

Many of the procedures used in conducting financial studies, such as regression, ARMA, and Granger Causality, require that a data series be stationary. Therefore, we must conduct a unit root test to verify that we are not violating this key assumption. If a series is found to be nonstationary, we can almost always make a simple adjustment to the series to make it become stationary. This adjustment is known as taking the first difference in the series. In more common terms, the adjustment involves converting the index into a return.

We will perform the unit root test in EViews. The file we will use to demonstrate the technique is "Country Return Data - 2." This dataset consists of time series data containing indexes of daily stock price levels for 13 world stock markets and the corresponding return on each index. Dates are listed in the rows, while the columns list each variable. Although each variable discussed will be explained in the chapter, additional information on each variable can be found in the Appendix.

14.2 PERFORMING A UNIT ROOT TEST

To open the "Country Return Data - 2" file in EViews, click "File," "Open," and then "Workfile."

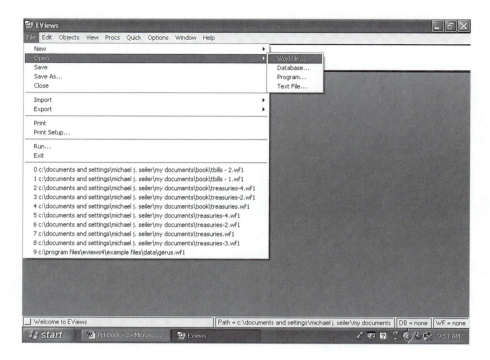

Select the file "Country Return Data - 2" by double-clicking on it. Alternatively, you could single-click on it and then click "Open."

After maximizing your window, your screen should look like this.

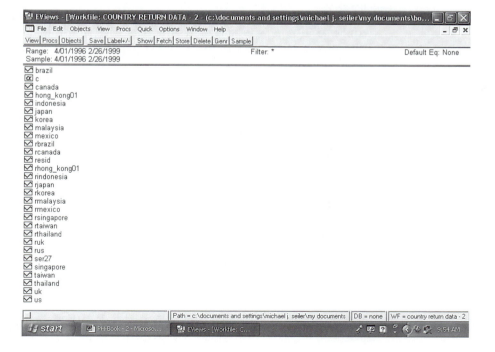

Let's focus on just the U.S. index of stock levels. That is, let's consider the variable "US." From this screen, double-click on the variable "US." You should see a spreadsheet containing just that variable.

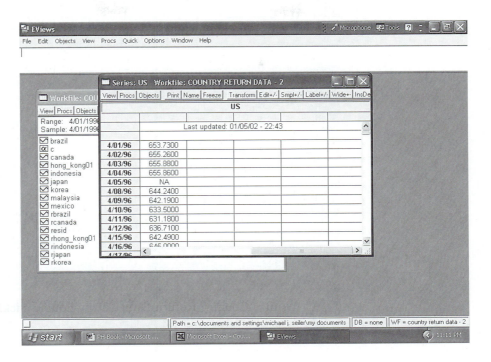

In the spreadsheet window, click "View" and then "Unit Root Test."

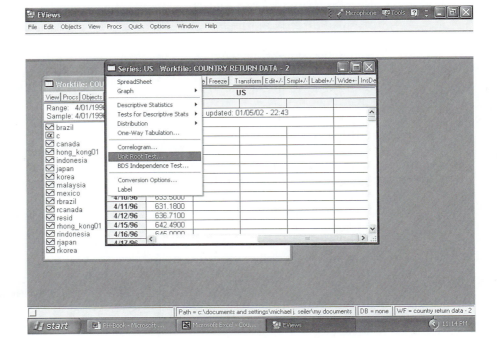

A "Unit Root Test" window will appear.

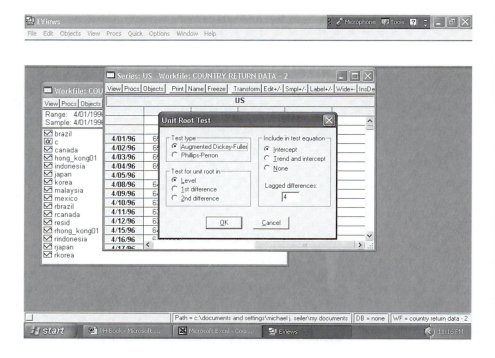

EViews uses two methods to perform the unit root test: Augmented Dickey-Fuller (ADF) and Phillips-Perron (PP). For now, let's focus on the ADF test.

Under the "Test for unit root in" box, you see the options "Level," "1st difference," and "2nd difference." "Level" means that you will consider the series "as is." In other words, no adjustments will be made to the series. In this case, the test would be performed directly on the index. If, however, "1st difference" is selected, EViews will adjust the series by taking the first difference in the series. This is analogous to calculating the return from the index as we did in Chapter 2. Finally, if we select "2nd difference," EViews will again take the difference of the series. In more common terms, it is equivalent to taking the first difference in the return. Taking a second difference is almost never necessary in practice.

Consider the "Include in test equation" box. The choices you have are "Intercept," "Trend and intercept," and "None." In Chapter 2, we established that a stock index will typically have an upward trend. Moreover, because an index typically does not start at zero (they usually start at 100), it will also likely have an intercept other than zero. Therefore, when dealing with indexes, as a general rule, you should select "Trend and intercept."

When dealing with a return series, only an intercept is typically present. That is, trends are not usually found in a return series. If the return series has a mean other than zero, then you should include an "intercept" term. However, if your return series has a mean very close to zero, you can select the button "None." As a general rule, you should select "Intercept" when testing a return series.

The final value to provide to EViews is the number of "Lagged differences" to include. The default value is "4." Picking this number is an example of where financial research becomes more of an art than a science. Although there are no hard and fast rules, two rules of thumb guide the number of lagged differences:

1. When you perform the ADF test, an "Akaike Information Criterion" and a "Schwarz Criterion" value will be reported. You can run the ADF test a few times, each time with a different number of lags, and rely on the results with the lowest reported values for the Akaike and Schwarz Criteria.

2. For the ADF test, the computer performs a regression. As in any regression, you should not leave nonsignificant variables in the final equation because it will bias the estimates on the other variables. The "Lagged difference" terms you include are extra explanatory variables in the regression. Therefore, if you try six lagged terms and they are all nonsignificant, you should not have them all in the equation. Instead, try four, then three, then two. It is OK to have a nonsignificant lag or two in your final test run, but you want to keep the number of nonsignificant lagged terms to a minimum.

Let's get back to the ADF test. We are ready to perform the unit root test on the variable, "US," which represents the U.S. index of stock prices. Because this is an index, we will select "Trend and intercept" from the "Include in test equation" box. Leave all other settings as they are. Your screen should look like this.

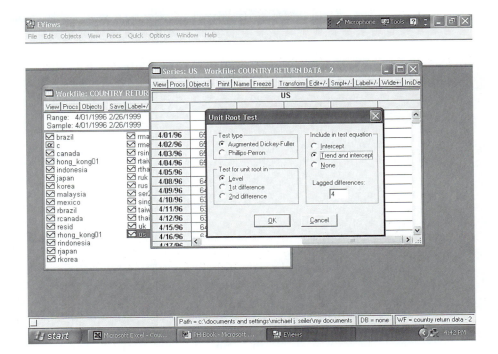

Click "OK" and the following screen will appear. I have pressed the "Maximize" button in the top-right corner of the window so it fills the entire screen.

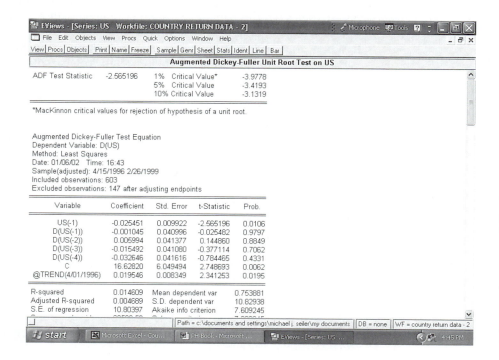

The key output is the "ADF Test Statistic" that is listed at the top of the page. The value is given as –2.565196. To the right, three critical values are provided, each corresponding to a higher level of significance. The critical (cutoff) values are –3.9778 (1%), –3.4193 (5%), and –3.1319 (10%). Picture these four values on the same line. Because the "ADF Test Statistic" lies to the *right* of the critical values, the series is found to be *nonstationary.*

For the sake of understanding, if the "ADF Test Statistic" had been –4.5289, then you would have concluded that the series was stationary at the 1% level of significance. Stated another way, you would have been 99% (100% – 1%) confident that the series was stationary. If the "ADF Test Statistic" had been –3.7853, you would have been 95% confident that the series was stationary. Finally, if the "ADF Test Statistic" had been –3.2514, you would have concluded that the series was stationary at the 90% level of confidence.

Consider the rest of the output. Recall that the number of "Lagged differences" terms to include in the ADF test is up for debate. We have chosen four terms because that is the default. But is this the right number? From the middle of the output, the coefficients on the four lagged terms, "D(US(-1))," "D(US(-2))," "D(US(-3))," and "D(US(-4))," are all nonsignificant. We know this because the p-values (EViews refers to p-values as "Prob." values) are all above .05. Therefore, it is likely that fewer than four "Lagged differences" terms are needed.

The ADF test was performed four more times, changing only the number of "Lagged differences" terms. The "Lagged differences" used were "3," "2," "1," and "0." Instead of the individual screens for each ADF test, the following table summarizes our findings.

Number of Lags	Number of Significant Lags	ADF Test Statistic	Conclusion	Akaike Criterion	Schwarz Criterion
4	0	−2.565	Not stationary	7.609	7.660
3	0	−2.656	Not stationary	7.607	7.650
2	0	−3.200	Stationary at 10%	7.580	7.614
1	0	−2.882	Not stationary	7.586	7.613
0	N/A	−2.766	Not stationary	7.584	7.604

Because none of the "Lagged differences" terms are significant, none should be included in the equation. The Schwarz Criterion confirms this conclusion. Its lowest value is associated with zero lags. For the Akaike Criterion, the selection of zero lags is associated with the second-lowest value. The "rules of thumb" seem to have converged relatively nicely to reach the conclusion that no lags are useful in conducting this unit root test.

As an interesting aside, when the unit root test is performed with zero lags, as we have done here, we are actually performing the Dickey-Fuller (DF) test, as opposed to the ADF test. That is, a DF test using any number of lags is an ADF test.

The final conclusion you should reach is that the index of U.S. stock prices is a *non-stationary* series.

Let's consider the first difference in the index "US." This test is performed the same way as before, with the exception that instead of selecting "Level" from the "Test for unit root in" box, you will select "1st difference." Note that we have used zero lags. If you want to verify the validity of doing this, you can repeat the (A)DF test using between zero and four lags. You will find zero lags to be the appropriate number.

Also, because we are taking the first difference in the series, it is no longer appropriate to assume that the series has a trend component. Therefore, you will need to select "Intercept" from the "Include in test equation" box. In this example, the choice between "Intercept" and "Trend and intercept" makes almost no difference at all. However, choosing between the two does affect the power of the unit root test, so you should get into the good habit of correctly choosing between the two.

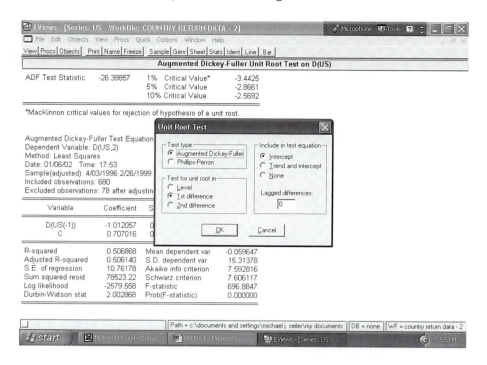

Click "OK." Maximize the "Output" window to see the following screen.

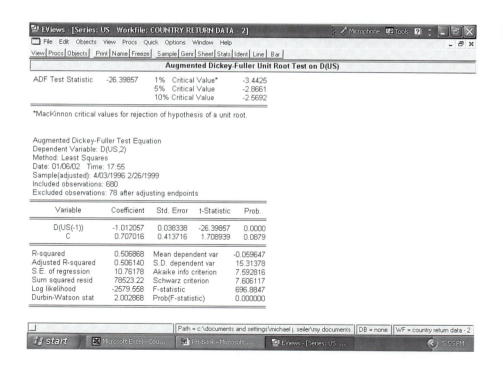

Because the "ADF Test Statistic" lies to the *left* of all three critical values, you should conclude that the series is now stationary.

To illustrate the linkage between the index and the return, perform the unit root test again, this time on the return series titled "rUS." Because the series is already differenced, select "Level" from the "Test for unit root in" box. Because the series represents a return, it is not appropriate to assume that the series has a trend component. Therefore, you will need to select "Intercept" from the "Include in test equation" box.

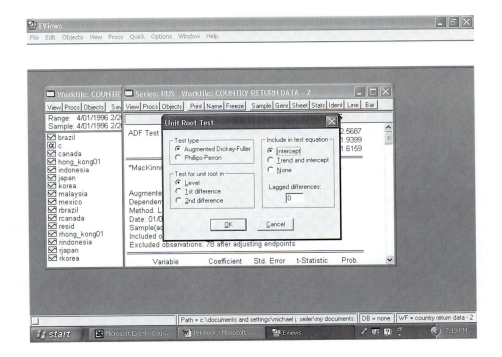

Click "OK" and maximize the resulting window.

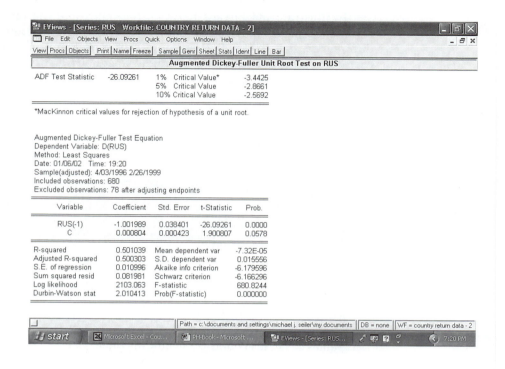

You will notice that the "ADF Test Statistic" is almost identical to the result when taking the first difference of the index. This makes sense because the return series comes from "differencing" the index of price levels. This is one of the reasons why you normally see studies performed using the returns on stocks rather than their price levels.

15

GRANGER CAUSALITY

15.1 PURPOSE OF GRANGER CAUSALITY

Correlation measures the degree to which two variables move together over a period of time. Correlation does not have anything to do with measuring a "cause-and-effect" relationship. That is, even if two variables are highly correlated, it does not at all imply that one variable causes the other. In fact, there are hundreds of examples where two variables have a high correlation but have absolutely nothing to do with each other.

Granger Causality is a technique commonly used to more rigorously examine if there exists a temporal cause-and-effect relationship between two variables.

As a way to understand Granger Causality, consider this example. Consider two variables "x" and "y." Current values of "y" (the dependent variable) are regressed against the following independent variables: past values of "y" and past values of "x." If these past values of "x" turn out to be significant, then "x" is found to Granger Cause "y."

Stated another way, Granger Causality tests whether past values of "x" significantly explain current values of "y" after controlling for past values of "y."

A third way to explain the concept is to say that we will see if current values of "y" can be explained by past values of "y." Then we will see if adding past values of "x" significantly help to further explain current values of "y." If past values of "x" significantly further explain current values of "y," then "x Granger Causes y."

The opposite effect is also tested. That is, thus far we have been asking if "x Granger Causes y." Granger Causality also measures the opposite effect: Does "y Granger Cause x"? It is possible that "x Granger Causes y," "y Granger Causes x," "neither one Granger Causes the other," or "both." That's right. You can find that each variable significantly Granger Causes the other.

To demonstrate Granger Causality, we will use the EViews file "Country Return Data - 2." This dataset consists of time series data containing indexes of daily stock price levels for 13 world stock markets and the corresponding return on each index. Dates are listed in the rows, while the columns list each variable. Although each variable discussed in this chapter will be explained in the text, additional information on each variable can be found in the Appendix.

15.2 PERFORMING GRANGER CAUSALITY

To open the "Country Return Data - 2" file in EViews, choose "File," "Open," and then "Workfile."

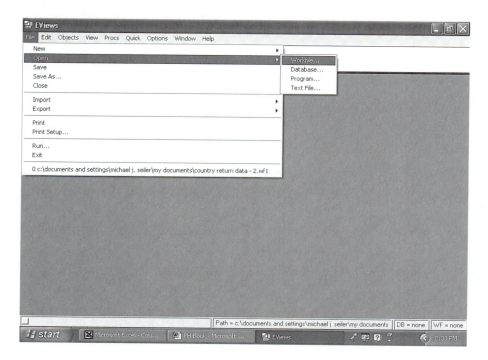

Select "Country Return Data - 2" and then click "Open."

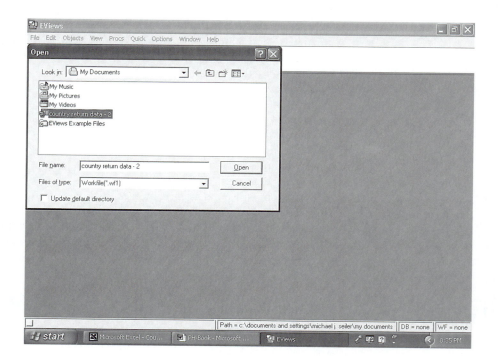

Maximize the screen and the file will appear as follows.

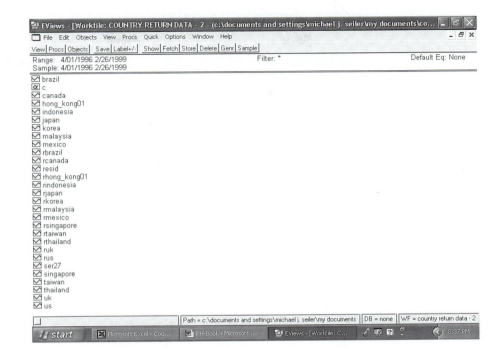

Let's test the Granger Causality relationship between the United States and the United Kingdom. One of the assumptions in Granger Causality is that the two series to be tested are stationary. Recall from Chapter 14 that we have already verified that the return series are stationary. For this reason, there is no need for us to repeat the unit root test here.

To select the two variables, click on one of the variables. To select the second variable, you must hold down the "Ctrl" key on your keyboard as you left-click your mouse button on the second variable. The variables we are selecting are "rUS" and "rUK." Now double-click on either variable. The following menu will pop up.

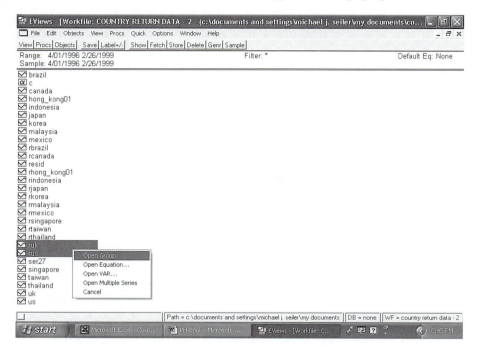

Click on "Open Group" and a spreadsheet will open showing the two return series. Maximize the window.

obs	RUS	RUK						
4/01/96	NA	NA						
4/02/96	0.002338	0.002713						
4/03/96	0.000946	-0.000912						
4/04/96	-3.05E-05	0.008154						
4/05/96	NA	NA						
4/08/96	NA	NA						
4/09/96	-0.003187	NA						
4/10/96	-0.013624	0.002339						
4/11/96	-0.003669	-0.006177						
4/12/96	0.008723	0.006018						
4/15/96	0.009037	0.006272						
4/16/96	0.003899	0.009139						
4/17/96	-0.005270	-0.005163						
4/18/96	0.003112	0.003960						
4/19/96	0.002266	0.009482						
4/22/96	0.004362	-0.001141						
4/23/96	0.005679	-0.005126						
4/24/96	-0.002166	-0.004026						
4/25/96	0.004144	0.000445						
4/26/96	0.000903	0.003528						
4/29/96	0.001071	-0.006176						
4/30/96	1.53E-05	0.002281						
5/01/96	0.000627	-0.003122						
5/02/96	-0.017258	-0.007808						
5/03/96	-0.002724	-0.006589						
5/06/96	-0.001279	NA						
5/07/96								

Click "File" and then "Granger Causality."

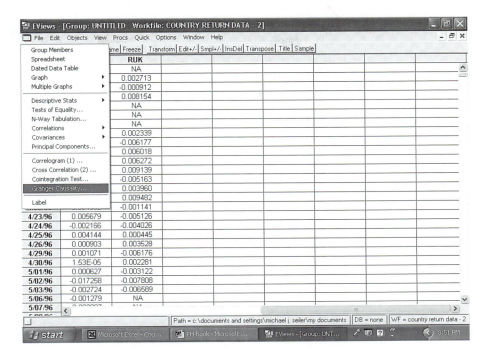

A window titled "Lag Specification" will appear. You must enter a number where it reads "Lags to include". For now, use "4" lags.

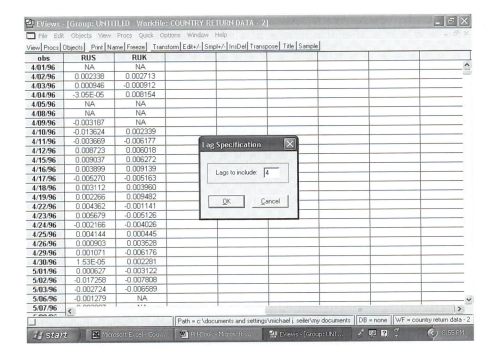

Click "OK." You will see the following window.

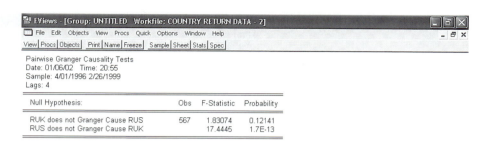

The key output you are interested in is the "Probability" associated with each of the two rows. "Probability" is the same as a p-value. As such, it is a measure of whether or not a variable is significant. For example, the first row, titled "RUK does not Granger Cause RUS," refers to whether or not the stock market of the United Kingdom Granger Causes the stock market of the United States. Because this value (0.12141) is *not* below .05, we conclude that the U.K. stock market does *not* Granger Cause the U.S. stock market.

The second row, "RUS does not Granger Cause RUK," indicates whether or not the U.S. market Granger Causes the U.K. market. Because the "Probability" (1.7E-13, which expands to 0.00000000000017) is below .05, we conclude that the U.S. market *does* Granger Cause the U.K. stock market.

In less statistical terms, this means that the U.K. market reacts significantly to relevant news from the U.S. market. However, the U.S. stock market does not significantly react to news from the U.K. stock market.

15.3 NUMBER OF LAGS

Determining the number of lags to use is another area where financial studies are more of an art than a science. Although there is no consensus as to the optimal number of lags, common sense would say to consider as many past observations as you think could reasonably explain the other variable.

Some researchers will tell you that it is better to use too many lags rather than too few. Although this may be true, I view it as only the lesser of two evils. Using too many lags will bias your test results. To understand why this bias will occur, I need to dig a little deeper into Granger Causality.

In our example, we used four lags to determine which series Granger Caused the other. Yet, in the "Output" window, you only saw one F-statistic associated with each directional test. Why did four lags result in only one output value (F-statistic)? The answer is that Granger Causality tests for the significance of all of the lagged values as a group. If the group of lagged values is jointly significantly different from zero, then Granger Causality is present.

The problem with using too many lagged values is that if the additional lags are not significant, it reduces the likelihood that all the lagged values, when taken as a group, will be significant. In short, selecting too many lags can cause you to conclude that Granger Causality is not present when it really is.

15.4 LIMITATIONS OF GRANGER CAUSALITY

Because of the calculations involved, Granger Causality assumes that the past can explain the future, but that the future cannot explain that past. On the surface, this sounds very reasonable. However, in finance, there are numerous examples where the future can cause the past.

Consider the reaction of the stock market when the Federal Reserve lowers interest rates. Theory states that the lowering of interest rates will cause an increase in stock prices. This is clearly a cause-and-effect relationship. However, this is a case where the "effect" often occurs *before* the "cause."

As you know, stock prices reflect the future expectations of investors. It is very often the case that the market fully anticipates not only the direction of an interest rate change, but also the magnitude of that change. If this is true, then stock prices will adjust today (effect) to reflect the expected interest rate change that will be announced tomorrow (cause).

Granger Causality is unable to correctly measure this relationship because it assumes forward temporal causation, or a relationship where the "cause" occurs before the "effect." Therefore, in our example, Granger Causality would conclude that stock price increases Granger Cause the Federal Reserve to lower interest rates. Clearly, this is not the case.

16

COINTEGRATION

~~~

16.1 PURPOSE OF COINTEGRATION

It is widely recognized that most economic time series are not difference stationary (contain a unit root). Recall from Chapter 14 that the test for this type of stationarity is the unit root test. If taking the first difference in the series causes it to become stationary, the series is said to be integrated of *order one*. If it is necessary to take the difference a second time (in order to eliminate the unit root), the series is referred to as being integrated of *order two*.

Several studies have shown that the common practice of taking the first difference (calculating the return) of the series can still lead to misspecification. As such, the use of economic time series returns in many procedures, such as linear regression, can produce biased or spurious results.

Interestingly, even if two or more series are shown to be integrated (nonstationary), it may be possible to combine them to create up to a $N - 1$ stationary series. These stationary series could then be used in subsequent methodologies to produce unbiased results. Integrated series of the same order that can be combined to create stationary series are called *cointegrated* series. The process of combining them is known as *cointegration*. Finally, the stationary series that are obtained are called *cointegrating vectors*.

Another beneficial application of cointegration occurs in the area of modern portfolio theory (MPT). MPT relates to how assets should be combined in a portfolio to maximize the level of return for a given level of risk or minimize the level of risk for a given level of return. MPT is based on correlations between assets (the covariance between the assets standardized by the standard deviation of the assets). The problem with correlation is that it is a static concept, meaning that it does not take into consideration the ordering of the time series. In contrast, cointegration takes the dynamic (intertemporal) relationship among the time series into consideration.

In MPT, if the correlation between assets is low, diversification benefits are possible. However, if a cointegrated relationship among the asset classes exists, the benefits derived from diversification are not accurately measured. Alternatively stated, MPT produces biased estimates of portfolio weights if an existing cointegration relationship exists but is ignored.

Finally, the result of finding a cointegrated relationship among asset classes creates the potential to identify a long-term relationship where not all of the asset classes (stocks, bonds, T-bills, real estate, gold, and so forth) are needed to achieve an optimal portfolio. This potential reduction in asset redundancy is important because it can allow a portfolio manager to focus on fewer asset types, thereby allowing more concentrated efforts into those that remain.

To demonstrate the concept of cointegration, we will refer to the dataset "cointegration data - 1." This dataset consists of time series data containing quarterly price levels and returns for stocks, corporate bonds, government bonds, and real estate. Dates are listed in the rows, while the columns list each variable. Although each variable discussed in this chapter will be explained in the text, additional information on each variable can be found in the Appendix.

16.2 PERFORMING A COINTEGRATION TEST

To open the "cointegration data - 1" file in EViews, click "File," "Open," and then "Workfile."

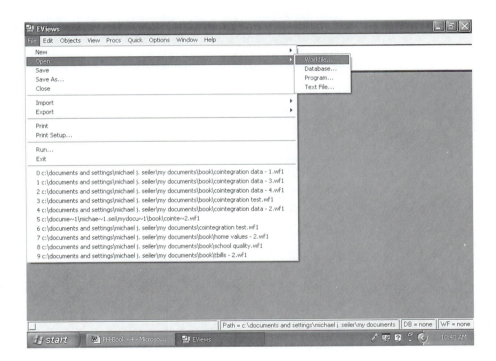

The following window will appear.

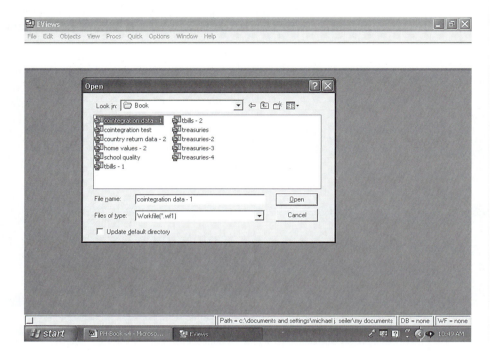

Select the file "cointegration data - 1" by double-clicking on it. After maximizing the window, you will see the following EViews Workfile.

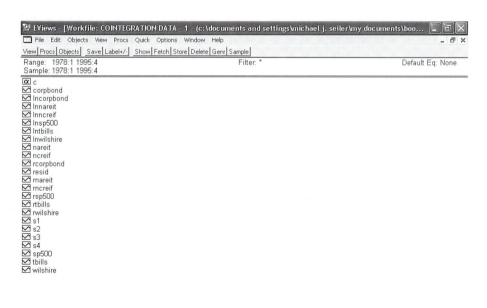

16.2.1 VERIFYING THAT THE SERIES ARE INTEGRATED

The goal of the cointegration test is to determine if two or more integrated (nonstationary) series can be combined to create (up to $N - 1$) stationary series. As such, before we perform the test, we must make sure that all series in the analysis are integrated and of the same order. Recall that this determination can be made by performing a unit root test. Specifically, we will perform an ADF test for stationarity.

Double-click on the variable titled "lnncreif." You will see the following EViews window.

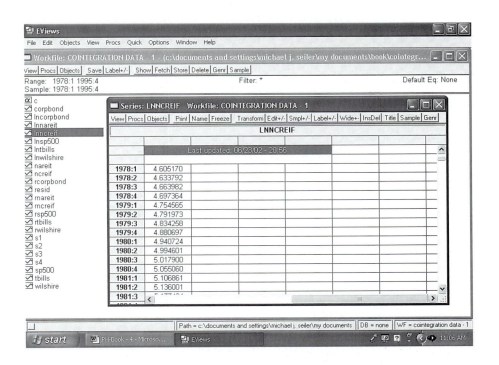

The variable "lnncreif" stands for the "natural log of the National Council of Real Estate Investment Fiduciaries (NCREIF) index." NCREIF is an unsecuritized commercial real estate index. That is, it measures the return on commercial real estate that is not traded in the public financial markets. The asset class is extremely illiquid and derives most of its return from income (as opposed to capital gains). Because it does not trade on public markets like a stock, it is not plagued with excessive price shocks (volatility due to noise trading and over- or underreaction). Perhaps most interestingly of all, the index values are based on appraisals rather than transactions. These are just a few of the most striking differences between this index and most other series. For these reasons (and many more not discussed here), it is no wonder why so much research has gone into trying to measure the extent to which, if any, unsecuritized real estate warrants inclusion in a mixed-asset portfolio.

Getting back to the ADF test, click "View" and then "Unit Root Test."

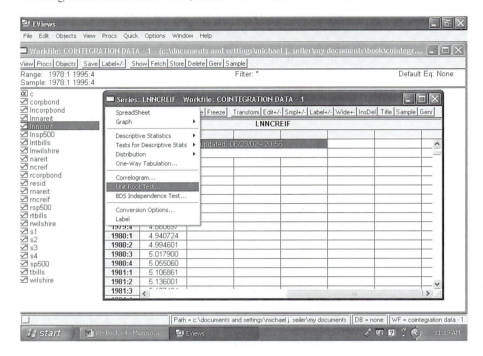

The following "Unit Root Test" window will appear.

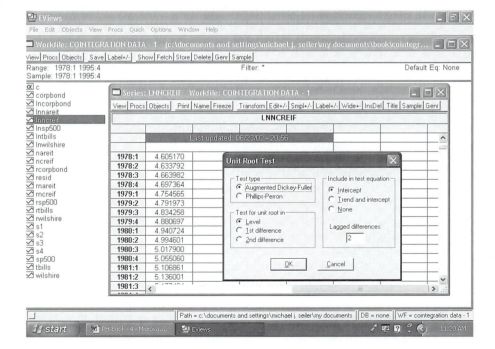

Under the box titled "Include in test equation," check the option labeled "Trend and intercept." Under the "Lagged differences" box, type in the value "4." We use this number of lags because it is widely known in real estate research that the NCREIF series is seasonal.

If you have correctly specified the options, your screen should look like this.

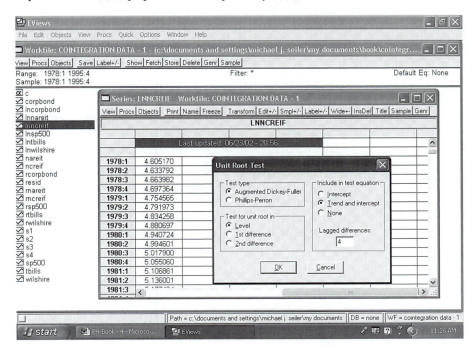

Click "OK" to perform the test. After maximizing the resulting window, your monitor should show the following output.

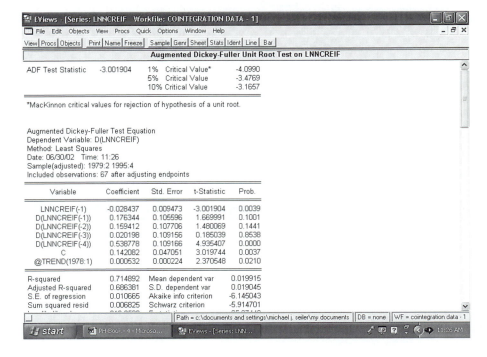

Because the ADF Test Statistic lies to the right of the three critical cutoff values, we conclude that the series is integrated (nonstationary). This means that it can be used in the test for cointegration.

We will use five different series in our cointegration analysis. The remaining four include: (1) "lnnareit," the natural log of the National Association of Real Estate Investment Trust (NAREIT) index of publicly traded real estate; (2) "lncorpbond," the natural log of the index of corporate bonds provided by Ibbotson & Associates; (3) "lnsp500," the natural log of the S&P 500; and (5) "lntbills," the natural log of U.S. Treasury bills.

For the sake of brevity, the ADF test will not be shown for the remaining four asset classes. However, each test was performed and each was found to be integrated of order one (nonstationary). As such, they can all be used in the test of cointegration.

16.2.2 CONTINUING WITH THE COINTEGRATION TEST

Now that the five series have all been found to be integrated of the same order, we are ready to perform the cointegration test. Start by selecting the five variables you wish to test. Specifically, start by selecting "lnncreif." This selection is done by left-clicking on the variable with your mouse. Next, while holding down the "Ctrl" key on your keyboard, left-click on the remaining four variables: "lnnareit," "lncorpbond," "lnsp500," and "lntbills," in that order.

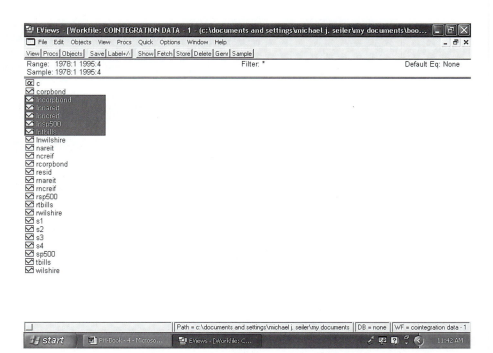

Now that all five variables are highlighted, double-click on the highlighted area. You will see the following window.

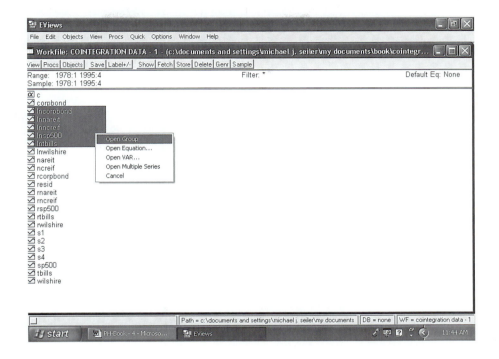

Select the choice "Open Group" by clicking it. You should now see a window that looks like a spreadsheet.

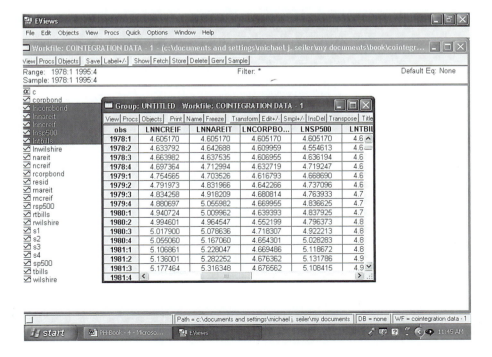

In the spreadsheet window, click "View" and then "Cointegration Test."

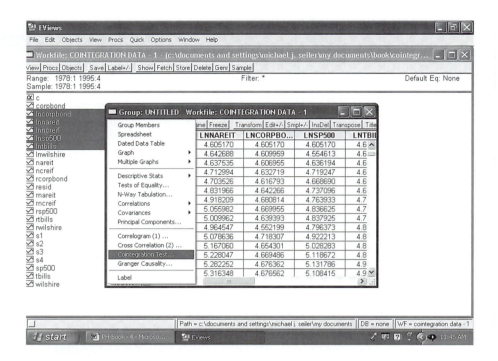

You will see a new window titled "Johansen Cointegration Test."

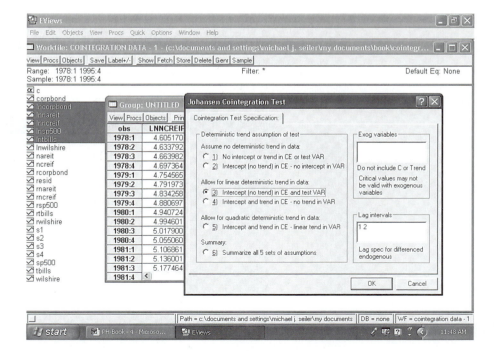

Three boxes must be specified in this window. For now, let's focus on the box marked "Lag intervals." When determining the number of lags to include, the intuitive choice, based on the appraisal-induced seasonality of the "lnncreif" series, is "4." Statistically, the Akaike Information Criterion and the Schwarz Criterion could be used to identify the optimal number of lags to include, as discussed in Chapter 14.

To change the number of lags from the default value of "2" to the appropriate value of "4," simply change the number as shown here.

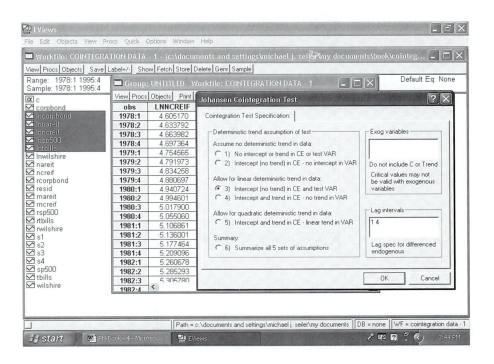

Consider the second box, "Exog variables." The abbreviation, "Exog," is short for "exogenous." In this box, we are to include the variables determined outside the model (exogenous variables). In most cases, you will not need exogenous variables. However, if you do need them, the most common variables to include are seasonal dummy variables, if they are appropriate. As previously discussed, the NCREIF series is widely recognized as having a strong seasonal component. For this reason, we must include the seasonal dummy variables in the model.

In our dataset, you will notice the variables "s1," "s2," "s3," and "s4." These variables are all seasonal dummy variables. That is, for "s1," a value of "1" is observed for all first quarters in the sample. A value of "0" is entered for the second, third, and fourth quarters of the year. Accordingly, for "s2," a "1" is entered for each row corresponding to the second quarter of each year; a "0" is entered for the first, third, and fourth quarters.

Enter all four dummy variables into the "Exog variables" list.

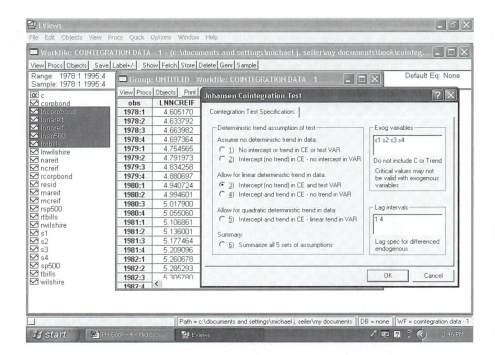

We are now ready to tackle the final box, "Deterministic trend assumption of test." There are five primary cases from which to choose. Each makes a slightly different assumption about the trend in the underlying data series. It is important to make the correct assumption, as each could result in a different number of cointegrating vectors. In general, use case 2 if none of the series has a trend. Case 3 is to be used if all of the series have a stochastic trend, whereas case 4 should be used if some of the series are trend stationary. Case 5 is rarely, if ever, used. It may produce a good in-sample fit, but it will not forecast well out-of-sample. If in doubt, select case 6. This selection will tell EViews to perform the test five separate times using each of the five different assumptions. The number of resulting cointegrating vectors will be summarized in a table for you.

We will now briefly discuss why case 1 is the appropriate selection for our analysis. Under this case, no trend is assumed in either the cointegrating equation (CE) or the vector autoregression equation (VAR) because the index values were specified as natural logs. Therefore, when the first difference in the index is taken, the result is a return series. Moreover, no constant is assumed in either the CE or the VAR because we have included four seasonal dummy variables. Any one of these four dummies can play the role of the constant in the equation. Alternatively stated, by including dummy variables, the procedure is estimated as if a constant is in the equation even though it is not explicit.

After completing these steps, the specification of your "Johansen Cointegration Test" window should be as follows.

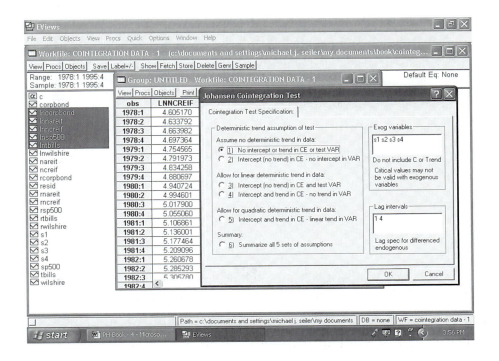

Click "OK" to perform the test. After maximizing the newly produced window and scrolling down a few lines, your screen should look like this.

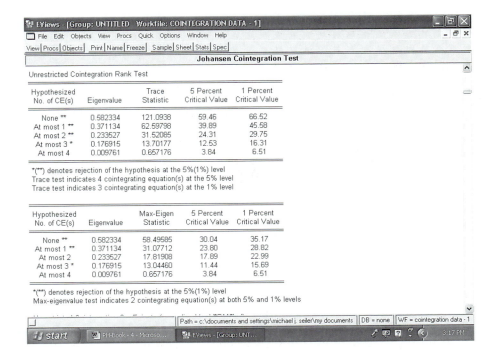

Two statistics are reported: the "Trace Statistic" and the "Max-Eigen Statistic (Maximum Eigenvalue Statistic)." Unfortunately, the two might yield conflicting results, as is the case here. The "Trace Statistic" concludes that three or four cointegrating vectors exist (depending on the required level of significance), whereas the "Max-Eigen Statistic" indicates that only two cointegrating vectors exist.

A logical explanation exists for these somewhat conflicting results. The critical values associated with the cointegration test reported by EViews do not incorporate the inclusion of exogenous variables. Because we have included four exogenous variables (the four seasonal dummy variables) in the analysis, the level of significance may be misleading, and therefore, the number of resulting cointegrating relationships might yield conflicting results.

Still, because there are five series in the analysis, we can conclude (under either measure) that these integrated (nonstationary) series can be combined to form at least two stationary series. That is, we can say that these series are cointegrated.

16.2.3   USING CENTERED (ORTHOGONALIZED) SEASONAL DUMMY VARIABLES

In recent years, it has been found that seasonal dummy variables should first be *centered* or *orthogonalized* before they are included in a cointegration analysis. If you fail to do so, the standard "0-1" seasonal dummy variable will change the mean and trend in the underlying series and possibly bias the results.

There are three ways to "center" or "orthogonalize" your seasonal (quarterly) dummy variables. The first is to manually go through each observation and subtract .25 from each observation. The second is to use a formula in Excel, which would be quite easy. The third way is to use a canned function in EViews. Because the dataset is already in EViews, we will use this final approach.

From the main EViews window, highlight the variable "s1" by single-clicking on it. Look for the button marked "Genr" towards the top of the screen. It is the tenth button from the left and the second from the right. The abbreviation "Genr" stands for "generate," as in "generate a series." Click this button and the "Generate Series by Equation" window will appear.

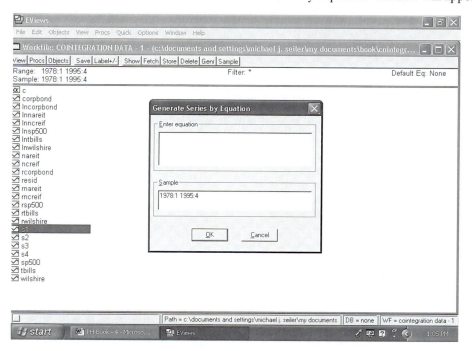

Under the box labeled "Enter equation," type in "s1c=@seas(s1)-1/4." The left-hand side of the equation, "s1c," is the new variable name we are about to create. It stands for "seasonal dummy variable 1 - centered." On the right-hand side of the equation, we start by using the function "@seas()," which tells EViews to create a seasonal dummy variable (based on the existing variable "s1"). To center the variable, we subtract .25 or "1/4."

As you know, the variable "s1" is already a seasonal variable. As such, we really do not need the redundant command "@seas()." That is, we could accomplish the same thing by simply writing "s1c=s1-1/4" in the box titled "Enter equation." The reason for showing you this command is to introduce the function that should be used for those situations where the seasonal dummy has not already been created.

In any event, type in either "s1c=@seas(s1)-1/4" or "s1c=s1-1/4" in the box marked "Enter equation."

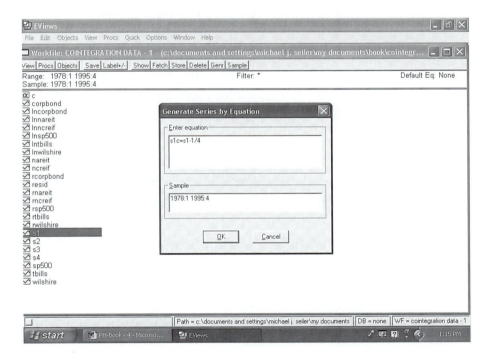

After clicking "OK," you will see the newly created variable "s1c" in the list among the previously existing variables. It is always a good idea to verify that EViews did what you thought it would do. To double-check the calculation, double-click on the new variable "s1c." A new spreadsheet window will appear titled "Series: S1C."

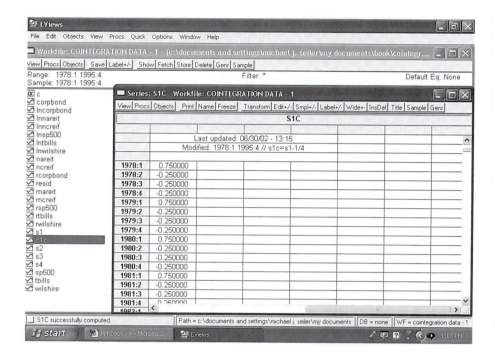

In the variable "s1," a "1" is observed for all first quarters and "0" elsewhere. In the "centered" series, "s1c," each value should be .25 lower. By looking at the values in the spreadsheet, we can now verify that EViews did perform the calculation correctly.

Center the three remaining seasonal dummy variables by following the procedure we just described. When you are done, you should have created the new centered (orthogonalized) seasonal dummy variables with the names "s2c," "s3c," and "s4c." Because we have adjusted the dataset, let's save it under the new name "cointegration data - 2." For the sake of brevity, the analysis will not be repeated using the centered seasonal dummy variables as exogenous variables. If you perform the test on your own, you will find the results to be different, but very much similar.

17

VECTOR AUTOREGRESSION

17.1 PURPOSE OF VECTOR AUTOREGRESSION

Vector autoregression (VAR) is used to model multiple variables that are linked together over time. Instead of specifying a dependent variable in terms of several other independent variables, the independent variables used in VAR are simply lags of the various interrelated dependent variables. For example, assume we recognize the existence of an interrelationship among five different time series: unsecuritized real estate, securitized real estate, stocks, corporate bonds, and government bonds. If we want to model the returns on unsecuritized real estate, we could model it as a function of lags of unsecuritized real estate, securitized real estate, stocks, corporate bonds, and government bonds. If we want to model the returns on stocks, we would include as independent variables lags in the series for unsecuritized real estate, securitized real estate, stocks, corporate bonds, and government bonds. In short, VAR bypasses the development of a structural equation by specifying a model in terms of lags in all the variables included in an interrelated system.

The following demonstration will go far in clarifying our understanding of this seemingly complex method of modeling a system of related time series. Consider the dataset "cointegration data - 1." This dataset consists of time series data containing quarterly price levels and returns for stocks, corporate bonds, government bonds, and real estate. Dates are listed in the rows, while the columns list each variable.

17.2 PERFORMING A VAR

To open the "cointegration data - 1" file in EViews, click "File," "Open," and then "Workfile."

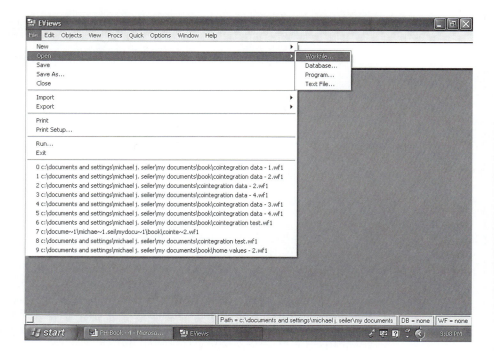

The following window will appear.

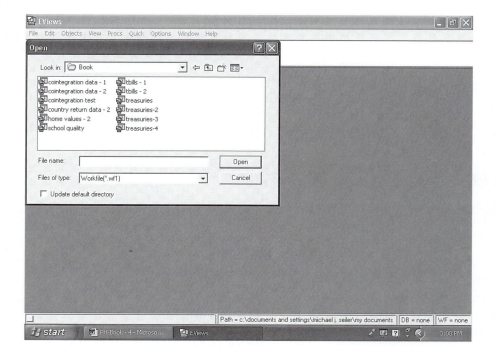

Select the file "cointegration data - 1" by double-clicking on it. After maximizing the window, you will see the following EViews Workfile.

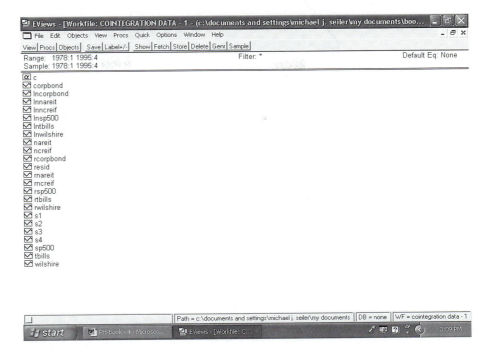

Select the following variables in this order: "rncreif," "rnareit," "rcorpbond," "rsp500," and "rtbills." To do so, left-click on the variable "rncreif." Then, while holding down the "Ctrl" key on your keyboard, left-click on "rnareit." Continue to hold down the "Ctrl" key and left-click on the remaining variables in the order indicated. When you are done, your screen should look like this.

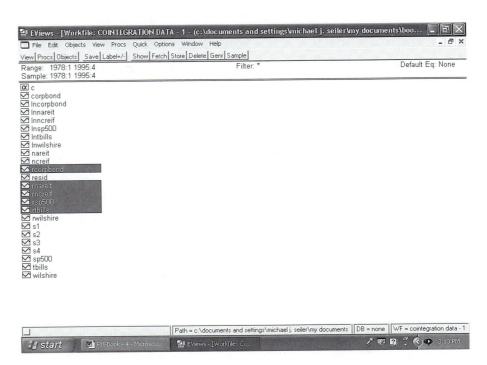

Double-click anywhere in the highlighted region. The following window will pop up.

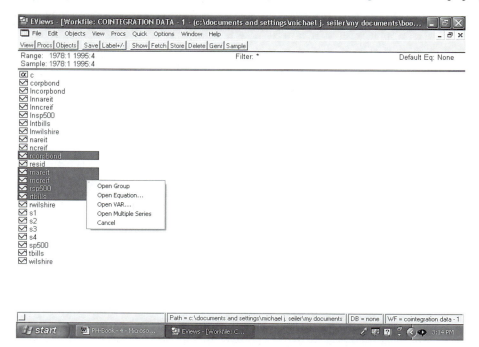

Select "Open VAR" by single-clicking on it. You should now see the window titled "VAR Specification."

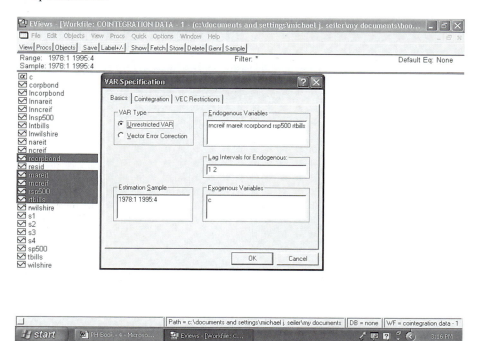

As explained in the chapter on cointegration, we must specify the number of lags as "4." Do this in the box marked "Lag Intervals for Endogenous." Also, under the box labeled "Exogenous Variables," we must identify the four seasonal dummy variables "s1," "s2," "s3," and "s4" and remove the "c."

After performing these steps, your screen should appear as follows.

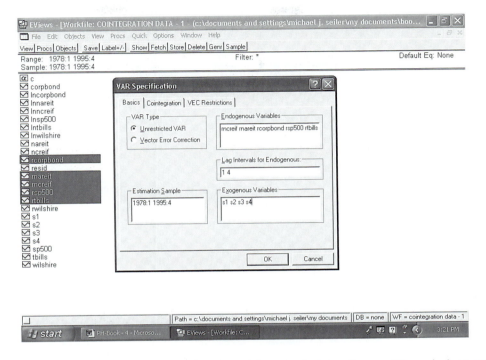

Click "OK" to perform the estimation. After maximizing the resulting window, you will see the top of the output.

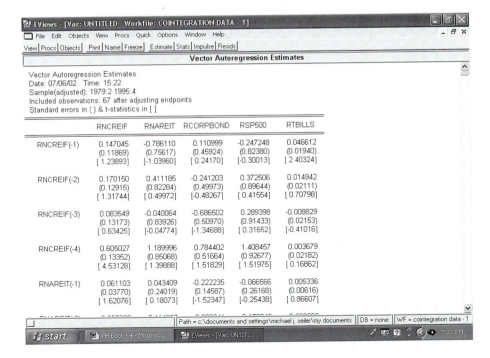

Each column represents a separate equation. The variable name at the top of each column is the dependent variable. The names in each row are the independent variables. The first number in each row is the regression coefficient. The second is the standard error. The third is the t-statistic.

Scroll down to the bottom of the window to view the remaining results.

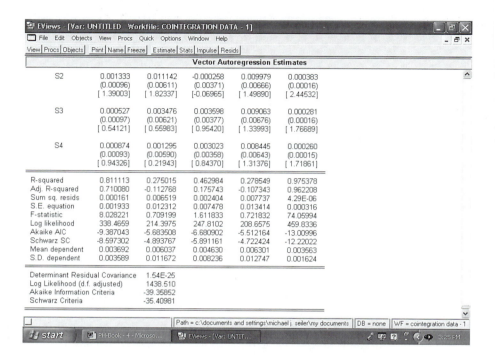

These results should be interpreted in the same way as any other regression results. For more details, refer to the chapter on regression.

18

VECTOR ERROR
CORRECTION

18.1 PURPOSE OF VECTOR ERROR CORRECTION

Once a group of series has been found to be cointegrated, a natural extension of VAR is the estimation of a vector error correction (VEC) model. A VAR is unrestricted and is used to model a system of stationary interrelated time series. A VEC model is a restricted VAR that is designed for use with integrated (nonstationary) series that are cointegrated.

The VEC incorporates the cointegrating relationship (which is a long-run equilibrium) amongst the variables by forcing the model to converge in the long-run. However, the VEC allows for deviations that are gradually corrected through a series of adjustments that are dictated by the long-run relationship. These adjustments are reflected in the cointegration term.

To aid in our understanding of how a VEC model is created, we will consider the dataset "cointegration data - 1." This dataset consists of time series data containing quarterly price levels and returns for stocks, corporate bonds, government bonds, and real estate. Dates are listed in the rows, while the columns list each variable.

18.2 PERFORMING A VEC

To open the "cointegration data - 1" file in EViews, click "File," "Open," and then "Workfile."

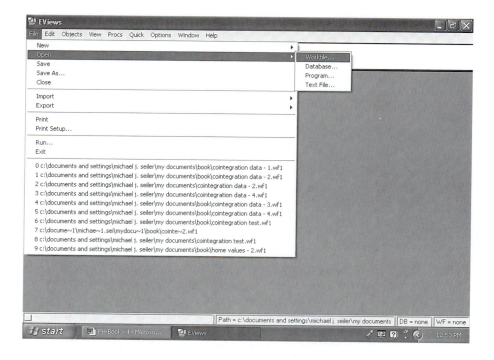

The following window will appear.

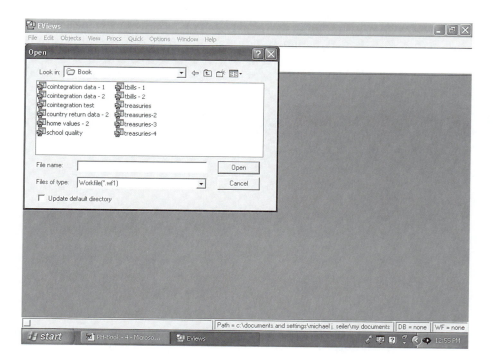

Select the file "cointegration data - 1" by double-clicking on it. After maximizing the window, you will see the following EViews Workfile.

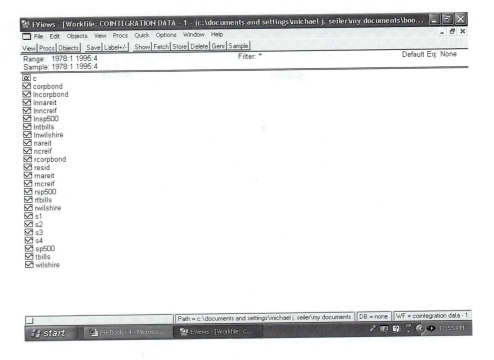

Select the variables in the following order: "lnncreif," "lnnareit," "lncorpbond," "lnsp500," and "lntbills." To do this, left-click on the variable "lnncreif." Then, while holding down "Ctrl" on your keyboard, left-click on "lnnareit." Continue to hold down the "Ctrl" key and left-click on the remaining variables in the order indicated. When you are done, your screen should look like this.

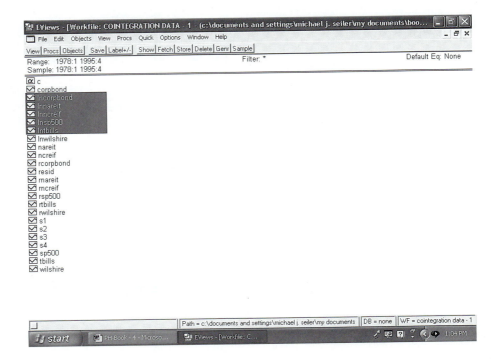

Double-click anywhere in the highlighted area. A small window will appear.

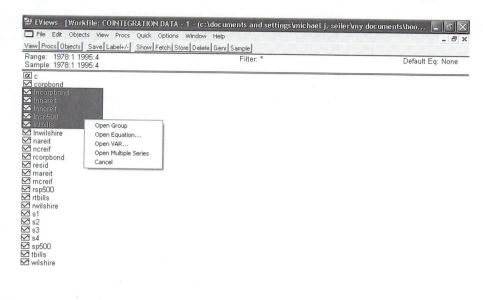

Select "Open VAR." A new window titled "VAR Specification" will open.

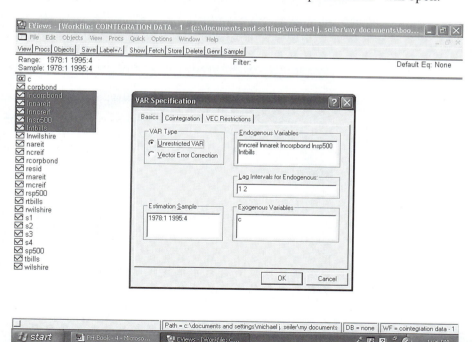

Under the section labeled "VAR Type," select the option "Vector Error Correction."

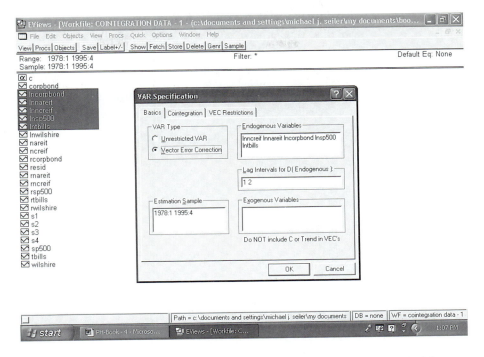

The next box, "Endogenous Variables," is already correctly specified because of the way we originally chose our variables. As explained in the chapter on cointegration, the appropriate number of lags to select is four. Therefore, type in the numbers "1 4" in the box labeled "Lag Intervals for D(Endogenous)."

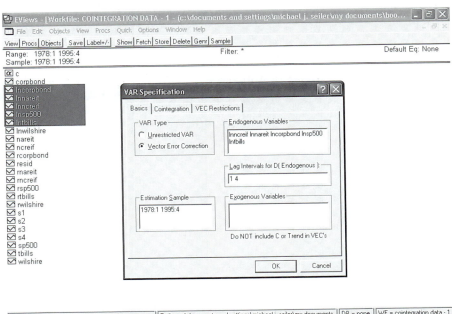

In the final box, titled "Exogenous Variables," type in the seasonal dummy variables "s1," "s2," "s3," and "s4." The justification for doing this was also explained in the chapter on cointegration. After you have entered the dummy variables, your window should look like this.

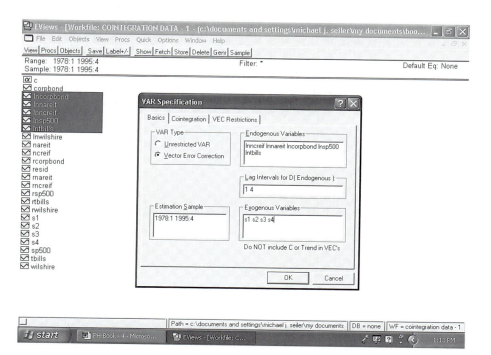

Now select the tab marked "Cointegration."

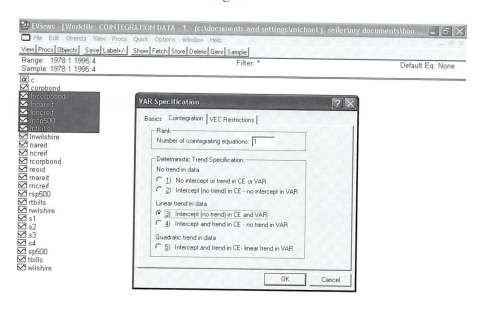

No matter how many cointegrating equations you identify when performing the Johansen test for cointegration, the test identifies the first vector as the most important cointegrating vector. This is because the first vector is the one associated with the highest Eigenvalue. For this reason, under the box titled "Rank," leave the "Number of cointegrating equations" equal to "1." Under the section labeled "Deterministic Trend Specification," select assumption "1." This assumption was justified in the chapter on cointegration.

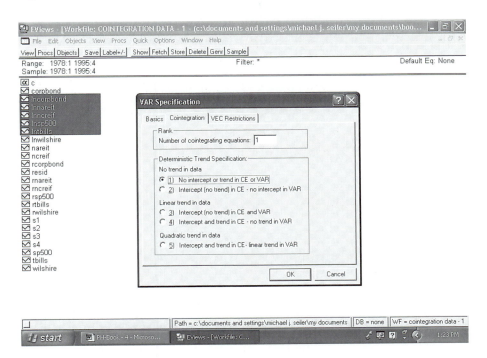

The VEC model is now completely specified. Click "OK" to estimate the model. After enlarging the newly created window, you should see the following screen.

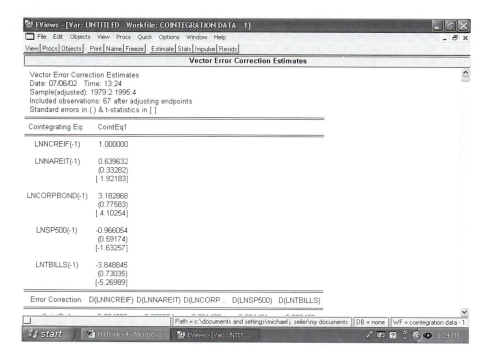

This first part of the output provides a cointegrating equation normalized by the variable "lnncreif." This equation shows the long-run relationships.

After scrolling down roughly one page, you will see the following output.

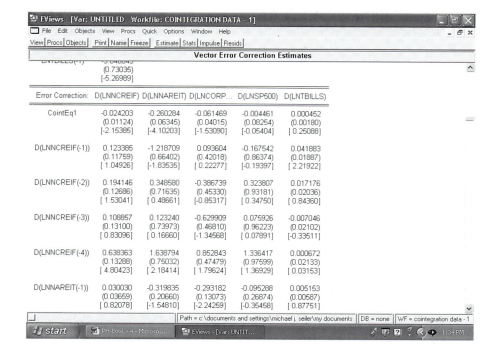

Each column in this table corresponds to a separate equation. The variable at the top of each column is the dependent variable. The variables in each row reflect the list of independent variables. Each independent variable has three numbers associated with it. The first number is the regression coefficient. The second number, which is given in parentheses, is the standard error of the estimate. Finally, the third number is the corresponding t-statistic.

The numbers of greatest interest correspond to the first independent variable, "CointEq1." "CointEq1" represents the error correction term. The more negative and significant the t-statistics, the more successful the VEC model.

Now compare these results to the results from the VAR model in the previous chapter. We see that the only VEC equation that is better than the VAR is the one associated with the NAREIT (securitized real estate) index. This conclusion was fully expected based on the observation that the only significant error correction term (denoted as "CointEq1" in the VEC) was the one for NAREIT.

In sum, because the VEC had a higher goodness of fit than the VAR for the NAREIT index, we can conclude that the existence of a cointegration vector allows us to improve our ability to specify returns on the NAREIT index.

19

ARCH/GARCH

19.1 PURPOSE OF ARCH/GARCH

A goal of many financial studies is to forecast the volatility of time series data. If volatility (e.g., in a stock) remained constant over time, this would be an easy task. You could simply observe past volatility through a measure such as standard deviation or variance and correctly assume that this past measure would apply in the future. Unfortunately, in finance, this is typically not the case. Instead, it is often observed that wide swings in the market are followed by more large swings. More formally, volatility appears to be serially correlated.

The observation that volatility is not constant over time is referred to as *heteroskedasticity*. The word *hetero* means "different" or "not the same." This is a problem for many statistical procedures that assume volatility is constant over time. In statistics, this assumption is referred to as *homoskedasticity* (*homo* means "the same"). If this assumption of homoskedasticity is violated, the interpretation of the results may no longer be accurate. For this reason, it is important to control for heteroskedasticity.

ARCH (Autoregressive Conditional Heteroskedasticity) and GARCH (Generalized Autoregressive Conditional Heteroskedasticity) are used to determine if a time series is plagued with heteroskedasticity. Moreover, ARCH/GARCH provides a way to correct or remove the unequal variance so that the series can be used in tests that assume homoskedasticity.

To illustrate the steps required to perform the test, we will consider the EViews Workfile "Tbills - 1." This file contains monthly time series data from February 1977 through November 2001 for 3-month Treasury Bills.

19.2 PERFORMING ARCH/GARCH

Once in EViews, open the file by clicking "File," "Open," and then "Workfile."

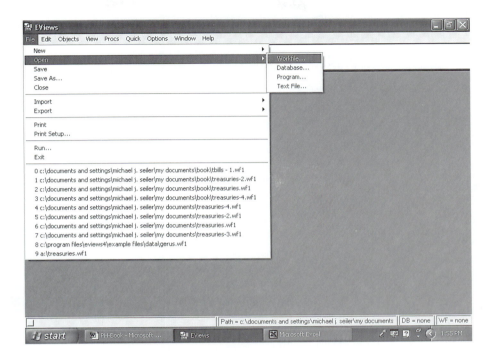

Select "Tbills-1" and then click "Open."

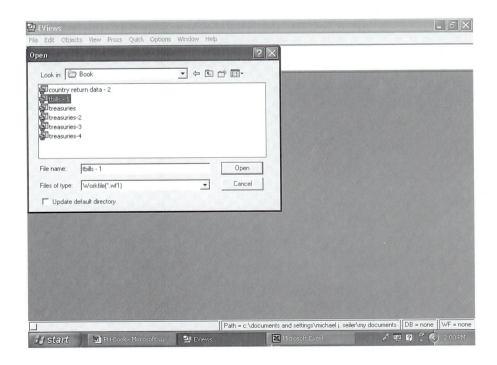

After maximizing, the following screen will appear.

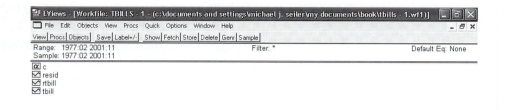

The variable "c" refers to a constant. The variable "resid" represents a residual. No matter what file you open, you will always see these two variables because EViews creates them automatically.

The title "tbill" is given to the nominal yield on a 3-month Treasury Bill, whereas "rtbill" is the return on a 3-month Treasury Bill. All data are monthly from February 1977 through November 2001.

To perform the ARCH/GARCH test, EViews requires you to highlight two variables. The variable of interest in our test is "rtbills." It does not matter which other variable you highlight. To select the first variable, simply use your mouse to left-click on it. To highlight the second variable, you must hold down the "Ctrl" key on your keyboard while you left-click on the second variable.

Once both variables are highlighted, double-click on them and a small menu will appear. Select "Open Equation" by clicking on it.

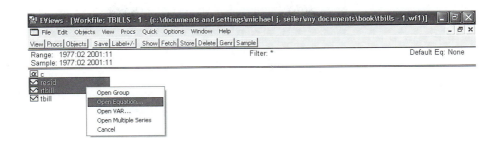

The following screen will appear.

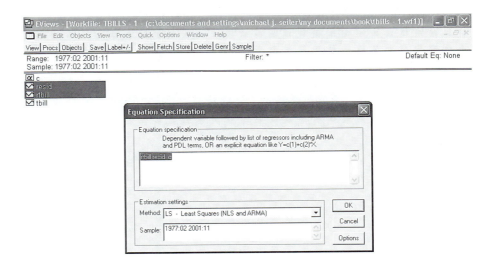

Under the "Estimation settings" area, you will see the "Method" box. Select the procedure "ARCH - Autoregressive Conditional Heteroskedasticity" from the pull-down menu.

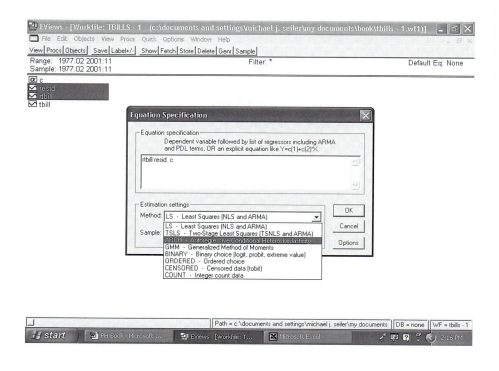

Click "OK."

At this point, we need to pause to understand the various required inputs. Under the "ARCH specification" box, you can specify the order, or number, of ARCH and GARCH terms to include.

Remember that you are trying to forecast or predict variance for the next period. To get the next period's variance, you will consider (1) the long-run average variance in the series, (2) the actual *observed* variance from the last period (the ARCH term), as well as (3) the *forecasted* variance from the last period (the GARCH term).

If the values entered for ARCH and GARCH both equal one, then only the last period's observed and forecasted variance will be considered. If values greater than one are entered, the model will look further back in time. It is extremely common to use values of one for both entries.

Next, consider the "Mean equation specification" box. Under the box title, you are told to enter the dependent variable (the one for which you are testing the presence of ARCH/GARCH; in our example this is "rtbill") followed by regressors and ARMA terms. Regressors and ARMA terms refer to additional variables that explain the returns on 3-month Treasury Bills. Without correctly identifying these, the ARCH/GARCH test will likely yield incorrect results. That is, if you fail to include relevant explanatory variables, you may conclude the presence of ARCH/GARCH where none exists.

The acronym ARMA is composed of two parts: "AR" and "MA." "AR" is short for "autoregressive" and "MA" stands for "moving average." In the chapter on autocorrelation, we examined the behavior of Treasury Bill returns and learned that the time series possesses high levels of serial correlation. That is, current residuals are highly correlated with their own past values. Moreover, if we were to conduct ARMA tests (which are beyond the scope of our focus here), we would conclude that the best measures to predict T-bill returns are a first-order AR term and first- and second-order MA terms.

For this reason, in the box titled "Mean equation specification," you will want to specify the dependent variable "rtbill" and follow it with the three ARMA terms "ar(1)," "ma(1)," and "ma(2)." Your screen should look like this.

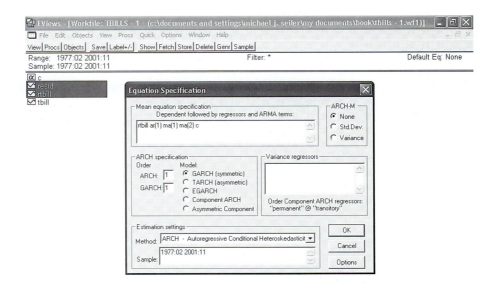

Do not concern yourself with the other boxes at this time. Click "OK" to generate the output.

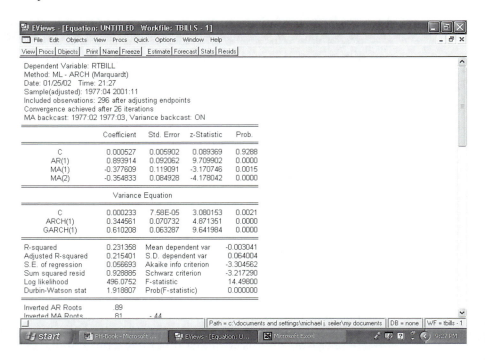

The output corresponding to the variables in the mean equation is shown in the top section of the table. You can see that the terms AR(1), MA(1), and MA(2) are all significant, as indicated by "Prob." values below .05. In fact, the "Prob." values are below .01, meaning that they are significant beyond the 99% level of confidence.

The two terms in the variance equation are ARCH(1) and GARCH(1). These two variables are also statistically significant. Therefore, we conclude that the T-bill return series violates the common assumption of homoskedasticity.

19.2.1 VERIFYING THE CORRECT MODEL SPECIFICATION

As previously discussed, if we incorrectly specified either the mean or variance equations, the ARCH/GARCH results could very well be flawed. Moreover, after performing this test, we want to be sure we have removed all the ARCH/GARCH effects. Fortunately, EViews has a series of diagnostic procedures we can use to make this determination.

19.2.1.1 The Mean Equation

To verify that the mean equation has been correctly specified, click "View," "Residual Tests," and then "Correlogram - Q-statistics."

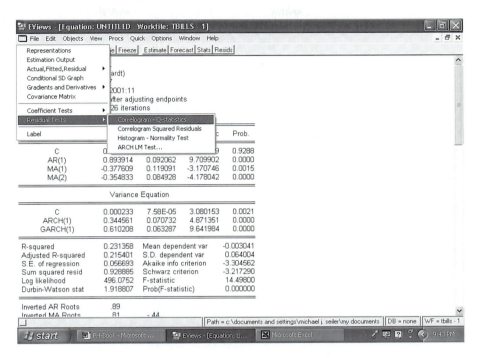

A screen will pop up asking you to specify the number of lags to consider. The default value is fine.

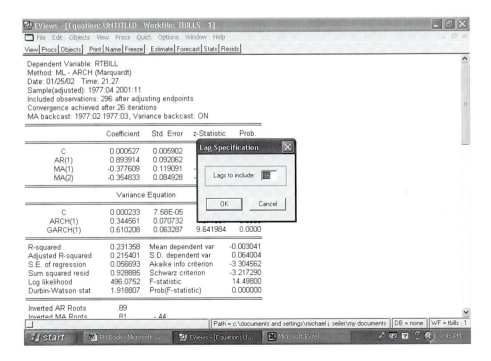

Click "OK."

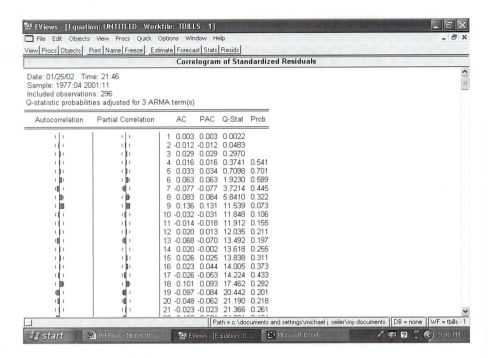

If the "Prob." values associated with the Q-stats are not significant (if they are above .05, as occurred here), you should conclude that the mean equation is correctly specified.

19.2.1.2 The Variance Equation

To verify that the variance equation has been correctly specified, click "View," "Residual Tests," and then "Correlogram Squared Residuals."

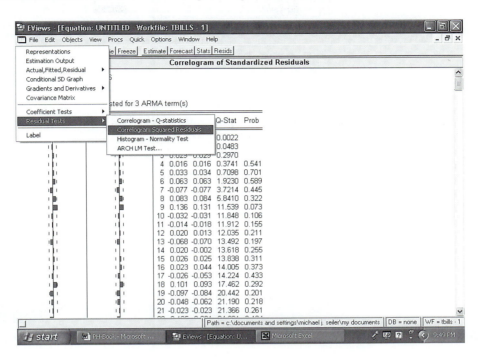

Again, the "Lag Specification" box will appear asking for the number of lags to include. The default value is fine.

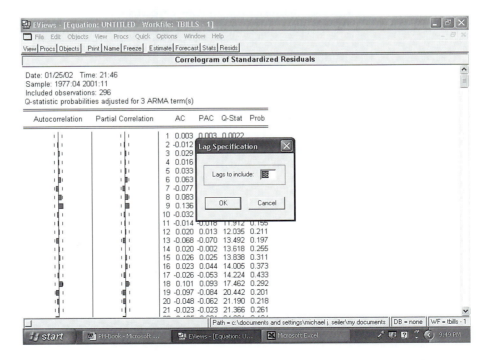

Click "OK."

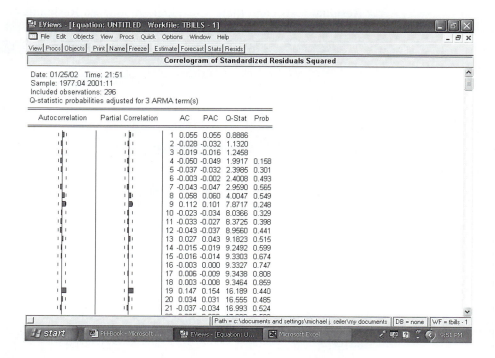

Because the "Prob." values associated with the Q-stats are not significant (if they are above .05, as occurred here), you should conclude that the variance equation is correctly specified.

19.2.1.3 Testing for ARCH Effects

If the variance equation is found to be correctly specified, all the ARCH effects should be gone. A more direct test for ARCH effects can be performed by clicking "View," "Residual Tests," and then "ARCH LM Test."

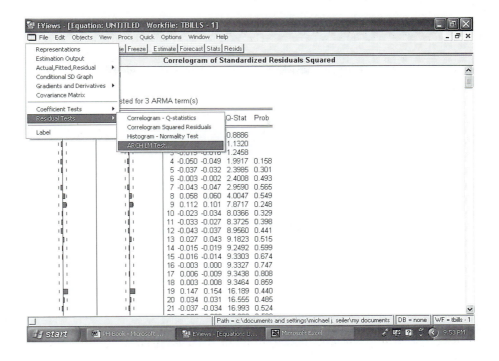

You will again be asked the number of lags to include. The default value is "1." Most researchers prefer that this test be performed at a higher order. Enter the number "4," then click "OK."

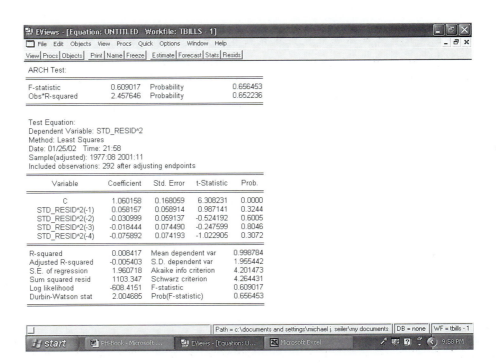

Because the "Prob." values associated with the four lagged terms "STD_RESID^2 (-1)," "STD_RESID^2(-2)," "STD_RESID^2(-3)," and "STD_RESID^2(-4)" are all nonsignificant, you should conclude that the ARCH/GARCH effects have been fully controlled for in the T-bill return series.

19.3 CREATING AN ADJUSTED SERIES FREE FROM ARCH/GARCH

Once you are satisfied that you have identified how to successfully remove all ARCH/ GARCH effects, you can go back to your original T-bill series and make a simple adjustment. The goal of making the adjustment is to be sure you have a series that does not violate critical assumptions when using the data to perform subsequent statistical procedures.

To create the adjusted series, click "Procs" and then "Make GARCH Variance Series."

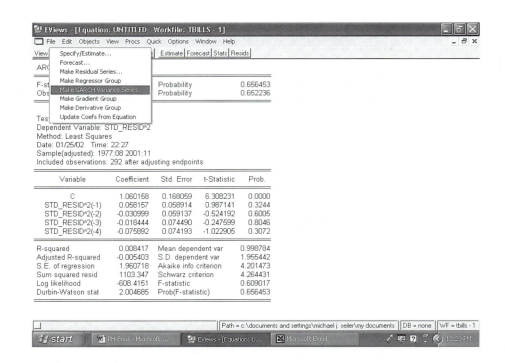

A newly created series titled "GARCH01" will appear. This series is the conditional variance.

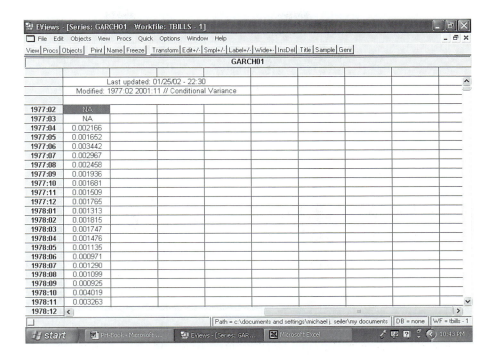

Go to the "Workfile" window in EViews by clicking "Window" and then "Workfile."

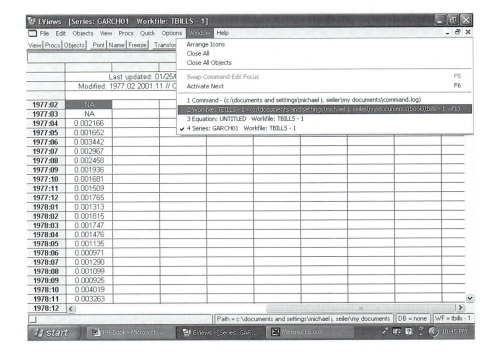

You will now see the new variable "garch01" in the list with the other variables.

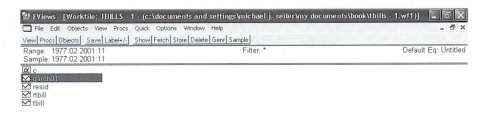

The final step required to create the adjusted series is to divide the T-bill return series, "rtbill" (which is found to possess ARCH/GARCH effects), by the square root of the conditional variance series "garch01."

To perform this calculation, click "Procs" and then "Generate Series."

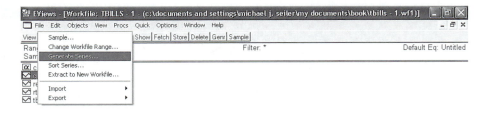

The following equation box will appear.

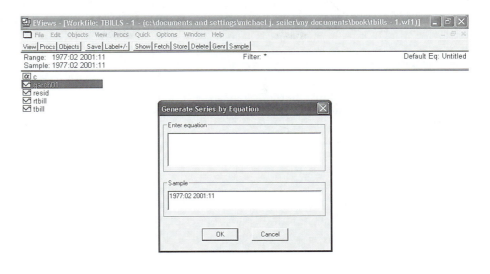

In the "Enter equation" box, enter the following formula:

$$atbill = rtbill/@SQRT(garch01)$$

The newly created variable is "atbill." The letter "a" stands for "adjusted."

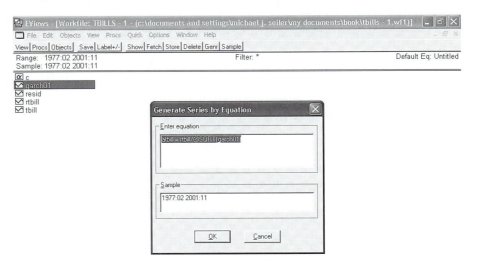

Click "OK" and you will see that the newly created variable "atbill" appears in the list with the other variables. This new series will be free from ARCH/GARCH effects. At this point, save the EViews Workfile as "tbills - 2" for future use.

19.4 VARIATIONS OF ARCH/GARCH

Like most methodologies, the basic ARCH/GARCH framework has been extended to apply to special situations. For example, ARCH/GARCH assumes that high observed variances are followed by further observations of high variance in the upward or downward direction. That is, you can expect to see the same amount of movement in either direction (a symmetric relationship; the same increase in volatility on either the up or down side).

This is not always observed with stock returns. Instead, it is often the case that a drop in stock prices is followed by larger volatility than an increase in stock prices by the same amount. That is, the effect is asymmetric, meaning it does not look the same in the upward and downward directions.

19.4.1 THRESHOLD ARCH

TARCH stands for "threshold ARCH." In this variation of ARCH/GARCH, downward movements in stock prices are treated separately from upward movements in prices. More formally, positive shocks to the system and negative shocks have different effects on conditional variance.

To perform this variation in EViews, you would perform the analysis the same way as for the traditional ARCH/GARCH. The only difference is that you should select the TARCH option instead of the GARCH option. When you examine the output, focus on the variable "(RESID<0)*ARCH(1)." If the "Prob." value is greater than .05, this means that good news (positive shocks) and bad news (negative shocks) have the same effect on future volatility. If the "Prob." value is less than .05, then the effect is asymmetric. That is, a downward movement in the market is followed by higher volatility than an upward movement of the same magnitude.

19.4.2 EXPONENTIAL GARCH

EGARCH stands for "exponential GARCH." EGARCH is extremely similar to TARCH in that it also tests for the asymmetric effect for good and bad news. The difference is that whereas TARCH assumes that the formula for the conditional variance is quadratic, EGARCH assumes that it is exponential.

To perform this variation in EViews, you would perform the analysis the same way as for the traditional ARCH/GARCH. The only difference is that you should select the EGARCH option instead of the GARCH option. When you examine the output, focus on the variable "RES/SQR[GARCH](1)." If the "Prob." value is greater than .05, this means that good news (positive shocks) and bad news (negative shocks) have the same effect on future volatility. If the "Prob." value is less than .05, then the effect is asymmetric. That is, a downward movement in the market is followed by higher volatility than an upward movement of the same magnitude.

19.4.3 ARCH-IN-MEAN

ARCH-M stands for "ARCH-in-mean." When specifying the mean equation in the traditional ARCH/GARCH model, you list the variables that should significantly explain or predict the mean. By doing so correctly, you are then able to measure the conditional variance, which is your goal. In some financial applications, however, the conditional variance itself is useful in predicting the mean. Stated another way, the expected return on the variable you are examining is a function of its expected risk. This concept is not new to people in finance who understand the concept of a risk-return tradeoff.

This ARCH-M variation is simply a potential additional variable to be entered into the "Mean equation specification" box. As such, it can be used with the traditional ARCH/GARCH (symmetric) test or with the TARCH or EGARCH (asymmetric) tests.

When you perform the test, your ARCH-M specification will, of course, appear in the mean equation part of the output (the top box). The ARCH-M variable will be labeled "GARCH." You will interpret it the same way you would any other variable. Thus, if the associated "Prob." value is above .05, it is not significant and should be removed from the analysis before you rerun the test.

19.4.4 COMPONENT ARCH

Most financial series are found to revert to their mean in the long-run. In the traditional GARCH model, mean reversion is assumed to occur at a constant rate over time. Component ARCH is a variation of the GARCH model in that it allows the mean of the series to revert at a varying level or at a nonconstant rate. For most readers, this is such a fine distinction that it does not warrant our attention.

19.4.5 ASYMMETRIC COMPONENT

The asymmetric component model is simply a combination of the component ARCH and the TARCH models. That is, it allows for a nonconstant reversion in the mean of the series as well as differential quadratic effects for positive and negative shocks to the series. Again, for most readers, this is a distinction so fine that it does not warrant our attention.

20

PROGRAMMING A BINOMIAL OPTION PRICING MODEL

20.1 PURPOSE OF A BINOMIAL OPTION MODEL

Two models are primarily used to value options: the Binomial option pricing model and the Black-Scholes option pricing model. The Binomial model is a discrete-time model, whereas the Black-Scholes is a continuous-time model. Both models are used to price call options and put options. A call option gives the buyer (who is said to hold a "long" position) the right to *buy* 100 shares of the underlying common stock at a predetermined price (the strike or exercise price) on (a European option) or before (an American option) a predetermined date (maturity). A put option is the exact opposite. A put option gives the buyer (who is said to hold a "long" position) the right to *sell* 100 shares of the underlying common stock at a predetermined price (the strike or exercise price) on (a European option) or before (an American option) a predetermined date (maturity).

20.2 PROGRAMMING A BINOMIAL EUROPEAN CALL OPTION

This chapter will consider only the Binomial option pricing model. As the name implies, the Binomial model assumes that the starting stock price can move in either of two directions, up or down, each period. For example, assume a stock is priced at $100. After one period, the price can go either above or below $100. To know how much above and below the stock price is assumed to move, we must calculate two values, "u" and "d." The first value, "u," is explained as the amount by which the stock price could go up. The second value, "d," is defined as the amount by which the stock price could go down. Mathematically, "u" and "d" are defined as:

$$u = e^{\vartheta \sqrt{\Delta t}} \tag{20.1}$$

and

$$d = 1/u \tag{20.2}$$

where

e = Euler's number = 2.71828 . . .
ϑ = implied (annualized) volatility expected over the life of the option
Δt = length of the discrete-time step = the number of years divided by the number of discrete time periods

Let's assume in our example that the implied volatility on this option is 20%, or .20. Moreover, let's assume the time to maturity for this option is 120 days. Finally, let's assume that there are 50 discrete time periods in our model. Therefore,

$$\Delta t = (120/365)/50 = .006575342$$

and

$$u = (2.71828 \ldots)^{(.20)(\sqrt{.006575342})} = 1.016349918$$

because $d = 1/u, d = .983913102$.

Thus, after one period, the price will either go up to $101.63 or down to $98.39. Let's build a Binomial call option model in Excel from an empty sheet. To do so, open Excel. Your blank spreadsheet should look like this.

Eventually, we will link all pricing models to the same sheet. To set this up ahead of time, let's title our various spreadsheets. Double-click on the tab marked "Sheet1." Relabel the sheet "cover" by typing over the old highlighted title.

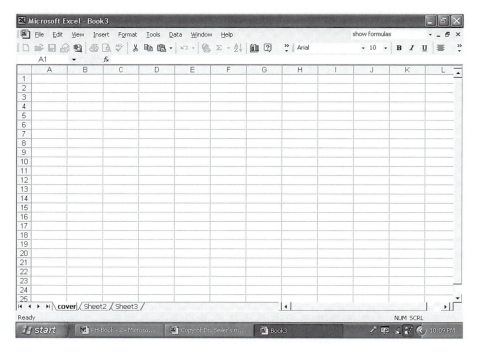

Give the following names to the next six sheets: "Bi_EuroCall," "Bi_EuroPut," "Bi_AmericanCall," "Bi_AmericanPut," "BS_nodiv," and "BS_div." These names correspond to the following option models: Binomial European call, Binomial European put, Binomial American call, Binomial American put, Black-Scholes model without dividends, and the Black-Scholes model with dividends, respectively.

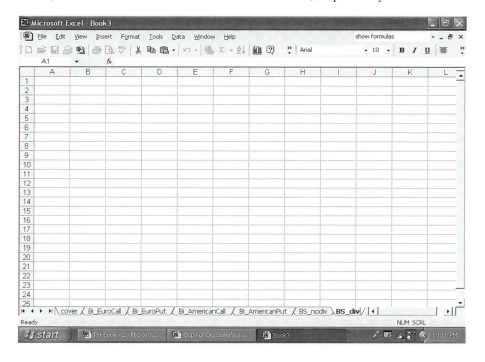

Save the Excel Spreadsheet as "Option Pricing Models" by clicking "File" and then "Save as." Name the file "Option Pricing Models."

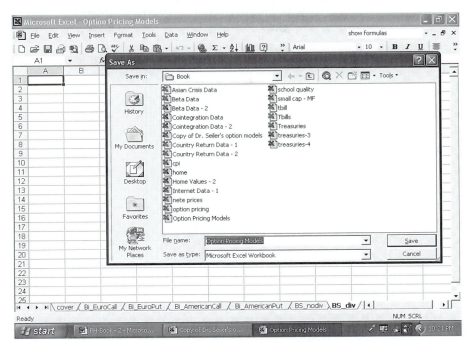

We are now ready to begin to complete the linked spreadsheets. Under the "cover" sheet, go to cell "A3" and type in the label "stock price." Below that, in cell "A4," type in the label "Exercise Price." Continue down column "A" by typing in the following headings: "volatility," "TTM(days)," "r(cc)," and "q(cc)." Your Excel spreadsheet should look like this.

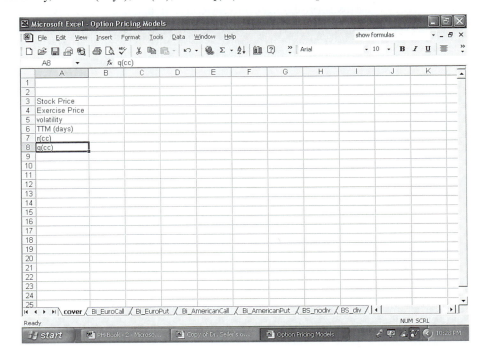

Next to these cells, type in the initial values of "100," "95," ".20," "120," ".05," and "0."

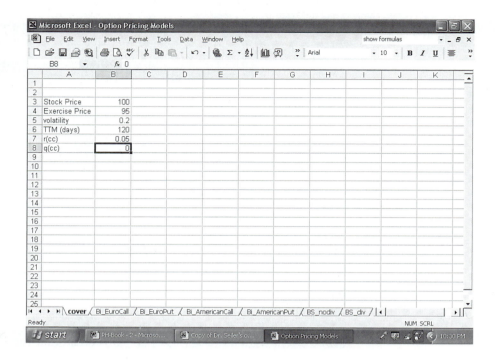

In cell "C6," type in the following Excel formula:

$$=TEXT(TODAY()+B6,\text{"mmm d, yy(ddd)"})$$

This formula is a courtesy/convenience used to identify the number of days until the option matures. It simply reports the date in the future that corresponds to the number of days you said the option has to mature. Remember that the last trading day for an option is the third Friday of the month in which it matures.

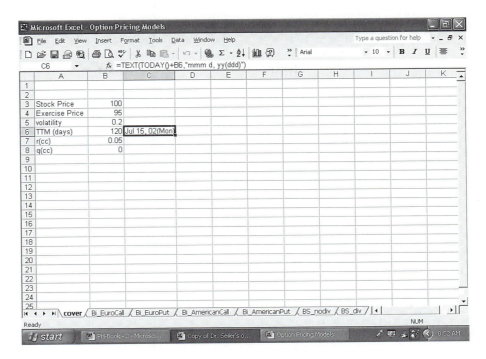

Starting in cell "E1," type in the labels as shown in the following screen.

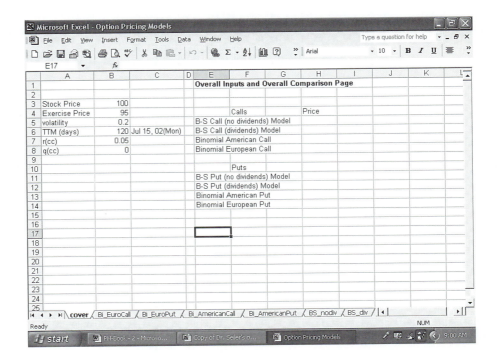

This "cover" sheet will serve as the page where all model prices can be compared at once. After we have programmed the subsequent sheets, we will be able to type in various inputs on the "cover" sheet and immediately see the resulting changes in the price of each option model on the same page.

Let's get back to the sheet titled "Bi_EuroCall." From cells "A45" through "A57," type the headings shown in the following screen.

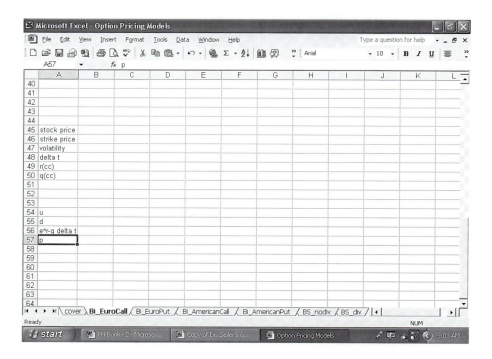

The labels in cells "A45"through "A48" have been previously defined. In cell "A49," the title "r(cc)" refers to the continuously compounded rate of return on the risk-free security (3-month T-bill). In cell "A50," the label, "q(cc)" refers to the continuously compounded dividend yield on the underlying common stock.

The cells "A45" through "A50" will read the values the user will type into the "cover" sheet. All we want to do here is borrow these same values. To get them from the "cover" sheet to this sheet, we simply type the command "+cover!B3." This command tells Excel to report the same value here as was given in cell "B3" from the sheet titled "cover." Enter this formula into cell "B45." Do the same for cells "A46" through "A50."

The only exception is cell "A48." On the cover page, the user only types in the number of days until maturity. What we need in the model is to convert this value to "delta t." This is easily done. Simply divide the number by 365, then again by the number of periods in the Binomial model. Your formulas should be typed in as follows, although all you should see are the numbers.

Let's determine the four values for the variables in cells "A54" through "A57." I have already shown the calculation for "u." In Excel, the formula is represented by typing:

$$=+EXP(B47*(B48^0.5))$$

Because "d" is simply "1/u," all you have to type in cell "B55" is "=1/B54." In cell "A56," the label "e^r-q delta t" can be represented in cell "B56" by the formula:

$$=+EXP((B49-B50)*B48)$$

The final variable, "p," is defined as the probability that the price will go up. Accordingly, "1−p" is the probability that the price will go down. Although we do not need to know "p" to calculate the price at each node, we will need to use it later to calculate the option price associated with the stock price at each node. We are only defining it now to round out the precalculations we will need to finish programming the model. Mathematically, "p" can be represented by the following formula:

$$p = \frac{e^{(r)(\Delta t)} - d}{u - d} \tag{20.3}$$

In Excel, the formula can be represented by the statement:

$$=+(B56-B55)/(B54-B55)$$

The formulas for each cell are shown in the following screen. Recall that only the resulting numbers will appear (unless you make Excel show you the formulas as I have done here so that you can see them all at once).

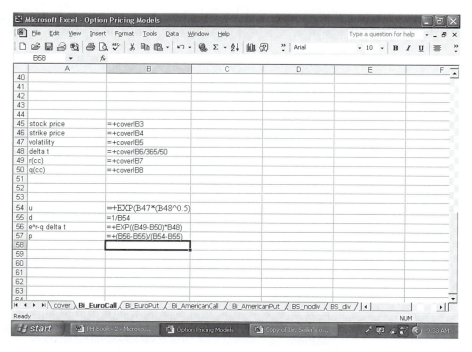

Now that we have the preliminary calculations out of the way, we can begin to build our stock prices at each node. Start by placing the current stock price in cell "C53." Because this price already appears in cell "B45," all you have to do is type "=+B45."

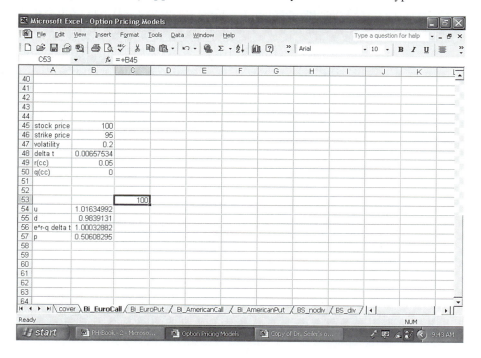

In cell "D52," type in the formula "=+C53*$B$54." This is the same as multiplying the initial stock price ("C53") by "u(B54)." To determine what the stock price will be when it goes down, multiply the initial stock price by "d." The corresponding formula that should be entered into cell "D54" is "=+C53*$B$55."

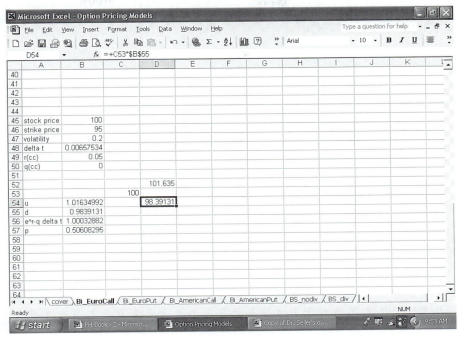

Just to make sure that we have the hang of it, do the same for cells "E51," "E53," and "E55." The formulas should be typed in as "=+D52*$B$54," "=+D54*$B$54," and "=+D54*$B$55," respectively. Your spreadsheet should appear as follows.

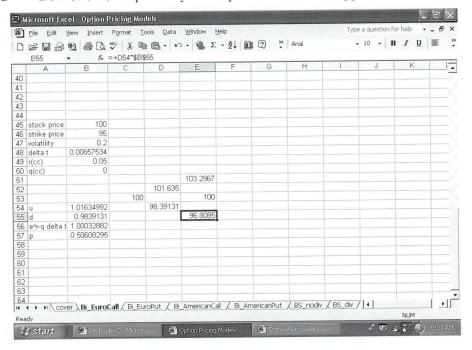

This process should continue until the stock prices at all nodes over the 50 periods have been filled in. Instead of retyping the formula each time, you will find it much easier to copy and paste the formula. For example, to complete cells "F50," "G49," "H48," and so on, simply go to cell "E51" and click "Copy." Then go to each of the three cells and click "Paste."

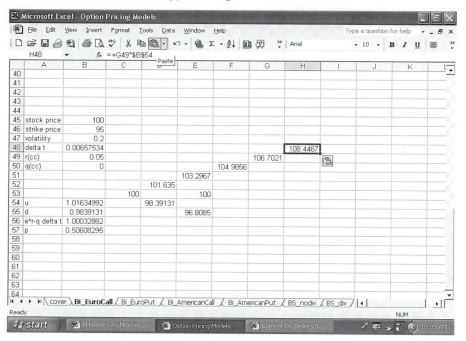

Creating a "macro" in Excel can reduce your workload even further. When you have completed filling in all the stock prices, your Excel spreadsheet should look like the following screen.

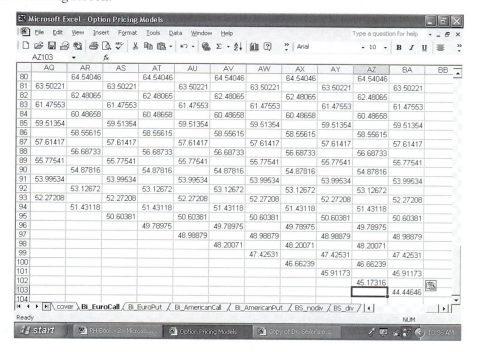

The second major step in the process is to calculate the corresponding option price at each node in the tree. To do this, it is necessary to start at the end and work your way back to the beginning.

At maturity, the value of the option is simply its intrinsic value. For a call option, this means that the value of the call is equal to either the difference between the stock price and the strike price or zero, whichever is greater. More formally, the relationship can be expressed as shown in Equation 20.4:

$$\text{Price of the call option} = \max(S - X; 0) \qquad \textbf{(20.4)}$$

where

$$S = \text{stock price}$$
$$X = \text{strike or exercise price}$$

In your Excel spreadsheet, go to cell "BA4." Here we will determine the price of the call for the node located in cell "BA3." In fact, the corresponding option prices associated with all the stock prices will be listed in the cells right below the stock prices. In cell "BA4," write the formula "=+MAX(BA3-$B$46,0)." You will see the amount 129.9898. If you continue, your spreadsheet will eventually be filled with numbers that will be difficult to differentiate from each other. For this reason, we will want to distinguish between stock prices and call prices. One easy way to do this is to color code the option price cells. Nothing stands out quite like dark red. To color code the option price, simply pull down the color codes and select red.

Your spreadsheet should look like this.

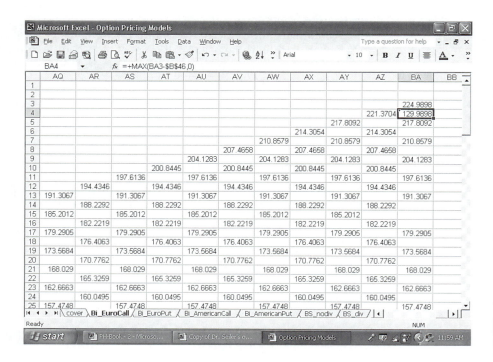

To calculate the option prices for the remaining stock prices in column "BA," simply copy the cell "BA4" and paste it in cells "BA6," "BA8," and so forth, all the way down to cell "BA104." When you are done, your spreadsheet will look like this.

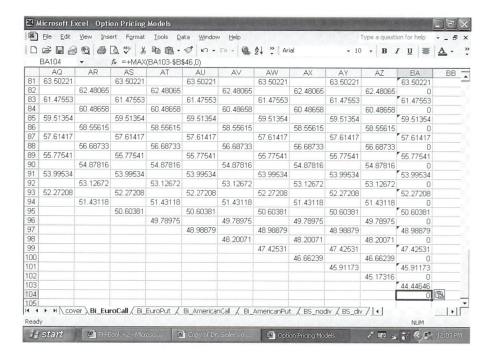

Now we need to calculate the option value for the stock prices in column "AZ." In cell "AZ5," we need to find the present value of the two possible option prices (cells "BA4" and "BA6"), keeping in mind that they have an unequal chance of occurring (weighted probability). Mathematically, this can be expressed as:

$$\text{call price} = [(c_1)(p) + (c_2)(1 - p)]e^{-(r)(\Delta t)} \qquad (20.5)$$

In Excel, the formula can be expressed as:

$$=+(BA4*\$B\$57+BA6*(1-\$B\$57))*EXP(-\$B\$49*\$B\$48)$$

Copy cell "AZ5" down to all option price cells in the column "AZ." When you are done, your spreadsheet should look like this.

Continue to copy this formula into the rest of the cells going all the way back to the beginning (cell "C54"). When you are done, your spreadsheet should contain black stock prices and red option prices for all nodes.

Microsoft Excel - Option Pricing Models

C54 = `=+(D53*$B$57+D55*(1-$B$57))*EXP(-$B$49*$B$48)`

	A	B	C	D	E	F	G	H	I	J	K	L
44												115.
45	stock price	100									113.8534	22.0
46	strike price	95								112.0219	20.29185	112.
47	volatility	0.2							110.2198	18.56488	110.2198	18.4
48	delta t	0.00657534						108.4467	16.89635	108.4467	16.80773	108.
49	r(cc)	0.05					106.7021	15.29261	106.7021	15.19797	106.7021	15.1
50	q(cc)	0				104.9856	13.76022	104.9856	13.65955	104.9856	13.55868	104
51					103.2967	12.30558	103.2967	12.19924	103.2967	12.09234	103.2967	11.9
52				101.635	10.93461	101.635	10.82331	101.635	10.71108	101.635	10.59793	10
53			100	9.652369	100	9.537145	100	9.420683	100	9.302938	100	9.1
54	u	1.01634992	8.462802	98.39131	8.344972	98.39131	8.225653	98.39131	8.104771	98.39131	7.982244	98.3
55	d	0.9839131	49569	96.8085	7.128989	96.8085	7.006663	96.8085	6.882487	96.8085	6.75	
56	e^r-q delta t	1.00032882		6.13201	95.25115	6.01006	95.25115	5.886173	95.25115	5.760223	95.2	
57	p	0.50608295			5.114557	93.71886	4.992909	93.71886	4.869237	93.71886	4.74	
58						4.200401	92.21121	4.080967	92.21121	3.959546	92.2	
59							3.391169	90.72782	3.275998	90.72782	3.15	
60								2.686638	89.26829	2.577795	89.2	
61									2.084548	87.83224	1.98	
62										1.58054	86.4	
63											1.16	
64												
65												
66												

cover / **Bi_EuroCall** / Bi_EuroPut / Bi_AmericanCall / Bi_AmericanPut / BS_nodiv / BS_div

The value in cell "C54," $8.46, is the price of the Binomial European call option. To report this value on the "cover" spreadsheet, simply select the tab marked "cover." Now go to cell "H8," and type in the formula "=+Bi_EuroCall!C54." You should see the price appear (8.462802).

Microsoft Excel - Option Pricing Models

H8 = `=+Bi_EuroCall!C54`

	A	B	C	E F G	H
1				Overall Inputs and Overall Comparison Page	
2					
3	Stock Price	100			
4	Exercise Price	95		Calls	Price
5	volatility	0.2		B-S Call (no dividends) Model	
6	TTM (days)	120	Jul 15, 02(Mon)	B-S Call (dividends) Model	
7	r(cc)	0.05		Binomial American Call	
8	q(cc)	0		Binomial European Call	8.462802
9					
10				Puts	
11				B-S Put (no dividends) Model	
12				B-S Put (dividends) Model	
13				Binomial American Put	
14				Binomial European Put	
15					
16					
17					
18					
19					
20					
21					
22					
23					

cover / Bi_EuroCall / Bi_EuroPut / Bi_AmericanCall / Bi_AmericanPut / BS_nodiv / BS_div

20.3 PROGRAMMING A BINOMIAL EUROPEAN PUT OPTION

Once the European call option has been programmed, it is extremely easy to program the European put option. In fact, all the cells are the same except for the option prices in the last column. Recall that the last column contains the intrinsic value formula for the option. For a put option, the intrinsic value is given by the strike price minus the stock price or zero, whichever is greater. Mathematically, it can be represented as:

$$\text{Price of the put option} = \max(X - S; 0) \tag{20.6}$$

where

$$S = \text{stock price}$$
$$X = \text{strike or exercise price}$$

We first need to copy all the work we have done for the Binomial European call option into the sheet for the Binomial European put option. To do so, highlight the area and click "Copy."

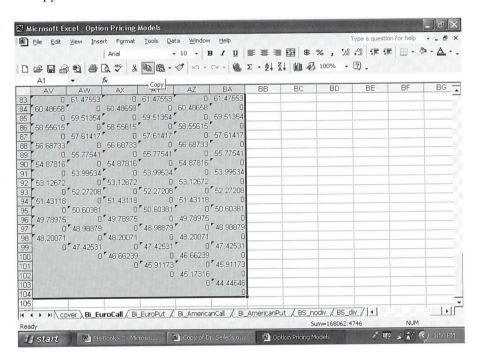

Go to the sheet titled "Bi_EuroPut" and click "Paste."

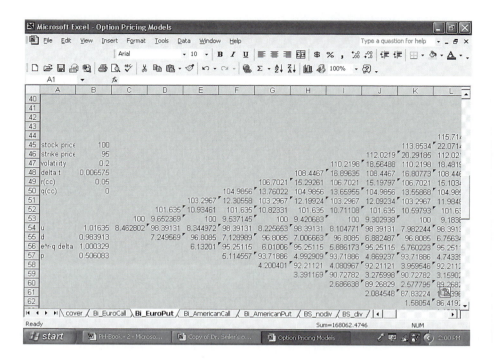

Go to cell "BA4" and change the formula to reflect the intrinsic value for a put option. The formula should be entered as "=+MAX($B$46-BA3,0)." Copy this formula all the way down column "BA" until you reach the last cell, "BA104."

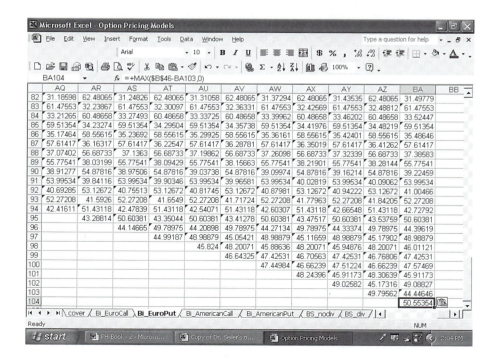

The price of the put option is again given in cell "C54." You also want this value to be reported on the "cover" sheet as we did before.

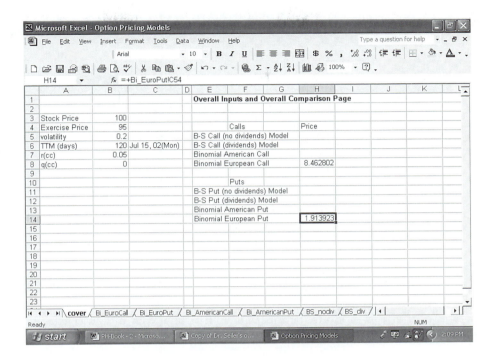

20.4 PROGRAMMING A BINOMIAL AMERICAN CALL OPTION

The difference between an American option and a European option is that an American option can be exercised before maturity. Early exercise will only occur if the price of the call option is less than its intrinsic value. When compared to the formulas for the European call option, the difference is very minor. Specifically, the last column, "BA," is the same. However, the option prices at all nodes before this last step need to be adjusted.

First, let's copy our work from the European call option to the sheet where we will show the American call option. To do so, first highlight the relevant area. Then click "Copy."

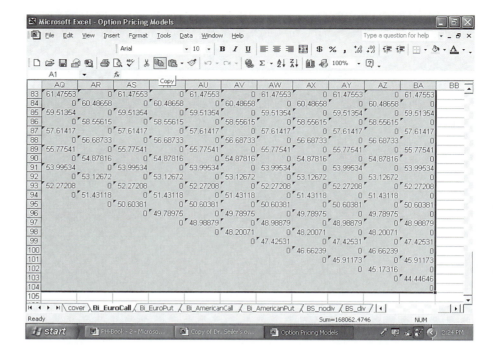

Go to the sheet titled "Bi_AmericanCall" and click "Paste."

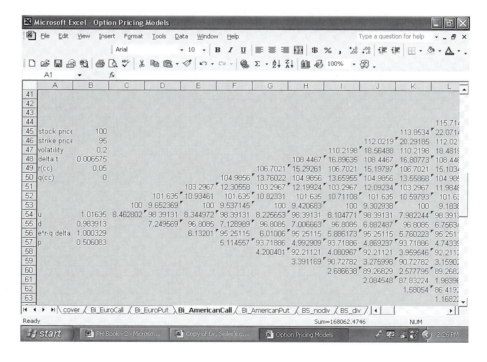

We are now ready to make the adjustment. The option prices in the column "BA" will be the same. Therefore, start in the second-to-the-last column, "AZ." In cell "AZ5," we want to take the maximum of the price of the call or the intrinsic value, whichever is greater.

The call price is formulated as:

$$(BA4*\$B\$57+BA6*(1-\$B\$57))*EXP(-\$B\$49*\$B\$48)$$

The intrinsic value is written as:

$$AZ4-\$B\$46.$$

Therefore, because we want the maximum of these two values, we need to write the combined formula as:

$$=+MAX((BA4*\$B\$57+BA6*(1-\$B\$57))*EXP(-\$B\$49*\$B\$48),AZ4-\$B\$46)$$

This formula should be typed into cell "AZ5." Next, copy this cell to all prior option price (red) cells until you reach the cell "C54." Your spreadsheet will look like this.

Now that we have programmed the model, we need to know when the call price becomes less than the intrinsic value. Go to cell "B51" and type in the following:

$$=+IF((D53*\$B\$57+D55*(1-\$B\$57))*EXP(-\$B\$4*\$B\$48)<(C53-\$B\$46),$$
$$\text{"Exercise!","Don't Exercise")}$$

This formula tells Excel to report the phrase "Exercise!" if the call price is less than the strike price and "Don't Exercise" if it is greater than or equal to the strike price.

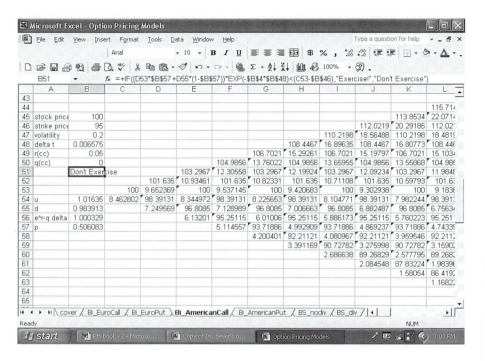

We need to report to the "cover" sheet (1) the Binomial American call option price and (2) the instruction either to "Exercise" or "Don't Exercise" the option. To do this, go to the "cover" sheet. In cell "H7" type: "=+Bi_AmericanCall!C54."

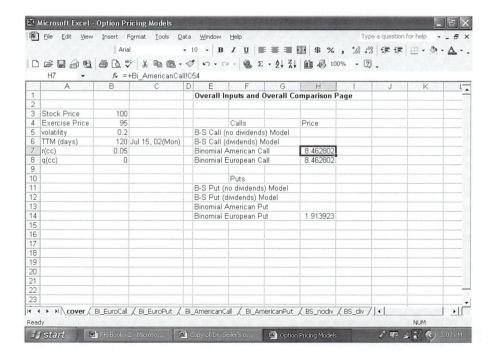

Then go to cell "I7" and type in the formula: "=+Bi_AmericanCall!B51."

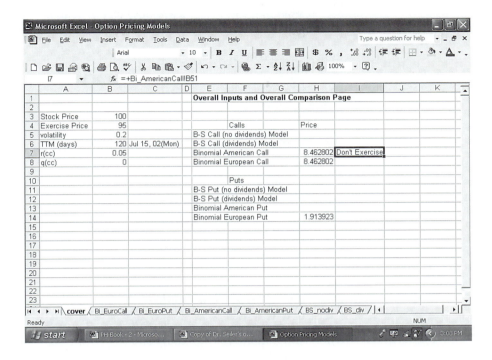

20.5 PROGRAMMING A BINOMIAL AMERICAN PUT OPTION

The Binomial American put option can be created from the Binomial European put model. As such, we need to copy the work we did for the European put model and paste it into the sheet for the American put model. To do so, go to the sheet labeled "Bi_EuropeanPut" and click "Copy." Then go to the "Bi_AmericanPut" sheet and click "Paste."

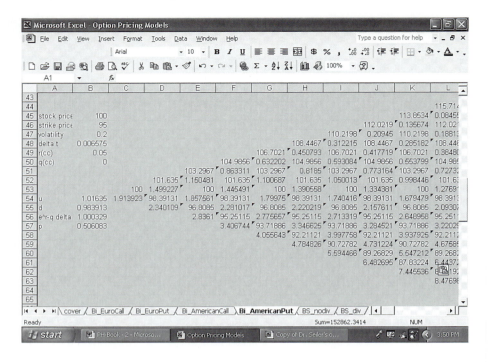

The last column, "BA," is the same for both models. The differences lay in the option price (red) cells before the last node. As we did for the call options, we need to adjust the formula to reflect the fact that early exercise is possible. For the European put option, in cell "AZ5," we priced the option using the formula:

$$=+(BA4*\$B\$57+BA6*(1-\$B\$57))*EXP(-\$B\$49*\$B\$48)$$

We now need to change it to:

$$=+MAX((BA4*\$B\$57+BA6*(1-\$B\$57))*EXP(-\$B\$49*\$B\$48),\$B\$46-AZ4)$$

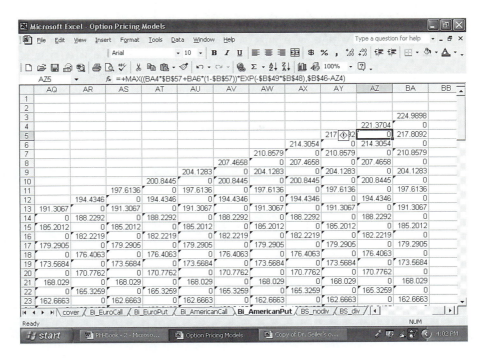

Complete the model by pasting this formula into each of the option pricing (red) cells before the last node. When you have finished, your model should look like the following screen.

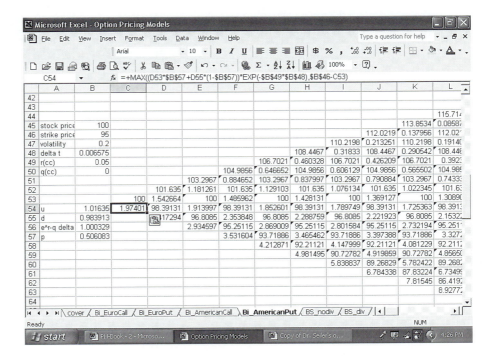

As with the American call option, we need to write a statement that will cause Excel to inform us of when it is ideal to early exercise our option. In concept, we would like to early exercise when the put price is less than the intrinsic value. In Excel, this can be expressed as:

$$=+IF((D53*\$B\$57+D55*(1-\$B\$57))*EXP(-\$B\$4*\$B\$48)<(\$B\$46-C53),$$
$$\text{"Exercise!","Don't Exercise")}$$

This formula should be typed into cell "B51," just as we did with the American call.

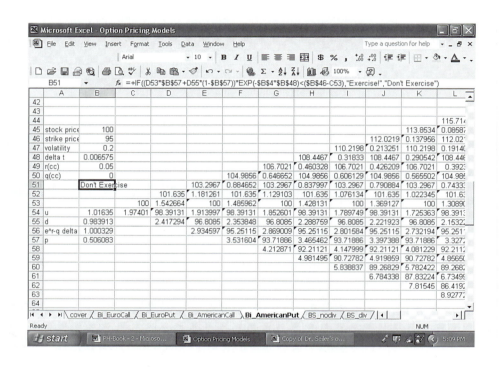

We need to report in our "cover" sheet (1) the price of the put and (2) the decision to early exercise or not. To do so, in the "cover" sheet, go to the cell "H13" and type in the following reference: "=+Bi_AmericanPut!C54."

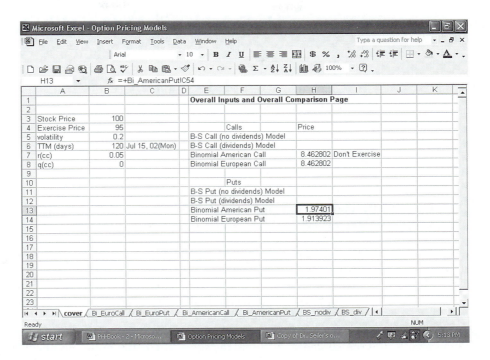

Report the decision to exercise or not by typing "=+Bi_AmericanPut!B51" in cell "I13."

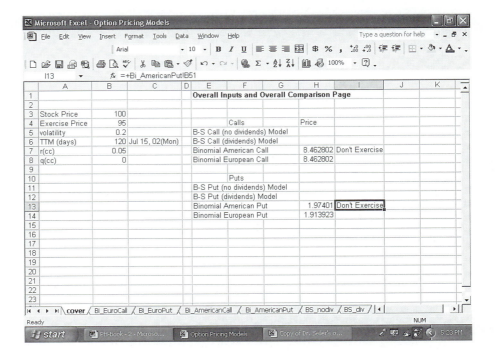

21

PROGRAMMING A BLACK-SCHOLES OPTION PRICING MODEL

21.1 PROGRAMMING A CALL OPTION WITHOUT DIVIDENDS USING BLACK-SCHOLES

The Black-Scholes model is a continuous-time model for pricing options. Established in 1973 by Fisher Black and Myron Scholes, it is the most popular model in use today. Moreover, it is the basis on which more advanced models are created.

In the previous chapter, we created the Excel file "Option Pricing Models." We will build on that file in this chapter.

Before we can begin to program the model, we need to label some of the cells in our spreadsheet. Go to the sheet titled "BS_nodiv" by clicking on the tab with the same name. In cell "A1," type the label "stock price." Continuing in cell "A2," type the label "strike price." The titles "volatility," "TTM," and "r(cc)" should be typed in cells "A3" through "A5," as shown in the following screen.

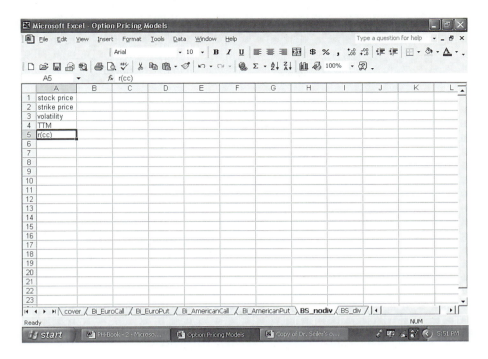

"TTM" stands for time to maturity and "r(cc)" stands for the continuously compounded rate of return on the risk-free asset (3-month T-bill). In cell "B1," we want to carry over the input value we used from the spreadsheet titled "cover." To do this, simply type in "=+cover!B3." To carry the strike price over in cell "B2," type in "=+cover!B4." Accordingly, for the variable "volatility," type in "=+cover!B5."

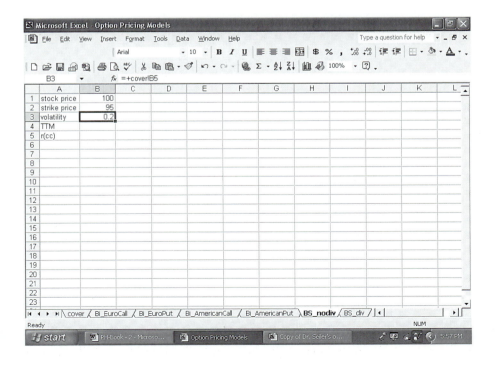

The variable "TTM" needs to be slightly adjusted from the value the ultimate user of our model will type in. That is, the user will type in the number of days until maturity. We need to take this value and divide it by the 365 days in the year. Therefore, the formula will be slightly altered. In cell "B4," type in "= +cover!B6/365."

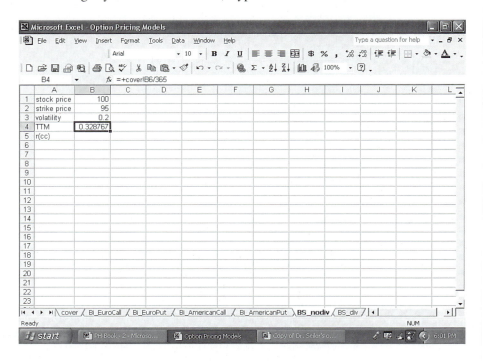

Finally, in cell "B5," type in "= +cover!B7."

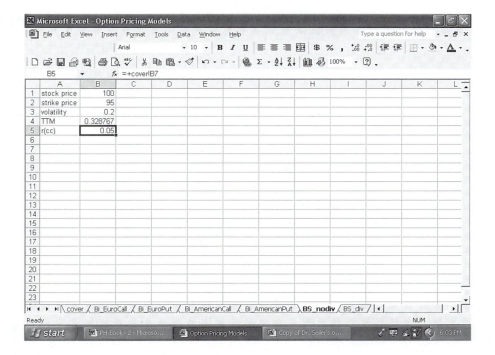

We are now ready to discuss the formula for the Black-Scholes model. The formula is given by:

$$C = S * N(d_1) - X * r^{-(r)(T)} * N(d_2) \qquad \textbf{(21.1)}$$

where

C = price of the call option
S = stock price
X = strike or exercise price
e = Euler's number = 2.71828 . . .
r = continuous compounded risk-free rate of return (3-month T-bill)
T = time to maturity (in years)
N = cumulative normal distribution

$$d_1 = \frac{\ln(S / X) + (r + 1 / 2 \, \vartheta^2)T}{\vartheta\sqrt{T}}$$

and

$$d_2 = d_1 - \vartheta\sqrt{T}$$

Getting back to the Excel model, let's create more titles. In cell "A8," type in the label "d1 =." In cell "A9," enter "N(d1) =." Similarly, in cell "A11," type in "d2 =." In cell "A12," enter "N(d2) =."

The formula for "d1" was just given. In the language of Excel, it can be expressed as:

$$= +(LN(B1/B2)+((B5+B3\wedge2/2)*B4))/(B3*B4\wedge0.5)$$

Enter the formula in cell "B8."

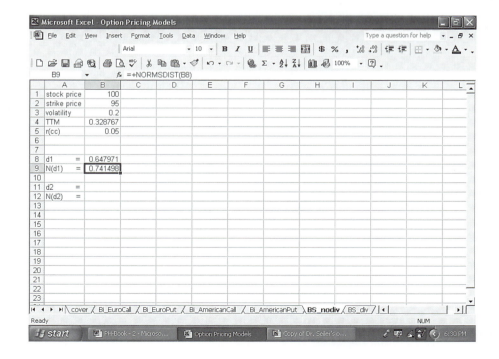

To create the cumulative normal distribution for "d1," an established Excel function can be used. In cell "B9," type:

$$=+NORMSDIST(B8)$$

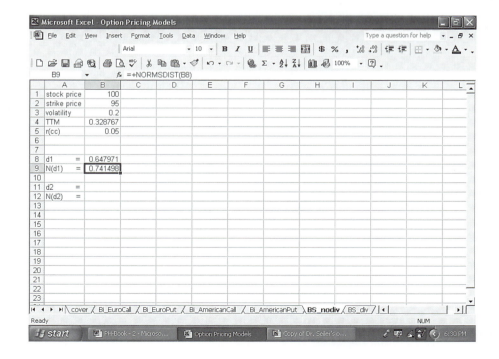

Now complete the formulas for "d2" and "N(d2)" in cells "B11" and "B12." The formulas should be written, respectively, as:

$$=+B8-B3*B4\wedge 0.5$$
$$=+NORMSDIST(B11)$$

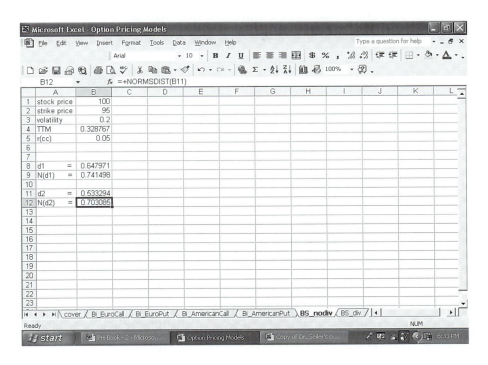

Now that the preliminary calculations are complete, we can calculate the price of the call option. Let's begin by creating a title in cell "D2." Let's title the cell "Call Price =." We will then place the formula for the call price in the neighboring cell, "E2." The mathematical formula for the price of a Black-Scholes call option was provided earlier. In Excel terminology, the formula can be represented by:

$$=+B1*B9-B2*EXP(-B5*B4)*B12$$

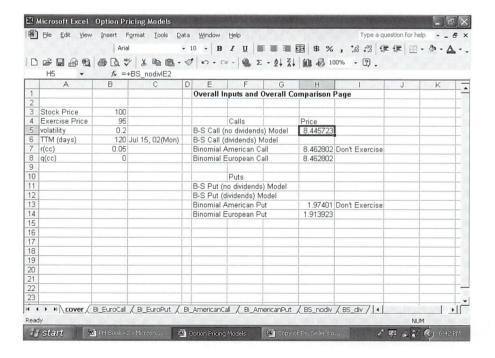

Based on our inputs, the price of the option is $8.445723. The last step is to report this value on the "cover" sheet. To do so, go to the spreadsheet titled "cover." In cell "H5" type "=+BS_nodiv!E2." You will now see the value reported on the "cover" sheet.

21.2 PROGRAMMING A PUT OPTION WITHOUT DIVIDENDS USING BLACK-SCHOLES

Not surprisingly, the call and put formulas are quite similar. The formula for the price of a put option is represented by the following equation:

$$P = X * e^{-(r)(T)} * N(-d_2) - S * N(-d_1) \qquad\text{(21.2)}$$

where

P = price of the put option
S = stock price
X = strike or exercise price
e = Euler's number = 2.71828 . . .
r = continuous compounded risk-free rate of return (3-month T-bill)
T = time to maturity (in years)
N = cumulative normal distribution

$$d_1 = \frac{\ln(S \ / \ X) + (r + 1 \ / \ 2 \ \vartheta^2)T}{\vartheta\sqrt{T}}$$

$$d_2 = d_1 - \vartheta\sqrt{T}$$

$$N(-d_1) = 1 - N(d_1)$$

and

$$N(-d_2) = 1 - N(d_2)$$

Getting back to the Excel model, let's first create a few titles where we can show our intermediate calculations. You will notice that the formulas for d_1 and d_2 are the same for both call and put options. Therefore, there is no reason to repeat them. However, the call option uses the values of $N(d_1)$ and $N(d_2)$ in its calculation, whereas the put option uses the values of $N(-d_1)$ and $N(-d_2)$. These can also be expressed as $1 - N(d_1)$ and $1 - N(d_2)$. For this reason, let's create the labels "1 - N(d1) =" and "1 - N(d2) =" in cells "D9" and "D12," respectively.

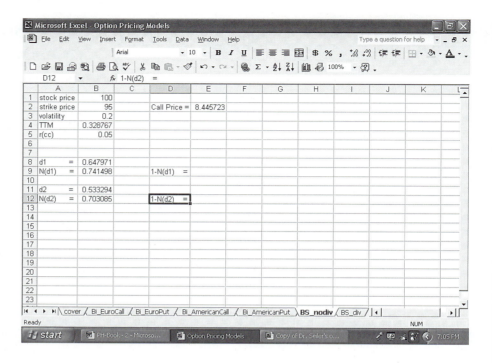

In cell "E9" write the formula as "=1-B9." Similarly, in cell "E12," type in "=1-B12."

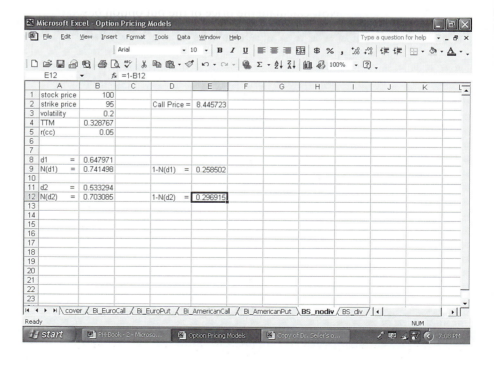

Now that all of the preliminary calculations are complete, we are ready to label and calculate the price of the put option.

In cell "D3," specify the label as "Put Price =."

Now calculate the price of the put option based on Equation 21.2. Using Excel terminology, the equation can be represented in cell "E3" as:

$$= +B2*EXP(-B5*B4)*E12-(B1*E9)$$

The last step is to report the price on the "cover" sheet. To do so, go to cell "H11" on the spreadsheet titled "cover" and type "=+BS_nodiv!E3."

21.3 PROGRAMMING A CALL OPTION WITH DIVIDENDS USING BLACK-SCHOLES

For corporations that pay dividends, the payments are typically made quarterly. However, when programming the Black-Scholes model, it is possible to specify whether the dividends are going to be paid in discrete amounts (quarterly) or continuously. The concept of a continuously paid dividend does not make much sense when including dividends into an option pricing model on an individual stock. However, when considering an index option, where not all stocks within the index pay dividends at the same point in time, the continuous dividend yield is very appealing.

21.3.1 CONTINUOUS DIVIDENDS

Fortunately, it is not difficult to incorporate continuously paid dividends into the Black-Scholes option pricing model. All we need to do is make a few simple adjustments to the model. To start, copy the cells we have already created from the "no dividend" case.

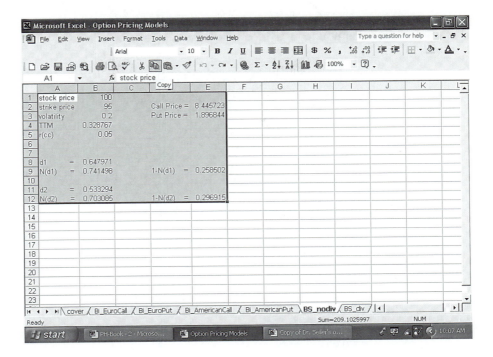

Click on the sheet titled "BS-div." In cell "A1," click "Paste."

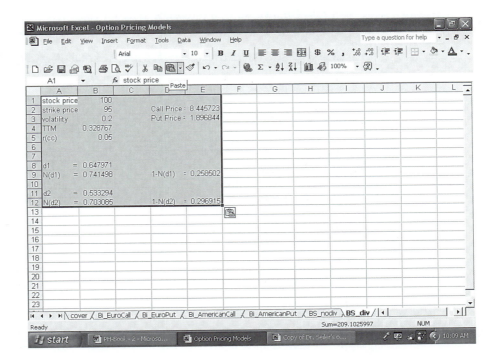

In cell "A6," type in the label "q(cc)." This title will represent the continuously compounded dividend yield on the stock index.

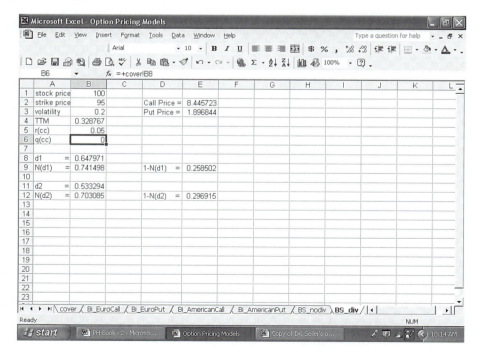

In cell "B6," we want to reference an input value from the "cover" sheet. Therefore, in cell "B6," type in the formula "=+cover!B8."

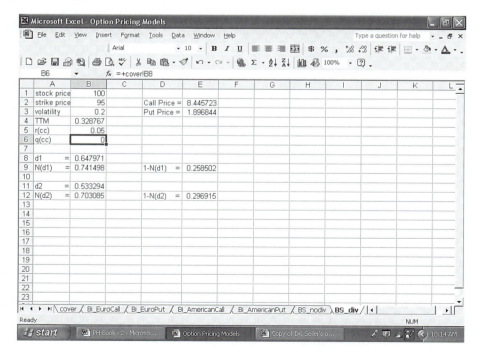

You will see the value "0" appear because this is the value on the "cover" sheet.

The next step is to adjust the stock price to reflect the continuously compounded dividend yield, "q(cc)." Before this next step is shown, it might help to explain why it is necessary. When you buy (take a long position in) a call option, you want the price of the underlying stock to go up. However, when a stock pays a dividend, the price will decrease by roughly the amount of the dividend (on the ex-dividend date). Therefore, your option becomes less valuable. The decrease in the value of the stock must be accounted for in the price of the option. To make this adjustment, we must complete the following steps.

In cell "A14," type in the label "Adjusted stock price."

The "Adjusted stock price" will be equal to the actual stock price minus the present value of the future dividends. Mathematically, the formula can be expressed as:

$$S = S * e^{-(q)(T)} \qquad \text{(21.3)}$$

In the language of Excel, the right-hand side of the formula is written as:

=B1*EXP(-B6*B4)

Therefore, in cell "C14," type "=B1*EXP(-B6*B4)."

The number "100" should appear. This number is the same as the unadjusted stock price only because we have the value "0" entered in as the dividend yield.

The next step is to use this newly created "Adjusted stock price" in the formula for the call option. The first place this adjustment is needed is in the calculation of "d1." Recall that the formula for *d1* can be expressed in Excel as:

$$=+(LN(\mathbf{B1}/B2)+((B5+B3\textasciicircum2/2)*B4))/(B3*B4\textasciicircum0.5)$$

This adjustment can be made in a number of ways. The way I find to be the least confusing is to change "B1" (the actual stock price) to "C14" (the adjusted stock price).

$$=+(LN(\mathbf{C14}/B2)+((B5+B3\textasciicircum2/2)*B4))/(B3*B4\textasciicircum0.5)$$

The final adjustment necessary to incorporate a continuously compounded dividend yield into the Black-Scholes call option is to make a slight adjustment to the formula for the call price itself. Recall that the formula for a call option is expressed mathematically as:

$$C = S * N(d_1) - X * e^{-(r)(T)} * N(d_2)$$

To adjust this formula to reflect a call option that pays a continuous dividend, all you need to do is substitute the "Adjusted stock price" for the actual stock price. Mathematically, the formula is rewritten as:

$$C = S' * N(d_1) - X * e^{-(r)(T)} * N(d_2) \tag{21.4}$$

Again, S' is defined as it was before. That is:

$$S' = S * e^{-(r)(T)}$$

In Excel, the "no dividend" call option price was expressed as:

=**B1***B9-B2*EXP(-B5*B4)*B12

All we have to do is change "B1" to "C14." Therefore, the formula to reflect continuous dividends is expressed as:

=**C14***B9-B2*EXP(-B5*B4)*B12

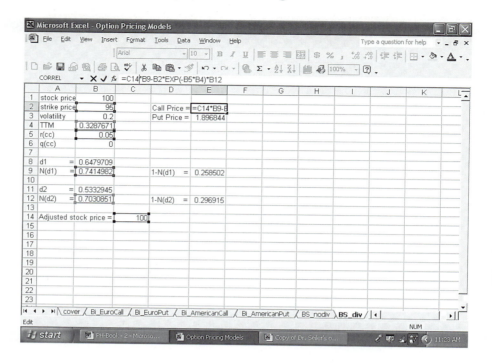

The model now fully incorporates a continuously compounded dividend yield.

21.3.2 DISCRETE DIVIDENDS

A *discrete dividend* is one that is paid periodically at different points in time. Alternatively stated, if a firm pays a dividend at the end of each quarter, this is known as a discrete dividend. Whether a dividend is paid continuously or discretely, the method of incorporating it into the model is the same. That is, it must be reflected in the "Adjusted stock price," "d1," and in the call price calculation.

The first step is to identify a place for the user to input the discrete dividends. Go to the sheet titled "cover." In cell "A19," type in the label "Dividends." In cells "B18" and "B19," type in the label "Days to ex-dividend." Finally, in cell "C19," type in the label "Present Value."

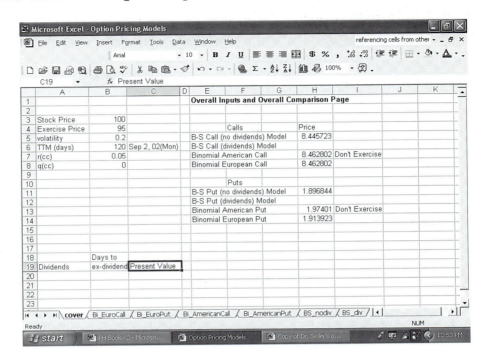

For now, let the dividends be equal to zero. Indicate this by typing in "0" for the cells "A20" through "A22."

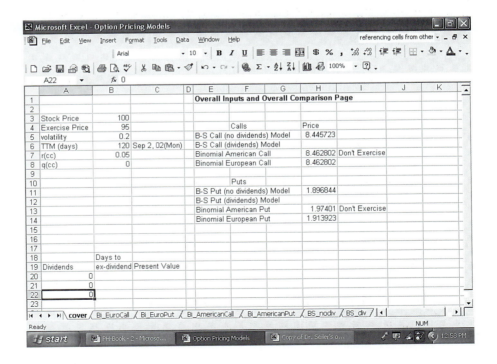

In cells "B20" through "B22," type in the number of days until the ex-dividend date. Because dividends are typically paid quarterly, these dates should be roughly 91 days apart. In general, you would forecast the dividends for the entire life of the option. In our example, assume three more dividends are to be paid. Further assume that the days until ex-dividend are 33, 124, and 215 days from now. Your cells should look like this.

We now need to calculate the present value of these dividends. The mathematical formula we need to do this can be expressed as:

$$PV = D * e^{-(r)(T)} \tag{21.5}$$

where

        PV = present value
        D = divided
        e = Euler's number = 2.71828 . . .
        r = continuous compounded risk-free rate of return (3-month T-bill)
        T = time to maturity (in years)

In Excel, the formula can be written as:

=A20*EXP(-$B$7*B20/365)

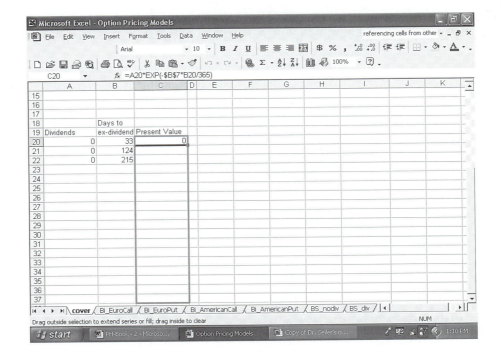

This "Present Value" formula should be copied down a number of rows so that it can be used for longer life options. To do so, simply left-click on your mouse and hold down the button as you drag down several rows. When you reach, say, cell "C37" release the left-hand mouse button.

The highlighted cells will show "0" because the dividends are all zero.

At this point, the user can go to the "cover" page and enter no dividends, continuous dividends, or discrete dividends. However, our model has not yet been programmed to handle discrete dividends. Let's do that now.

Recall that the way to incorporate dividends into the model is through the "Adjusted stock price." This incorporation will, in turn, trickle down through "d1" and ultimately into the "call price" calculation.

It is possible to create another sheet in Excel to do this. However, the most efficient way is to make a simple adjustment to the existing formula for the "Adjusted stock price." As previously illustrated, the Excel formula used to calculate the Adjusted stock price for a continuously compounded dividend is:

$$=B1*EXP(-B6*B4)$$

In this formula, "B6" represents the dividends as a single value. However, when discrete dividends are paid, a range of values must be considered. In Excel, the formula would be written as:

$$=B1-SUM(C20:C37)$$

Instead of using another sheet, it is much more efficient and user friendly to incorporate either continuous or discrete dividends into the same formula (or cell). To do so, under the worksheet titled "BS_div," go to cell "C14," where the "Adjusted stock price" (which already incorporates continuous dividends) has already been created. Adjust the formula by typing in the following:

$$=\text{IF(SUM(cover!C20:cover!C37)=0,B1*EXP(-B6*B4),}$$
$$\text{B1-SUM(cover!C20:cover!C37))}$$

This lengthy command tells Excel that the "Adjusted stock price" should reflect either discrete dividends or continuously compounded dividends. The user should know not to include both discrete and continuous dividends at the same time. However, if the user makes the mistake of including them both, this expression tells Excel to consider *only* discrete dividends. In essence, this command does not allow the user to make the mistake of entering both discrete and continuous dividends.

As a courtesy to the user, go to the "cover" worksheet and type "*NOTE: If both **discrete and continuous dividends are entered, ONLY DISCRETE dividends will be used.**" in cell "A16."

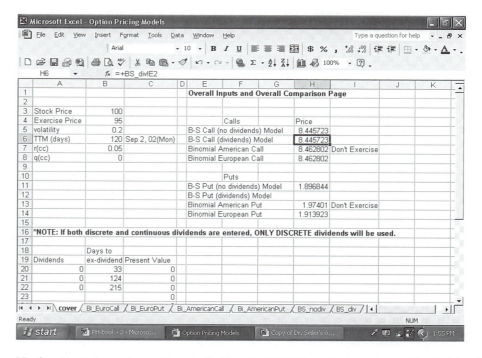

To be consistent, we should report the results from including dividends on the "cover" sheet. To do so, go to cell "H6." Type in the command "=+BS_div!E2" to reference the relevant worksheet and cell.

Notice that the price without dividends ("H5") and the price with dividends ("H6") are the same. This is only the case because both the continuous dividend yield and the discrete dividends are set to zero. As such, the models are effectively the same.

21.4 PROGRAMMING A PUT OPTION WITH DIVIDENDS USING BLACK-SCHOLES

As you might guess, programming a put option to reflect dividend payments requires only a minor adjustment to the calculations we have already done for the call option models.

21.4.1 CONTINUOUS DIVIDENDS

Because the "Adjusted stock price" has already been created and because "d1" has already been changed to reflect the adjusted stock price, only the formula for the put price has to be changed to fully incorporate continuous dividends. The formula for the "no dividend" case was expressed in Excel as:

$$=+B2*EXP(-B5*B4)*E12-(\mathbf{B1}*E9)$$

All we need to do now is substitute the Adjusted stock price for the actual (or unadjusted) stock price. The new price of the put option is written as:

$$=+B2*EXP(-B5*B4)*E12-(\mathbf{C14}*E9)$$

Type this formula into cell "E3."

The put model now fully incorporates a continuously compounded dividend yield.

21.4.2 DISCRETE DIVIDENDS

Discrete dividends are incorporated into put options the same way they are incorporated into call options. As such, we have already done this. At this point, all we need to do is report the price of the put option (which now accounts for all three cases of "no dividends," "continuously compounded dividends," or "discrete dividends") on the "cover" sheet.

To do this, go to cell "H12." Type in the command "=+BS_div!E3" to reference the relevant worksheet and cell.

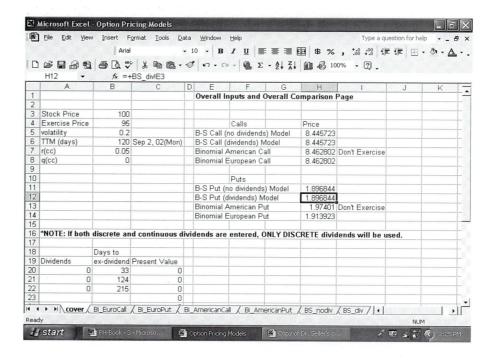

Notice that the price without dividends ("H11") and the price with dividends ("H12") are the same. This is only the case because both the continuous dividend yield and the discrete dividends are set to zero. As such, the models are effectively the same.

21.5 UNDERSTANDING THE EFFECTS OF INPUTS ON CALL AND PUT OPTIONS

Now that we have successfully programmed the various option pricing models, it is possible to examine the relationships between the six key input variables (stock price, exercise/strike price, volatility, time to maturity, the risk-free rate, and dividends) and the option values. To understand each effect, we will change only one input at a time while leaving the others constant. All inputs will be changed from the "cover" worksheet only. As we will see, the relationships are not the same for both call and put options.

21.5.1 STOCK PRICE

When you buy (take a long position in) a call option, you want the stock price to go up. Therefore, the greater the stock price, the greater the option price will become. When you buy (take a long position in) a put option, you expect the stock price to go down. Thus, if stock prices go up, put prices go down. That is, there is a negative relationship between stock prices and put option values.

Turning to the model, the starting stock price is set at $100. The corresponding option prices are: Call = $8.44; Put = $1.89.

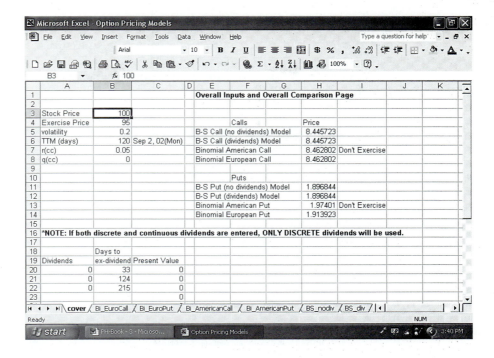

In cell "B3," change the stock price to "$110."

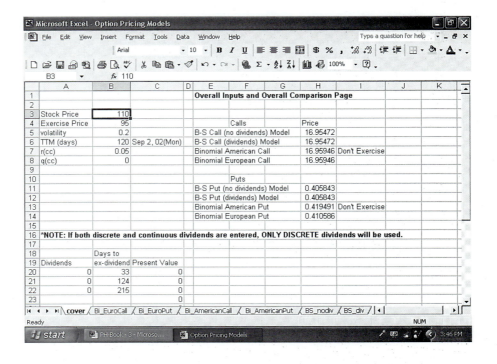

As expected, the call price went up (from $8.44 to $16.95) and the put price went down (from $1.89 to $0.40).

21.5.2 EXERCISE (OR STRIKE) PRICE

The lower the exercise price relative to the stock price, the more valuable the call option. This is because the option will be more toward "in-the-money." For a put option, the reverse is true. Using the original input values, go to cell "B4," and type in an exercise price of "$100."

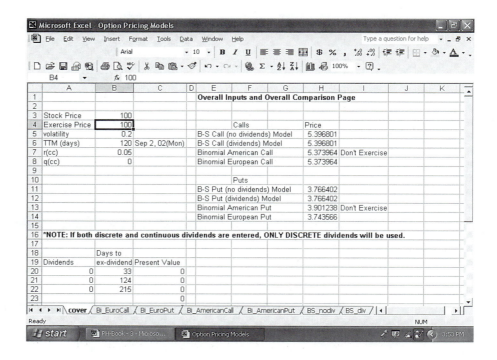

As anticipated, the call price went down from $8.44 to $5.39. Moreover, the put price went up from $1.89 to $3.76.

21.5.3 VOLATILITY

Volatility is a measure of how much the price of the underlying asset's (stock's) value moves over time. To understand the effect of volatility on a conceptual basis, consider the purchase of an out-of-the-money call. You need the price of the stock to move (specifically, to go up) in order for the option to eventually pay off. Without volatility, there is no change in the price, and your option will expire worthless. However, if the price of the stock is extremely volatile, there is a greater chance that it will eventually exceed the strike price.

A similar example applies to a put. You need the stock price to go down below the strike price or it will expire out-of-the-money (which would make it worthless). In either a call or a put, the greater the volatility, the greater the value of the option.

In cell "B5," change the original input for volatility from "0.2" to "0.8."

Notice that the price of both the call and the put increased as hypothesized. Specifically, the call option increased in value from $8.44 to $21.00, whereas the value of the put increased from $1.89 to $14.45.

21.5.4 TIME TO MATURITY

The number of days before the option matures is positively related to both call and put options. To see why, consider a call option that is out-of-the-money by $10. If the time to maturity is only 1 *day,* the odds are very much against the stock price going up by at least $10 in one trading session. Therefore, this option should have little to no value. However, if the stock has 1 *year* to go up by $10, then there is a much greater chance of it happening. Therefore, the option should have more value. Of course, the same analogy can be applied to a put option where you want the price to go down within a certain amount of time.

To measure the impact of time to maturity on option values, type in the value of "300" in cell "B6."

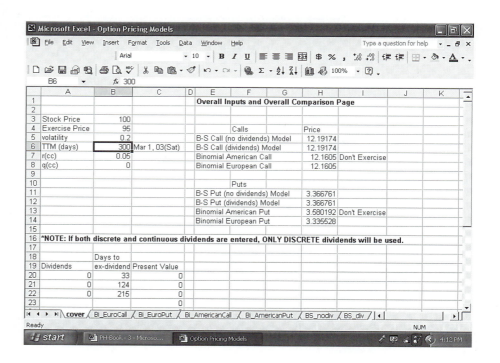

The price of the call increased from $8.44 to $12.19, whereas the price of the put went from $1.89 to $3.36.

21.5.5 RISK-FREE RATE

People typically have a more difficult time guessing the relationship between the continuously compounded risk-free rate of return and option values. Instead of using formulas (which we could have done to illustrate all of these relationships), I prefer to explain it as follows.

In the Black-Scholes model, the underlying stock price is assumed to grow at the risk-free rate. When you buy (take a long position in) a call option, you want the price of the stock to go up. Because the rate at which it is assumed to go up is equal to the risk-free rate, then the higher the risk-free rate, the more the stock price will go up. Therefore, the greater the value of the option.

The reverse is true for a put option. Because you want the price to go down, a higher risk-free rate works against you when you buy (take a long position in) a put option. As such, there is a negative, or inverse, relationship between the risk-free rate and put options.

To illustrate this relationship with our models, change the risk-free rate from ".05" to ".10" in cell "B7."

As you can see, the price of the call went up from $8.44 to $9.55. The put price decreased from $1.89 to $1.48.

21.5.6 DIVIDENDS

Whether they are paid continuously or discretely, dividends are negatively related to call prices and positively related to put prices. When a stock goes ex-dividend, the price of the stock should decrease by roughly the amount of the dividend (holding all other factors constant).

When you buy (take a long position in) a call option, you want the stock price to go up. Therefore, the payment of dividends works against you. Conversely, when you buy (take a long position in) a put, you want the price of the stock to go down. Thus, the payment of dividends works in your favor.

To illustrate, in cell "B8," change the value of "q(cc)," the continuously compounded risk-free rate of return, from "0" to ".04."

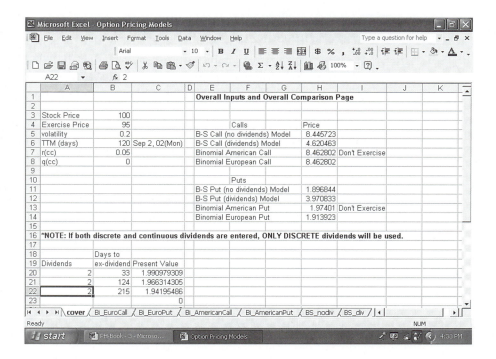

Notice that the price of the call went down from $8.44 to $7.50 ("H6"). The value of the put increased from $1.89 to $2.25 ("H12").

The relationship between dividends and option values can be seen through a change in the discrete dividends as well. In cells "A20" through "A22," type in "2."

Under this different example, the value of the call decreased from $8.44 to $4.62, whereas the put option increased in value from $1.89 to $3.97.

The directional effects of the six key input variables are summarized in the following table.

	Stock Price	Strike (or exercise) Price	Volatility	Time to Maturity	Risk-free Rate	Dividends
Call option	+	−	+	+	+	−
Put option	−	+	+	+	−	+

22

SECTIONS IN A FINANCIAL STUDY

A financial study includes the following sections: cover page, abstract, introduction, literature review, data, methodology, results, summary and conclusions, references, and tables. In this chapter, we examine the sections of the financial study and describe the required elements in each.

22.1   COVER PAGE AND ABSTRACT

The financial report should begin with a traditional cover page that includes the title of the paper, your name, the date, and appropriate contact information. Following the cover page, an abstract should appear. An abstract is a paragraph or two that conveys the purpose and findings of the study.

22.2   INTRODUCTION

The introduction serves two purposes. It should provide a nontechnical overview of what you are examining in the paper. It should also provide the rationale for examining your topic so that the reader understands why your research is important.

22.3   LITERATURE REVIEW

The next section in your study is the literature review. By reviewing past studies that relate to your research, you will be able to demonstrate that your research offers something new. You will try to show that you are filling in a gap in the research literature by (1) examining something that has never before been examined, (2) using better data to answer a question that has been studied in the past, or (3) using a more appropriate or sophisticated methodology than what has been used in the past. This is a very critical step in the research process. No one will want to read your study if someone else has already done what you are proposing to do.

22.4 DATA

The data section will be the easiest part of the paper to write. Simply state the *exact* data sources and fully describe the data that you have used to test your hypotheses. This section can be placed before or after the methodology section. All other sections should be in the order presented here.

22.5 METHODOLOGY

In the methodology section, you will describe how you will answer your research question. You will present your hypotheses and the exact models to be tested. Sound and appropriate statistical procedures must be used here.

22.6 RESULTS

In the results section you will present the results of your study. Place your results in easy-to-read tables at the end of the paper (not in the middle). Each table should be placed on a separate page. In the text, fully interpret and discuss the finding(s) shown in each table. Take the reader slowly step-by-step through the findings and make sure that the results flow logically.

Each table should be able to stand alone. This means that each table should be titled and labeled in enough detail so that a reader could understand it without reading the results section.

Do not attach *all* of your computer output. You must *summarize* the important results and report *only* what the reader needs to see.

22.7 SUMMARY AND CONCLUSIONS

In the summary and conclusions, you should highlight the major finding(s) of your study using nontechnical language. Do *not* introduce new results here. This section is a summary of what you have already fully explained to the reader in the results section. After highlighting your major findings, interpret what all of it means. What should the reader conclude from your study? Any reader should be able to read just the introduction and the summary and conclusions and have a good feel for the study you have completed. If they want more specific information, they can refer to the other sections of the paper where you describe the data, methodology, and results.

22.8 REFERENCES

After the summary and conclusions, list all of the references used in the paper on a separate page. If you did not mention a source in the text, do not list it in the references. This is not a bibliography. You should *not* include your actual (full-text) sources. Instead, save them separately for your own future use. Include a source in the references *if* and *only if* you refer to the source in the paper. For example, if in the paper you write, "Johansson, Seiler, and Tjarnberg (1999) find that . . ." then you would provide the source in the references as:

Johansson, Fredrik, Michael J. Seiler, and Mikael Tjarnberg, "Measuring Downside Portfolio Risk: All VaRs For Equities Are NOT Equal," *The Journal of Portfolio Management*, Fall 1999, 26:1, 96–107.

22.9 TABLES

Following the references, number your tables and place them in order, being sure that no two tables appear on the same page. Refer to Section 22.6 and Chapter 23 for more information on table format.

23

BRINGING OUTPUT INTO
MICROSOFT WORD

<hr>

No matter what software you use to generate your output, you will want to present your results by placing the tables in a word processing file such as Microsoft Word.

23.1 BRINGING SPSS OUTPUT INTO MICROSOFT WORD

For the sake of demonstration, we will insert an output table from the ANOVA analysis that was done in Chapter 8 using the "Home Values - 1" dataset. To bring SPSS output into Word, follow the three easy steps presented here.

First, when you go to the SPSS "Output" window, you will see all of the tables you have generated thus far. It will look like this.

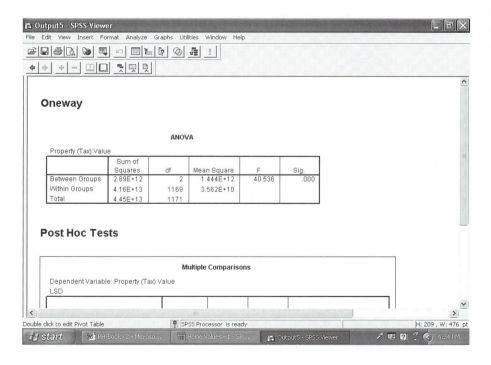

To select the table you wish to bring into Word, simply left-click on it. Your screen will now look like this.

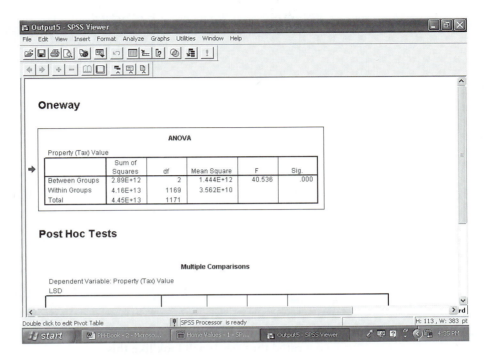

The red arrow and the box surrounding your table indicate that it is selected.

The second step to bringing the output into Word is to right-click and select "Copy Objects."

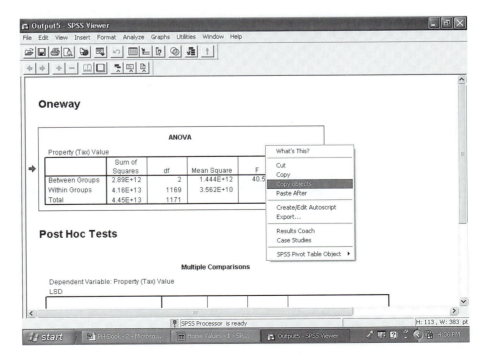

Our third and final step is to go into Word and click "Paste." The table will appear as follows.

ANOVA					
	Property (Tax) Value				
	Sum of Squares	*df*	*Mean Square*	*F*	*Sig*
Between Groups	2.89E+12	2	1.444E+12	40.536	.000
Within Groups	4.16E+13	1169	3.562E+10		
Total	4.45E+13	1171			

If you want to adjust the table in any way, do so in SPSS before you paste it into Word. It is much easier to manipulate the table in SPSS. To adjust the table while it is still in SPSS, double-click on the table. Next, double-click on the cell you want to change. For example, let's say you want to spell out the word "Sig." as "Significant." Select the table and then the column. Once the column is selected, type "Significant." The screen will appear as follows.

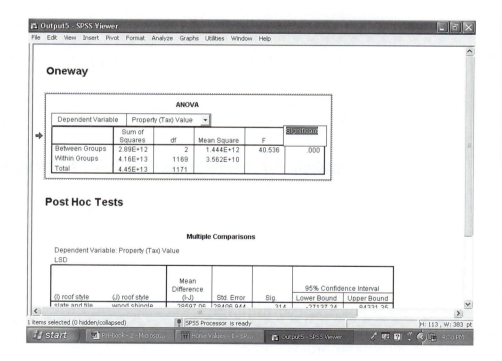

After typing in the full word, the "Output" window will look like this.

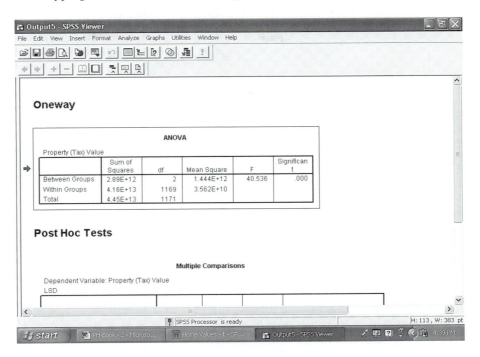

When changing titles in SPSS, you may notice that the new titles wrap around and no longer appear clean and professional. To get them to look professional again, you can resize the table by double-clicking on it after it has already been selected. Your table will appear with a thicker box.

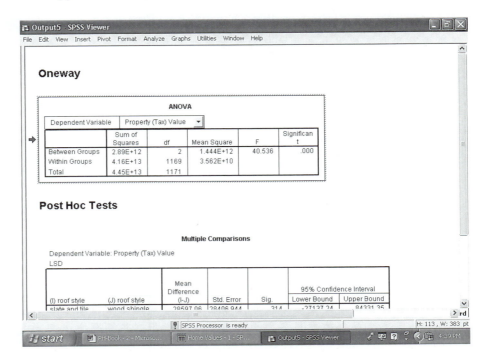

If you place your mouse on the vertical bar to the right of the column "Significant," you can left-click and drag the bar further to the right to expand the column. Do so and your screen will look like this.

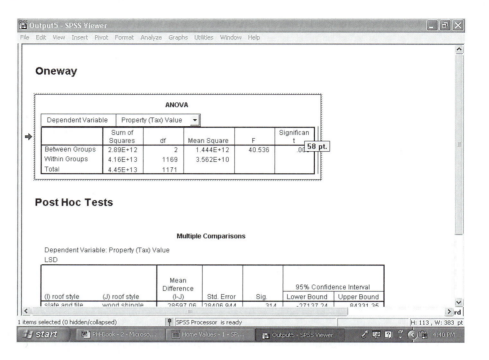

When you are satisfied the column is wide enough, release the left-hand mouse button. The entire word should now appear on one line.

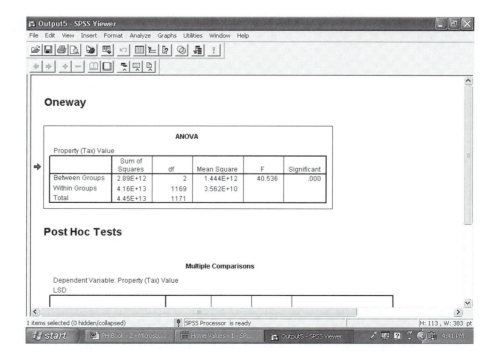

You can then copy the table into Word as was described earlier. Again, the steps are (1) right-click on the table, (2) left-click on "Copy Objects," (3) enter Word and click on the "Paste" icon. The finished table will look like this.

ANOVA					
	Property (Tax) Value				
	Sum of Squares	df	Mean Square	F	Significant
Between Groups	2.89E+12	2	1.444E+12	40.536	.000
Within Groups	4.16E+13	1169	3.562E+10		
Total	4.45E+13	1171			

23.2 BRINGING EXCEL OUTPUT INTO MICROSOFT WORD

For the sake of demonstration, we will insert an output table from a salary study I performed. To bring Excel output into Word, follow the four easy steps described here.

First, select the part of the Excel worksheet you wish to bring into Word by highlighting the area.

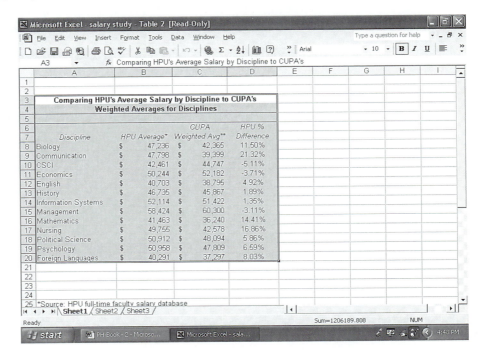

The second step is to click the "Copy" icon in Excel.

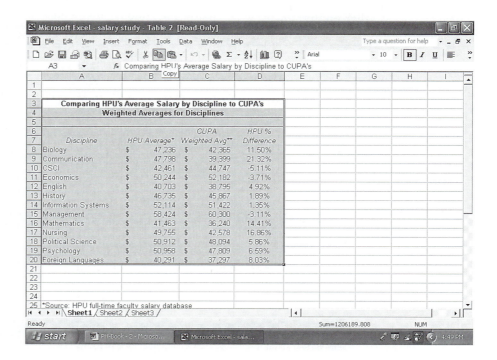

The third step is to enter Word and click "Edit" and then "Paste Special."

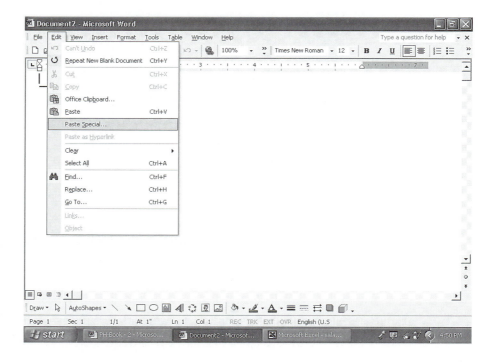

Select "Microsoft Excel Worksheet Object." Click "OK."

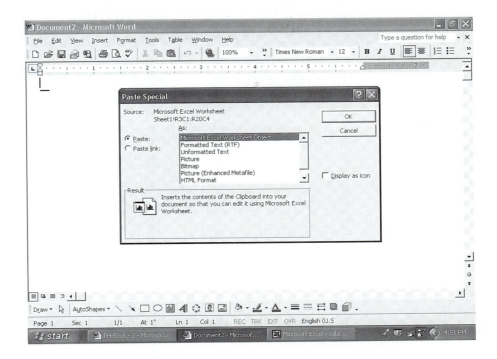

The object will appear in Word as follows.

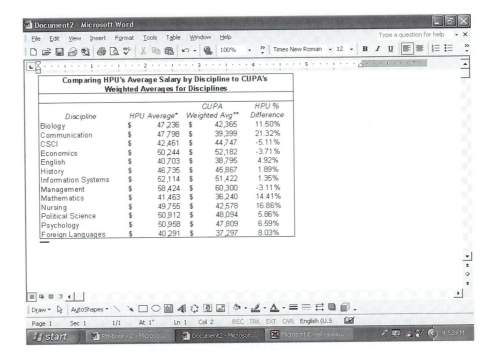

The fourth step is to resize the object. Objects are often too large for the Microsoft Word page. In this situation, it is necessary to resize the object. You can resize an object by left-clicking (and holding down) in the lower-right-hand corner of the object and then moving the mouse to reduce or increase its size. Here, I show how to reduce the size of an object.

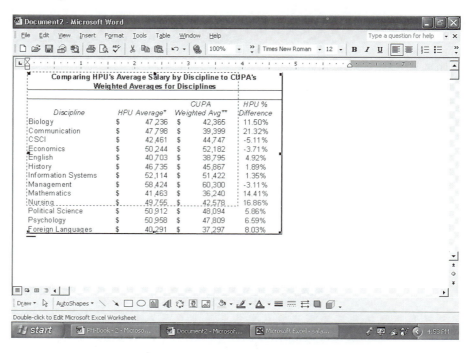

After you release the mouse button, the object will be smaller.

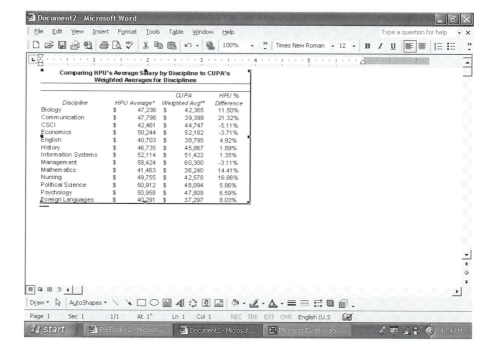

You can reposition an object by positioning the mouse over the object and then depressing and holding down the left-hand mouse button. Next, just move the mouse to where you want to reposition the object. This action only moves the object, it does not change its size.

23.3 BRINGING EVIEWS OUTPUT INTO MICROSOFT WORD

For the sake of demonstration, we will bring into Word an output table from a 2SLS procedure performed in EViews. To bring EViews output into Word, follow the three easy steps described here.

First, in EViews, highlight the area you want to bring into Word.

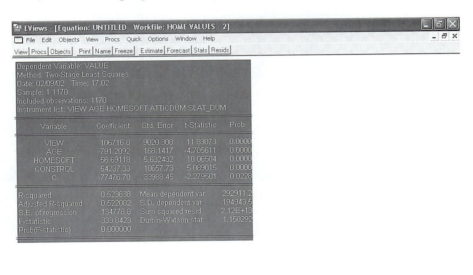

Second, right-click with your mouse and select "Copy."

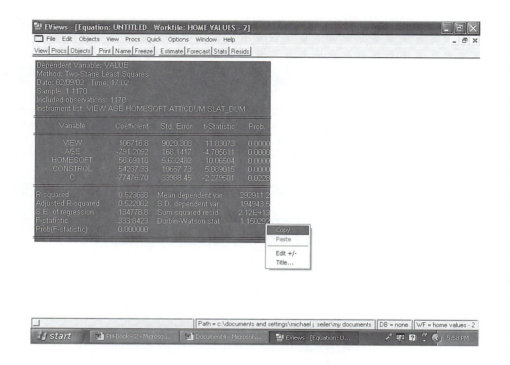

The window "Copy Precision" will appear. Choose the option "Formatted - Copy numbers as they appear in table."

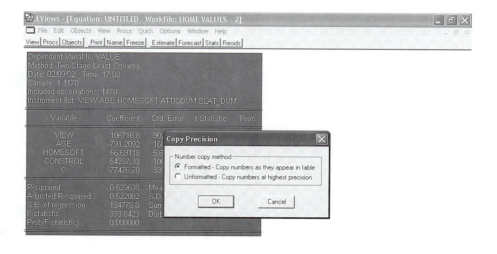

The third and final step is to enter Word and click "Paste."

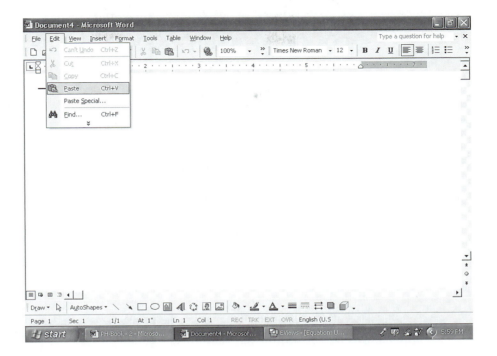

Your Word file will look like this.

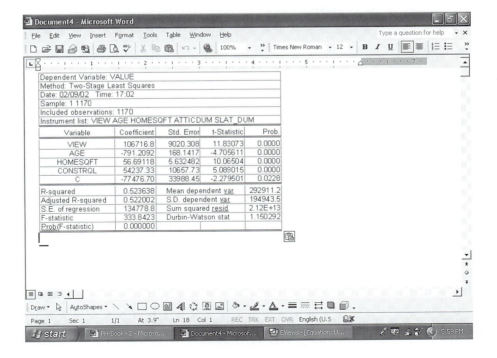

APPENDIX

DATASET DESCRIPTIONS

ASIAN CRISIS DATA

This time series dataset contains daily return data for three world stock markets: the United States, Japan, and Hong Kong. For each market, returns are provided for the period preceding the Asian crisis (April 2, 1996 through December 31, 1996), as well as the period following the Asian crisis (April 2, 1998 through December 31, 1998).

Variable List	Definition
rusb	Return on the U.S. stock market before the crisis
rjapanb	Return on the Japanese stock market before the crisis
rhkb	Return on the Hong Kong stock market before the crisis
rusa	Return on the U.S. stock market after the crisis
rjapana	Return on the Japanese stock market after the crisis
rhka	Return on the Hong Kong stock market after the crisis

BETA DATA - 1

This time series dataset contains the monthly yield on 3-month Treasury Bills, the value of the S&P 500 Index, and stock prices (adjusted for stock-splits) for both Microsoft and Netegrity from January 1998 through December 2001.

Variable List	Definition
date	Date (month and year)
sp500	S&P 500 Index values
tbill	Nominal T-bill yield
microsft	Microsoft's stock price
netegrit	Netegrity's stock price

BETA DATA - 2

This time series dataset contains the monthly yield on 3-month Treasury Bills, the value of the S&P 500 Index, and stock prices (adjusted for stock-splits) for both Microsoft and Netegrity from January 1998 through December 2001. It also contains the returns and excess returns for the S&P 500, Microsoft, and Netegrity.

Variable List	Definition
date	Date (month and year)
sp500	S&P 500 Index values
tbill	Nominal T-bill yield
micro	Microsoft's stock price
nete	Netegrity's stock price
r_sp500	Return on the S&P 500 Index
r_tbill	Return on T-bills
r_micro	Return on Microsoft
r_nete	Return on Netegrity
er_micro	Excess return on Microsoft
er_sp500	Excess return on the S&P 500 Index
er_nete	Excess return on Netegrity

COINTEGRATION DATA - 1

This time series dataset contains the quarterly price levels and returns for stocks (S&P 500 and Wilshire 5000), corporate bonds, government bonds, and real estate (NCREIF and NAREIT) from the first quarter of 1978 through the fourth quarter of 1995.

Variable List	Definition
ncreif	NCREIF index of unsecuritized real estate
nareit	NAREIT index of securitized real estate
corpbond	SBBI index of corporate bonds
sp500	S&P 500 Index
tbills	U.S. Treasury Bill index
wilshire	Wilshire 5000 stock index
lnncreif	Natural log of the NCREIF index of unsecuritized real estate
lnnareit	Natural log of the NAREIT index of securitized real estate
lncorpbond	Natural log of the SBBI index of corporate bonds
lnsp500	Natural log of the S&P 500 Index

Variable List	Definition
lntbills	Natural log of the U.S. Treasury Bill index
lnwilshire	Natural log of the Wilshire 5000 stock index
rncreif	Return on the NCREIF index of unsecuritized real estate
rnareit	Return on the NAREIT index of securitized real estate
rcorpbond	Return on the SBBI index of corporate bonds
rsp500	Return on the S&P 500 Index
rtbills	Return on the U.S. Treasury Bill index
rwilshire	Return on the Wilshire 5000 stock index
s1	A seasonal dummy variable for the first quarter of the year
s2	A seasonal dummy variable for the second quarter of the year
s3	A seasonal dummy variable for the third quarter of the year
s4	A seasonal dummy variable for the fourth quarter of the year

COINTEGRATION DATA - 2

This time series dataset contains the quarterly price levels and returns for stocks (S&P 500 and Wilshire 5000), corporate bonds, government bonds, and real estate (NCREIF and NAREIT) from the first quarter of 1978 through the fourth quarter of 1995. It also contains centered seasonal dummy variables for each quarter of the year.

Variable List	Definition
ncreif	NCREIF index of unsecuritized real estate
nareit	NAREIT index of securitized real estate
corpbond	SBBI index of corporate bonds
sp500	S&P 500 Index
tbills	U.S. Treasury Bill index
wilshire	Wilshire 5000 stock index
lnncreif	Natural log of the NCREIF index of unsecuritized real estate
lnnareit	Natural log of the NAREIT index of securitized real estate
lncorpbond	Natural log of the SBBI index of corporate bonds
lnsp500	Natural log of the S&P 500 Index
lntbills	Natural log of the U.S. Treasury Bill index

Variable List	Definition
lnwilshire	Natural log of the Wilshire 5000 stock index
rncreif	Return on the NCREIF index of unsecuritized real estate
rnareit	Return on the NAREIT index of securitized real estate
rcorpbond	Return on the SBBI index of corporate bonds
rsp500	Return on the S&P 500 Index
rtbills	Return on the U.S. Treasury Bill index
rwilshire	Return on the Wilshire 5000 stock index
s1	A seasonal dummy variable for the first quarter of the year
s2	A seasonal dummy variable for the second quarter of the year
s3	A seasonal dummy variable for the third quarter of the year
s4	A seasonal dummy variable for the fourth quarter of the year
s1c	A centered seasonal dummy variable for the first quarter of the year
s2c	A centered seasonal dummy variable for the second quarter of the year
s3c	A centered seasonal dummy variable for the third quarter of the year
s4c	A centered seasonal dummy variable for the fourth quarter of the year

COUNTRY RETURN DATA - 1

This file consists of time series data containing indexes of daily stock price levels for 13 world stock markets. Dates are listed in the rows. Columns list each variable.

Variable List	Definition
Date	Data are from April 1, 1996 through February 26, 1999
US	S&P 500 Index
UK	FT 100 Index
Mexico	IPC Index
Brazil	Bovespa Index
Japan	Nikkei 300 Index
Hong Kong	Hang Seng Index
Singapore	Singapore Straits Times Index
Taiwan	Weighted Composite Index
Korea	Korea Composite EX
Indonesia	Jakarta Composite Index
Thailand	Bangkok SET Index
Canada	Toronto 300 Composite Index
Malaysia	Kuala Lumpur SE Stock Index

COUNTRY RETURN DATA - 2

This file consists of time series data containing indexes of daily stock price levels for 13 world stock markets *and* the corresponding return on each index. Dates are listed in the rows. Columns list each variable.

Variable List	Definition
Date	Data are from April 1, 1996 through February 26, 1999
US	S&P 500 Index
UK	FT 100 Index
Mexico	IPC Index
Brazil	Bovespa Index
Japan	Nikkei 300 Index
Hong Kong	Hang Seng Index
Singapore	Singapore Straits Times Index
Taiwan	Weighted Composite Index
Korea	Korea Composite EX
Indonesia	Jakarta Composite Index
Thailand	Bangkok SET Index
Canada	Toronto 300 Composite Index
Malaysia	Kuala Lumpur SE Stock Index
rUS	Return on the S&P 500 Index
rUK	Return on the FT 100 Index
rMexico	Return on the IPC Index
rBrazil	Return on the Bovespa Index
rJapan	Return on the Nikkei 300 Index
rHong Kong	Return on the Hang Seng Index
rSingapore	Return on the Singapore Straits Times Index
rTaiwan	Return on the Weighted Composite Index
rKorea	Return on the Korea Composite EX
rIndonesia	Return on the Jakarta Composite Index
rThailand	Return on the Bangkok SET Index
rCanada	Return on the Toronto 300 Composite Index
rMalaysia	Return on the Kuala Lumpur SE Stock Index

FACULTY EVALUATIONS - 1

This cross-sectional dataset contains the student evaluations of 11 professors in the Department of Finance at a 4-year university in the Midwest. The first 34 questions relay the responses of each student. The remaining seven variables were added to provide additional characteristics of the class and professor.

Variable List	Definition
q01	Year in school
q02	Undergraduate major
q03	Undergraduate GPA
q04	Graduate GPA
q05	Undergraduate degree from
q06	Number of courses (GRAD)
q07	Fairness
q08	Thinking
q09	Responsible
q10	Knowledgeable
q11	Helpful
q12	Original
q13	Enthusiasm
q14	Critical thinking
q15	Listener
q16	Humorous
q17	Likes teaching
q18	Confidence
q19	Professor rank vs. others in the university
q20	Professor rank vs. others in the college of business
q21	Standards
q22	Course materials 1 - stimulating?
q23	Course materials 2 - relevant?
q24	Written assignments
q25	Magnitude of work
q26	Course value
q27	Course content
q28	Syllabus
q29	Challenging
q30	Teaching methods
q31	Course objectives
q32	Class organization
q33	Course expectations
q34	Amount learned
tenured	Professor tenured
research	Research oriented
time	Day or night class
req_elec	Required or elective
mba_und	MBA or undergraduate
fullpart	Part-time or full-time
profname	Professor name

FACULTY EVALUATIONS - 2

This is the same dataset as "Faculty Evaluations - 1" except that this dataset has been cleansed of identifiable coding errors.

FACULTY EVALUATIONS - 3

This is the same dataset as "Faculty Evaluations - 2" except that six new variables have been created. The first three were created automatically by SPSS when a factor analysis was performed. The second three are summated scale variables that we created based on output from the same factor analysis. These six variables are described below.

Variable List	Definition
fac1_1	REGR factor score 1 for analysis 1
fac2_1	REGR factor score 2 for analysis 1
fac3_1	REGR factor score 3 for analysis 1
summfac1	Summated-scale factor 1
summfac2	Summated-scale factor 2
summfac3	Summated-scale factor 3

HOME VALUES - 1

This dataset contains cross-sectional data relating to home attributes for 1,172 properties located in Cuyahoga County, Ohio.

Variable List	Definition
value	Cuyahoga County property tax value (of the home)
view	0 = home has no view of Lake Eire (is an adjacent property) 1 = home has a lakefront view of Lake Erie
constrql	A rating of the home's construction quality ranging from 1 to 6
age	The age of the house (in years)
roofstyl	1 = slate and tile 2 = wood shingle 3 = asphalt shingle
basement	0 = has only a slab or crawl space 1 = has a full basement
aircond	1 = central air 2 = window unit air conditioner 3 = no air conditioner
attic	1 = fully finished attic 2 = unfinished attic 3 = no attic
rooms	Total number of rooms in the home
bedrooms	Number of bedrooms in the home
baths	Number of bathrooms in the home
fireplac	Number of fireplaces in the home
homesqft	Total living space in the home (in square feet)
lotsize	Lot size (in square feet)
frontage	Length of linear lake frontage (in feet)

Variable List	Definition
ac_dum	0 = no air conditioning 1 = air conditioning
atticdum	0 = no attic 1 = attic
roof_dum	0 = a style other than asphalt shingle 1 = asphalt shingle

HOME VALUES - 2

This is the same dataset as "Home Values - 1" except that it contains only 1,170 properties because of changes made throughout the book.

INTERNET DATA - 1

This dataset contains time series data on the yield on Aaa rated corporate bonds, Baa rated corporate bonds, 3-month Treasury Bills, 30-year Treasury Bonds, and the CPI from February 1977 through December 2001.

Variable List	Definition
Date	The month and year
Aaa	The yield on Aaa rated corporate bonds
Baa	The yield on Baa rated corporate bonds
Tbond	The yield on 30-year Treasury Bonds
Tbill	The yield on 3-month Treasury Bills
CPI	Consumer Price Index (CPI)

PREDICTIVE ABILITY

This dataset contains cross-sectional data relating to 247 mutual funds. For each of the funds, the returns for 1998 and 1999 are given as well as the resulting rankings. Finally, the predicted mutual fund rankings, associated with five industry analysts, are listed.

Variable List	Definition
ticker	Ticker symbol
fundname	Fund name
rtn1999	Actual return during 1999
rtn1998	Actual return during 1998
rank1999	Actual rank during 1999
rank1998	Actual rank during 1998
analyst1	Predicted rank in 1999 by analyst 1
analyst2	Predicted rank in 1999 by analyst 2
analyst3	Predicted rank in 1999 by analyst 3
analyst4	Predicted rank in 1999 by analyst 4
analyst5	Predicted rank in 1999 by analyst 5

TBILLS - 1

This file contains monthly time series data from February 1977 through November 2001 for 3-month Treasury Bills.

Variable List	Definition
rtbill	Return on Treasury Bills
tbill	An index of nominal Treasury Bill yields

TBILLS - 2

This file contains monthly time series data from February 1977 through November 2001 for 3-month Treasury Bills. Additional variables have been created and saved.

Variable List	Definition
atbill	An adjusted Treasury Bill return series free from ARCH/GARCH effects
garch01	A series of conditional variance created by EViews
rtbill	The return on Treasury Bills
tbill	An index of nominal Treasury Bill yields

GLOSSARY

Abnormal return in an event study, the difference between actual return and expected return.

Akaike Information Criterion a measure used to determine the optimal number of lags to include for a series.

American option an option that can be exercised at any point on or before maturity.

Analysis of Variance (ANOVA) a test to determine if the means of more than two variables are the same as the overall mean.

ARCH (Autoregressive Conditional Heteroskedasticity) a method to determine if a time series is plagued with heteroskedasticity. Moreover, it provides a way to correct or remove the unequal variance so the series can be used in tests that assume homoskedasticity.

ARCH-in-Mean (ARCH-M) an additional ARCH/GARCH/TARCH/EGARCH specification to be used when the expected return on the variable under examination is a function of its expected risk.

Asymmetric Component model a combination of the Component ARCH and the TARCH models; that is, it allows for a nonconstant reversion in the mean of the series as well as differential quadratic effects for positive and negative shocks to the series.

At-the-money refers to the situation where the option has a zero payoff (ignoring commissions) if the option were exercised immediately. For either a call or a put option, it refers to a situation where the stock's price is equal to the exercise price.

Augmented Dickey-Fuller (ADF) a procedure used to test for stationarity.

Autocorrelation measures the degree to which a single series moves relative to its own lagged values over time.

Bear market a market characterized by a general decrease in prices.

Beta the covariance between a stock and the market divided by variance on the market. Beta is a measure of a firm's systematic risk and a measure of how a stock's excess returns move relative to the excess returns on the market.

Binomial Option Pricing Model a discrete time model used to price put and call options.

Black-Scholes Option Pricing Model a continuous time model used to price put and call options.

Bull market a market characterized by a general increase in prices.

Call option gives the buyer (who is said to hold a "long" position) the right to buy 100 shares of the underlying common stock at a predetermined price (the strike or exercise price) on (a European option) or before (an American option) a predetermined date (maturity).

Cointegrating equation (CE) once normalized, a CE shows the long-run relationships among the included variables.

Cointegration nonstationary series that can be combined to create (up to n-1) stationary series.

Communality in factor analysis, communality reports the percentage of variance within each variable that is explained by the resulting factors.

Component ARCH a variation of the GARCH model in that it allows the mean of the series to revert at a varying level or at a nonconstant rate.

Condition indexes used to identify the presence of multi-collinearity. Values above 30 (some statistics books recommend the more restrictive cutoff value of 15) can be problematic.

Contagion effects in an event study, contagion means not being able to distinguish between two effects because both occurred around the same period of time.

Continuous (Ratio) data continuous (or ratio) data are the same as interval data except they have a fixed zero point. A common example is a stock's return.

Continuous dividends dividends that are paid at a frequency equal to the smallest unit of time imaginable (continuously). The concept of a continuously paid dividend does not make much sense when including dividends into an option pricing model on an individual stock. However, when considering an index option where not all stocks within the index pay dividends at the same point in time, the continuous dividend yield is very appealing.

Correlation measures the degree to which two variables are associated with or related to each other.

Cumulative abnormal return (CAR) in an event study, CAR is simply the sum of the abnormal returns (ARs) for each day in the event window.

Cumulative TSAR in an event study, cumulative TSAR is simply the sum of the total standardized abnormal returns (TSARs) for each day in the event window.

Difference stationary a term used to describe a nonstationary series that can be made stationary by taking the (first, second, etc.) difference in the series.

Discrete dividends dividends paid periodically at different points in time (typically quarterly in the United States). Discrete dividends are used when an option model is based on an individual stock.

Dummy variable a nominal variable that has only two classifications or categories.

Endogenous variables variables determined inside the model.

Error correction term in a VEC model, the term represents deviations that are corrected gradually through a series of adjustments dictated by the long-run relationship. The more negative and significant the t-statistics, the more successful the VEC model.

Estimation period in an event study, the period of time over which no event has occurred. It is used to establish how the returns on the stock should behave in the absence of the event.

Estimation period firm residual in an event study, it is the actual return on the stock minus the expected return on the stock—given the relationship between the stock and the market.

European option an option that can be exercised only at maturity.

Event clustering in an event study, where the firms in the sample have event dates that are very close together.

Event date in an event study, the time when the market first learns of the relevant, new information.

Event study a methodology used to measure how a firm's stock price reacts to new information.

Event window in an event study, the number of trading periods (usually days) examined preceding and following the event date.

Event window market residual in an event study, it is the return on the market over the event window minus the average return on the market over the estimation period, squared.

Excess return the return in "excess" of the risk-free rate.

Ex-dividend date occurs 4 days before the date of record. These 4 days provide enough time for the sale of the common stock to be reflected in the stockholder list by the date of record. On the ex-dividend date, the price of the stock should decrease by roughly the amount of the dividend provided all other factors are constant.

Exogenous variables variables determined outside the model.

Exponential GARCH (EGARCH) a variation of ARCH/GARCH that tests for the asymmetric effect for good and bad news. EGARCH assumes the formula for the conditional variance is exponential.

Factor analysis a statistical technique where many variables can be statistically grouped or reduced to just a few factors.

Factor loadings in factor analysis, loadings measure the strength of the relationship between the variable and the factor onto which it loads. The greater the absolute value of the factor loading, the more important the variable is in representing the factor.

Factor scores in factor analysis, it is possible to save newly created factors, or groupings of variables, as new variables. The values for these new variables are known as factor scores.

First-order autocorrelation the degree of correlation between adjacent time series data values.

GARCH (Generalized Autoregressive Conditional Heteroskedasticity) a method to determine if a time series is plagued with heteroskedasticity. GARCH provides a way to correct or remove the unequal variance so the series can be used in tests that assume homoskedasticity.

Granger Causality a technique used to determine whether a temporal (a relationship over time) cause-and-effect relationship exists between two variables.

Heteroskedasticity the observation that volatility is not constant over time.

Homoskedasticity the observation that volatility is constant over time.

In-the-money if the option were exercised immediately, in-the-money refers to the situation where it has a positive payoff (ignoring commissions). For a call option, it refers to a situation where the stock's price is greater than the exercise price. For a put, it refers to a situation where the stock's price is less than the exercise price.

Independent samples t-test a type of t-test where the goal is to determine if there is a significant difference between the mean of two variables that belong to separate groups (or independent samples).

Information coefficient a measure used to determine the level of predictive ability.

Initial public offering (IPO) the first time a company offers its shares of stock to the public.

Interval data ordinal data where the differences between each observation are constant. Interval data also differ from ordinal data in that interval data have an arbitrary zero point.

Intrinsic value for a call option, intrinsic value means the value of the call is equal to either the difference between the stock price and the strike price, or zero, whichever is greater. For a put, it is equal to either the difference between the strike price and the stock price, or zero, whichever is greater.

Kendall's tau-b a correlation test designed for use with nonmetric data when a large number of observations fall into a small number of categories (thereby resulting in a large percentage of ties).

Lag an adjustment made to a time series where each observation is moved back in time a certain number of periods.

Leakage in an event study, leakage describes an environment where someone involved with, for example, a merger (lawyers, board members, analysts, etc.) leaked the news to someone who ultimately purchased shares of stock in the target firm.

Levene statistic a test used to determine if the variance associated with two different variables is equal or not.

Long position in options, a long position is said to be held by the person who buys the option.

Market return approach in an event study, this approach assumes the mean of the stock's return over the event window is expected to be the same as the mean of the market's return over the event window.

Maximum eigenvalue statistic a test statistic used to determine the number of cointegrating equations.

Mean return approach in an event study, this approach assumes the mean of the stock's return over the event window is expected to be the same as the mean over the estimation period.

Metric data consists of both continuous (ratio) and interval data.

Multicollinearity when one independent variable can be expressed or represented by a linear combination of the others.

Multiple regression a procedure used to predict or explain one variable (the dependent variable) using more than one variable (the independent variables).

National Association of Real Estate Investment Trust (NAREIT) index a securitized (publicly traded) real estate index.

National Council of Real Estate Investment Fiduciaries (NCREIF) index an unsecuritized commercial real estate index; that is, it measures the return on commercial real estate that is not traded in the public financial markets.

Natural log a logarithm with a base of *e*.

Nominal data a variable where numbers are arbitrarily assigned to identify or classify categories.

Nonmetric data consists of both ordinal and nominal data.

Normal return in an event study, what the return on the sample of stocks would be in the absence of the event.

Oblique (Oblimin) rotation in factor analysis, it is a factor rotation method where the axes about which the factors are rotated are not maintained at right angles. Moreover, the resulting factors are allowed to be correlated.

One sample t-test a type of t-test where only one variable is involved. The goal is to determine if the mean, or average, of that variable is significantly different from some fixed value (a constant).

Ordinal data indicates the relative position of each observation, but does not consider the magnitude of the differences between them. That is, ordinal observations are not set equally apart from each other.

Orthogonal (Varimax) rotation in factor analysis, it is a factor rotation method where the axes about which the rotation occurs are maintained at right angles. This method minimizes the number of factors onto which a single variable has a high loading. Orthogonal rotation results in factors that are not correlated with each other.

Orthogonalized (centered) seasonal dummy variable a seasonal dummy variable that has 1/4 subtracted from each observation in the time series.

Out-of-the-money if the option were exercised immediately, out-of-the-money refers to the situation where it has a negative payoff (ignoring commissions). For a call option, it refers to a situation where the stock's price is less than the exercise price. For a put, it refers to a situation where the stock's price is greater than the exercise price.

P-value (probability value) a measure of the level of significance. It can be thought of as the break-even alpha value. More formally, it is the probability of falsely rejecting the null hypothesis when it is true. Alternatively, this is your probability of committing a Type I error.

Paired samples t-test a type of t-test where the goal is to determine if there is a significant difference between the means of two groups that are linked (or paired) in some way.

Partial autocorrelation measures the autocorrelation in a time series with lower-order effects removed.

Phillips-Perron (PP) a procedure used to test for stationarity.

Proxy (or Control) portfolio return approach in an event study, this approach is just like the market return approach, except instead of using the market (S&P 500) as the expected return on each stock, an industry return should be used.

Put option gives the buyer (who is said to hold a "long" position) the right to sell 100 shares of the underlying common stock at a predetermined price (the strike or exercise price) on (a European option) or before (an American option) a predetermined date (maturity).

Return the natural log of the price this period (t) divided by the price from last period (t-1).

Risk-adjusted return approach in an event study, this approach defines abnormal returns as the difference between the actual return and the expected return, where the expected return for each of the days in the event window is predicted using a regression.

Risk-free rate the return earned on a security that has no risk. It is commonly approximated by the yield on a 3-month Treasury Bill.

Schwarz Criterion a measure used to determine the optimal number of lags to include for a series.

Seasonal dummy variable a dummy variable where a 1 is assigned for a particular season or quarter of the year; otherwise the variable is 0.

Second-order autocorrelation measures the correlation between the series' values and those lagged by exactly two periods.

Short position in options, a short position is said to be held by the person who writes the option.

Simple regression a procedure used to predict or explain one variable (the dependent variable) using only one variable (the independent variable).

Single index market model (SIMM) in an event study, SIMM is a version of the risk-adjusted return approach where only one independent variable is used in the regression to establish normal returns.

Spearman's rho a correlation test designed for use with nonmetric data when a large number of observations do not fall into a small number of categories.

Standard normal distribution a normal distribution with a mean of zero and a standard deviation of one.

Standardized abnormal return (SAR) in an event study, CAR is the abnormal return standardized (divided) by the standard deviation of the abnormal return.

Stationarity a condition where the mean and autocovariances of a series do not depend on time.

Strike (or exercise) price a predetermined price at which the person who holds the long position can buy (call) or sell (put) the shares of the underlying asset.

Summated scale in factor analysis, it is possible to define the series for a resulting factor as the average value of each of the variables in the factor.

Systematic risk risk that cannot be removed through diversification (nondiversifiable risk).

T-test a test to determine if the means (averages) of two variables are significantly different from each other.

Third-order autocorrelation measures the correlation between series values and those lagged by exactly three periods.

Threshold ARCH (TARCH) a variation of ARCH/GARCH where downward movements in the series are treated separately from upward movements. More formally, positive shocks to the system and negative shocks have different effects on conditional variance. TARCH assumes the formula for the conditional variance is quadratic.

Ticker symbol letters used to identify securities in the financial markets without having to refer to the security's full name.

Time to maturity the number of days before the option matures.

Tolerance a statistic whose values below .10 indicate the presence of multicollinearity.

Total risk systematic risk plus unsystematic risk.

Total standardized abnormal return (TSAR) in an event study, TSAR is simply the sum of the standardized abnormal returns (SARs) across all firms for each day in the event window.

Trace statistic a test statistic used to determine the number of cointegrating equations.

Trend stationary a term used to describe a nonstationary series that can be made stationary by regressing on time.

Two-Stage Least Squares (2SLS) regression a regression that requires two steps because the explanatory (predictor) variables are not truly independent (or exogenous).

Uniqueness in factor analysis, uniqueness reports the percentage of variance within each variable that is not explained by the resulting factors.

Unit Root Test a procedure used to determine if a series is stationary.

Unrotated Component Matrix in factor analysis, it identifies the relationship between the individual variables and factors onto which they load.

Unsystematic risk (diversifiable risk) risk that can be removed through diversification.

Variance inflation factor (VIF) a statistic whose values above 10 indicate the presence of multicollinearity. It is also the reciprocal of tolerance.

Variance proportions used to identify the presence of multicollinearity. If at least two of the variables in the analysis have a variance proportion value above .90 (associated with a condition index above 30), the model has excessive multicollinearity.

Vector autoregression (VAR) a procedure used to model numerous variables that are linked together over time. Instead of specifying a dependent variable in terms of several other independent variables, the independent variables used in VAR are simply lags of the various interrelated dependent variables.

Vector error correction (VEC) model a restricted VAR and is designed to be used with integrated (nonstationary) series that are found to be cointegrated.

Volatility a measure of the fluctuation in the price of an asset.

Wald-Wolfowitz Runs test a nonparametric test for autocorrelation.

INDEX